SAILING SABBATICAL

A Family Adventure

DR. KAREN ERIKSEN

ISBN-10: 1495473244
ISBN-13: 9781495473241

Library of Congress Control Number: 2013912506
CreateSpace Independent Publishing Platform
North Charleston, South Carolina

For my husband, the love of my life, for my high-spirited, darling children and my wonderful parents

Contents

Prologue

Ratty was right. He knew it all along. It isn't about getting someplace. It is simply messing about in boats.

Bored? Frustrated? Feel like you're stuck in a rut, doing the same thing day after day? Whole magazines are now dedicated to de-stressing our lives, finding our inner selves, slowing down to avoid burnout or worse. In our fast world of information overload, micro-managed parenting, and nonstop social activities, many long for a calmer existence to get their headspace back. To escape the every-day, some people phone their mums or reminisce about their weddings. Some middle-aged professional men are looking for chal-lenges and adventures that will push them mentally and physically. There is always cycling or mountain climbing—or living in a foreign city. A lot of work- and life-weary people dream about a sabbatical to get some magic back into their lives. Sailing away onto the big, wide ocean ticks a lot of boxes for "late gap year" aspirants, like us.

This book might appeal to four groups of people: Those who are planning a sabbatical with children (part 1), those who want to take their family on a longer sailing trip and are interested in the Mediterranean (part 2), those who want to cross oceans (part

3), and our friends who are curious to know what it really was like, this big trip of ours. I hope that each group will get something out of the book and gain useful insights for similar ventures. The book also offers lots of practical tips.

It took us years of planning to make these eighteen months possible. Our little family set out from Australia on an escape from everyday life with a precise objective: for the four of us to live 24/7 with each other without the framework, creature comforts, and endless minutiae and activities that dominate modern family existence. Our stay in Denmark was necessary to secure the kids' European passports while connecting them to their Viking roots.

But for our ten months on the boat in 2012 we had an additional agenda. That year was going to be an extra special year for our family, a lucky year, in which John and I celebrated ten years of marriage, I turned fifty, and Finn turned ten. We were excited but also a bit worried. We would be away, with the boat our home, living in cramped conditions on a few square metres with three generations, see uncountable countries, experience other cultures and food, and finally conquer an ocean, the biggest challenge. A real family adventure.

For our family, going away was about living our dream before it was too late, but also dealing with the hard yards involved. It meant financial and organisational challenges as well as emotional ones. We wanted to rediscover the value of things in our lives that we often take for granted. John and I had similar expectations and goals for this journey. I wanted John to relax from his stressful work life and spend some quality time with the children before they turned into difficult teenagers. I also wanted him to get a better feeling for his Asperger son's eccentricities. Personally I couldn't wait to get out of my mundane but exhausting routines of school runs, shopping, kids activities, and organising our lives.

John also felt there were only a few precious years left where the children still enjoyed our company and didn't yearn to be with their friends. He had enjoyed a shorter sabbatical before and remembered how good it felt to own his own time rather than his employers', not to race and catch up all the time. He had crossed the Atlantic before, so didn't need that T-shirt, but he was keen to explore regions in the Mediterranean and Caribbean that he hadn't seen. Of course there were practical concerns. Would we have enough money to go now? Would John be able to re-establish himself at work after a year? What about health insurance? Would we be able to handle our big boat by ourselves?

The children, Finn and Lizzie, were very accepting about living in a foreign country and on the boat for a period, but they were not particularly thrilled. However, Finn with his Aspergers needed a break from the heavy demands of school life and the occasional bullying. We had sent Lizzie to school too young, and this break would offer a perfect opportunity to help her with her learning and, after our return, pull her back one year. Away from peer pressure and mass media we hoped our children would be free to be kids a little longer. We were ready!

Here are the kids' top five destinations as a taste of our travels:

Finn
Montenegro
Guernsey
Marmaris/Turkey
Mallorca
Gibraltar

Lizzie
Montenegro
Turgutreis/Turkey
Guernsey
Paris
Istanbul

PART ONE

FIRST WORK,
THEN PLAY

CHAPTER 1.

DENMARK, NOT ITALY

Gitte from the Danish consulate in Sydney couldn't have been more helpful or friendly. But she saw no way around it. If we wanted the children to keep their Danish passports with all the European Union work and living implications for their future we would have to live in Denmark for twelve months. Officially that was necessary before the kids turned twenty-one, but what parent can drag a sulky teenager anywhere, let alone to a country where he doesn't speak the language and doesn't know anybody? So it had to happen fast, possibly the following year while the economic climate was bad and husband John's law firm could spare him for a year. We left the consulate in a sombre mood. People dream about a year in Italy or follow Peter Mayle's footsteps to Provence. Even Mallorca attracts some weary "sabbaticalists" or retirees. But Denmark?

So why do the children have Danish as well as Australian citizenship? This is slightly complicated. My Danish grandfather had married a Hamburg girl and settled in Germany in the 1930s. As Germany is not keen on dual citizenship their children, one of them my father, stayed Danish—although my father was born and lived in Germany most of his life. Same with me: Danish father, German mother, born in Germany, but I remained a Dane. So my children also got a Danish passport in addition to their Australian one. We had no family in Denmark, only a holiday connection, and I only spoke very little Danish. But that passport was my children's entry ticket into the EU, and in our fast and international world we considered this very important.

We are one of these intercultural families, if you can call a German-Danish-Australian mix being of different cultures. I certainly believe so. You know us Germans, we are a bit officious. And the Danes are majorly quirky. The Australians are just nice people, so not a bad mix. John, a true Sydneysider, and I had met at the Swan Cup 2000 sailing regatta in Porto Cervo, Sardinia. He was helping his friend Stephen campaign his new Swan 48 *Loki*, and I was racing my Swan 40 *Bella Gioia* with some German friends.

When the race week was over and John spent the last three month of his six-month sabbatical travelling around Europe, I joined him in Rome, Paris, Madrid, and elsewhere for weekends. It was all very romantic. We had a lengthy "honeymoon" before we were even married. In 2001, a year after we met, I sold up in London and moved to Sydney. We had Finn in 2002 and Elizabeth (Lizzie) in 2005. Sailing remained our passion, and we took my parents and the kids on a cruise every Northern summer.

A year in Denmark, with the kids at school and John and I huddling in front of the fire with not a lot to do because he couldn't work there as a lawyer or, in fact, as anything? As it turned out, John had to stay home anyway. As an Australian, he would have to go through a family reunification process equalling the gruelling Australian immigration. And would be taxed with the sky-high Danish tax rates. And the best for last: he would have to learn Danish, not an easy feat for a man who has lived in a mostly German-speaking family for ten years without really picking the language up. So he decided to give the adventure a miss and continue in his job instead. But the problems we encountered in getting a visa for John as an Australian confirmed the importance of the kids keeping a European passport.

"Why would you bother to go there, let them lose the passport," one of my Australian girlfriends said. Another male friend agreed he wouldn't go to Norway (it's Denmark, mate) just for the kids. But having both come from families where our postwar parents worked extremely hard and had done everything to give us children a better start, we had no doubt we owed it to our offspring, Finn Einar, nine, and Elizabeth (Lizzie) Carla, six, to keep the European door open for them.

The Coles in Stade, Germany

The preparations began. I started to realize the harsh realities of the dream of an overseas sabbatical. The computer hummed nonstop while I researched our options on the Internet. Where would we live, where would there be good schools, could we keep a boat there? What about our house, could we rent it out and for how much? What about our stuff? The dog? I started to come to grips with the harsh realities of converting the dream into a sabbatical. We were realistic; we would need two years of lead time.

Then there was the language. My Danish was halfheartedly learnt in my late teens thirty years ago, and although I could still read some, speaking was another matter. So I joined a Danish course offered by the Danish church in Pennant Hills, and as the drive was too long, after a while I took private lessons. Progress was slow. Finn also started out with Danish lessons at the church once a month, and eventually he and Lizzie joined my Danish teacher's grandchildren with some young teachers at her house for a few months.

But even the Danish children's stories on CDs in the car would not make us fluent enough in this difficult language to cope with school and everyday life, I feared. Also the cost of living in one of the most expensive countries in the world was scary. We would have to rent a flat or a house, but the Copenhagen real estate sites were not very encouraging; we clearly couldn't afford to live there. What about Århus? My grandfather was from there, or Sønderborg, close to the German border and my parents?

I started doing my homework more seriously. Pauli, our eight-year-old labradoodle, could be taken into Europe with a few vaccinations and a lot of paperwork. Getting her back into Australia was harder, but not impossible. The quarantine period could be as short as four weeks. While we were in Denmark, she could stay with my parents in Stade, a medieval town north of Hamburg on the Elbe River. Maybe she could force them into a regular exercise regime.

The house needed to be rented out for the period we were away. Rental prices seemed good as there was a shortage of rentable houses in our suburb, Hunters Hill. John decided to keep working for the first nine months while we were in Denmark to have money coming in and to avoid the family reunification hassle and the Danish winter.

New Plans

I gave Gitte from the consulate another call to clarify John's situation and asked how long he could legally visit us. Ninety days every six months in the EU, as it turned out. A few days later Gitte's voice chirped from our answer phone, excitedly announcing that unbeknownst to the consulate, citizenship laws had changed in Denmark and we now only had to stay there for three months. Hurrah! This changed about everything. Though we were really keen for the kids to connect to their heritage, if we could stay for only a few months then expensive Copenhagen would become a feasible option. John was also concerned that the other towns we had considered would be too small, and chances were we would be lonely.

The kids and I could spend the winter in the Danish capital, one of the world's greatest cities, while John was still working and would join us for the European spring. We could do six months there, hopefully enough time for the kids to get to know their roots. If John's firm would let him take a one-year sabbatical, we could then hop onto the boat and sail around the Mediterranean, homeschooling the kids. Then across the Atlantic into the Caribbean, a very ambitious plan, but the world was our lobster. We were elated. A winter in the wonderfully interesting Danish capital would be educational for the children and fun for me. My parents could visit by train as often as possible. My father spent his apprentice years in Copenhagen in the fifties, and our family had visited the lively city often.

CHAPTER 2.

HOW DID YOU NOT SPOT THIS BEFORE?

Finn

A fter talking to his group at work, John had a lengthy conversation with his managing partner, and things were looking positive. If he put good systems into place and was available by phone or e-mail it looked as if he could take twelve months off.

But there were a few spanners in the works, as happens with complex plans like this. It was that time of the year, just before Christmas, school report time, year 2. Our son had never been an easy child, but this year we were relaxed, had gotten frequent positive updates from his capable teacher, and expected quite a good report. We intended to hand that in as part of an application for a private high school.

And there it was—the big white envelope. All marks about average, but the negative summary at the end of the report took us by complete surprise. So a meeting with our son's teacher was called for on the last day of school. She explained the report to us but also elaborated on his sometimes unusual behaviour in the classroom.

He was very set on classroom routines, she said, didn't cope with change that well, was prone to meltdowns, interrupted her often. He had, on the other hand, an amazing wealth of knowledge, but sometimes had problems concentrating and finishing his work. Hence some of the average results. Recess and lunch were problem times, and they had resorted to sending him to the library to avoid conflict with his peers.

I was stunned. Why had nobody all year mentioned to me that there were problems in the school yard? Tears welled up and I said: "I really don't know what is wrong with him sometimes." The teacher looked uncomfortable and then said, "Have you had a look at Asperger yet?" My husband turned to me with a big question mark on his face.

Asperger syndrome is a high functioning autism named after Austrian paediatrician Hans Asperger who described children with problems in nonverbal communication in a thesis in 1944. Children with Asperger syndrome, as it is now called, don't understand how people feel, and they don't get social cues. They use their intellect rather than intuition to deal with normal social situations.

Those children often have remarkable knowledge in one field of interest and a fantastic memory, very true for our boy, who is a walking dictionary. Their language can be quite formal. We had been proud of our son's astounding vocabulary in English and German; now we know it is part of the syndrome. Aspergers kids are often seen as eccentric or odd and get easily bullied. They get overwhelmed by the demands of daily life. The concentration necessary to function normally and the accompanying anxiety lead to mental and physical exhaustion. Their subsequent frequent meltdowns can cause their peers to distance themselves, especially as they get older. Gross motor skill problems or clumsiness can also be a problem. When the majority of the boys in the school yard played handball, our boy with his lack of coordination became isolated. Children with Aspergers also often have difficulties with criticism and imperfection. And take everything literally. In my quest to pinpoint our boy's behaviour I had read about ADHD, Tourette, OCD, and Aspergers but had come to no conclusion about him.

It was December 23, not easy to get referred with suspected autism or Aspergers for a proper diagnosis soon. There was no doubt we were in shock. Autism is the big, scary *A* of children's conditions. Who hasn't seen *Rain Man*? The diagnosis of Aspergers as one form of autism had lifelong ramifications. We went through denial, despair, lots of tears, and helplessness.

"Why did you not spot this before?" the man of the house said.

"Because the criteria never fit," I defended myself. "He is way too sociable."

In terms of getting a specialist appointment we were lucky: a brilliant young psychologist connected to Australian Asperger guru Tony Atwood had just moved to Sydney from Brisbane. A miracle, his list was not full yet, and he could see us in early February. Both my son and I filled out lengthy questionnaires, and he got tested for hours, amongst other things having to explain portrait photos of people with different facial expressions.

I thought he did quite well, but the verdict was "textbook Aspergers" and led to frequent psychologist sessions. The psychologist tried to make him understand his emotions, anger, and frustration and help him deal with them in an appropriate manner. "No more meltdowns," was the mantra. But the main help had to come from us.

But how about the big trip, all our plans? Many Aspergers help books suggest you should leave your "Aspie" at home as much as possible, where he feels safe. Travelling disrupts their routine, they say. We had been lucky in our ignorance; the kids had frequent flyer cards from birth and had visited their grandparents in Germany every European summer. So Finn was used to leaving home for a big trip every year.

The health professionals assured us that our travels would be the best thing for him. To have to adapt to changing environments all the time would be hard for him, but being in a safe family environment in Copenhagen, in my hometown, and on the boat the trip would be a big positive. We were off!

CHAPTER 3.

THE PLANNING STAGE – MINOR DETAILS NEEDED SORTING OUT

"No matter where you might go or how dramatically you might change things, there is no escape from the familiar frustrations of the everyday."
Mike Litzow[1]

John had sailed *Senta*, our Swan 46, from North America to Germany the previous summer for us to have the boat available in Northern Europe for coming sailing seasons. Clearly with our changed plans we didn't need the boat in Denmark or Northern Europe in winter, and we preferred to cruise around the Med for a summer.

---

1 Mike Litzow, *South from Alaska*, Sydney 2011

Senta **in the shed in Rendsburg, Germany**

So after more research and price quotes we decided to have the boat trucked to Slovenia and start our sailing adventure in spring after our winter stay in Copenhagen. Fellow sailor Mike Litzow, quoted above, said that the act of buying an actual boat on an actual budget ends the romantic part of sailing. So true! From then on it is endless lists of repairs, maintenance, spare parts, and other organisational issues. A never ending outflow of money.

The school issue was resolved easily—so we thought. Right in the middle of Copenhagen next to the university was a grand old German-Danish school connected to an ancient German cathedral, the Sankt Petri Skole, which was happy to accept our children for the period planned, Lizzie into kindergarten, Finn into year 3.

Sankt Petri Kirke, Copenhagen

However, we found renting a home for us harder than anticipated. The websites for furnished executive rentals showed amazing, glitzy places in central Copenhagen, but not at all within our
budget. Most normal flats were available unfurnished, meaning
completely empty, without washing machine, fridge, etc., and were
only available for longer periods. I had wanted to find something
before we arrived in Denmark to avoid hotel costs and stress, but
the web just showed nothing suitable.

Then one day a distant acquaintance suggested we look on sab-
baticalhomes.com, which specializes in university lecturers roam-
ing the globe. There were two flats in Copenhagen on that website,
and one looked perfect. Located in Christianshavn, a picturesque
waterfront suburb in central Copenhagen, it had two bedrooms and
looked beautiful. I sent an e-mail straight away. This was meant to
be, as it turned out.

Tina and Heiko were young university professors with two children, and Tina was going to lecture in the United States for a year. She was English-Australian, and he was from my university town Hamburg. In this world of three degrees of separation it turned out his father had been a work colleague of mine in Hamburg in the '90s. Their nine-year-old daughter Maibritt went to the German school, and we could use all their belongings in their absence, like bicycles, bedding, and kitchen contents. It could not have been better.

Back at home we had several estate agents survey our house and also put a small ad into the school newsletter. A few families had traipsed through the house without us coming to an agreement. Then we had an evening phone call, and an hour later a handshake sealed a deal with a nice Hunters Hill family looking to rent while they were building a house. Perfect!

The Adventure can Begin!

As I was doing the organising and planning of the big move, the enormity of it was more real to me than to the kids or John. When they would say, "In next year's school concert I am going to wear that costume," I would have to say, "We will be in Denmark then." That phrase came out often, as the children had to get used to the idea of parting from their friends and the school.

I was sad about that too. The school was a huge part of our lives, and I enjoyed walking the kids up there every day and chatting to my girlfriends. The teachers were great; the kids were in a good routine. It would be starting from scratch in Denmark with the language problems on top. Also we would be without John for months, as he had to live with his brother until he could join us in the European spring.

Also I was not looking forward to packing up the house into which we had moved only four year earlier and which we loved. But whose house doesn't need a good clean out and shedding of some stuff, also a great opportunity. Getting our things over to Europe in an economical way was another matter. It would be hard to choose what to take.

Our last Christmas in the house arrived, and my parents travelled to Australia as in the years before. Then the boxes started to fill. The run-up to the big trip was really hard. The packing went in stages; the good plates were packed away after a last big dinner party, the kids' toys into boxes after the Easter school holidays, and on and on it went. We were lucky that our good friends Malcolm and Claire were in Europe with their children over the two weeks before our departure so we could stay in their house. A huge farewell dinner with friends and lots of children at the Hunters Hill Club the night before our departure left us sentimental but also happy that we would come back to a great community and lovely set of friends.

Packing up

Chapter 4.

Kids – See Asia!

"Asia is not going to be civilized after the methods of the West. There is too much Asia, and she is too old." Rudyard Kipling

In my last year of high school I had compared the tiger economies of Hong Kong and Singapore in my main subject, geography. I was fascinated by the British colony, had read a lot about it, loved *Noble House* by James Clavell, and on a flight back from Australia in the late 1980 stopped over in Hong Kong for a few days. Then the strangeness of an Asian city and its street-smart inhabitants had overwhelmed me, even scared me.

But in May, before our Denmark adventure, we wanted to stop in Hong Kong for a few days to expose the kids to Asia. Australia and China are so closely linked now that it looked as if our children's future would to a great extent be made by China. We had never broken up our journey to Europe before, and this would be the last opportunity for a while.

Hong Kong was fantastic, we all just loved it. Possibly the best city break we have ever had, certainly with the kids. Why were we so taken by the former British colony? Was it the obvious mix of Asia and Europe, a city unlike other Asian capitals, completely safe and non-threatening, prosperous and clean? Or was it the luxurious accommodation at the Intercontinental organised by our friend Paul, where we enjoyed the panoramic view of Hong Kong Island from our rooms?

Aberdeen Harbour

I think mainly it was the very busy harbour that delighted us, watching freighters, tugboats, sampans, and ferries during the day and the magical light display at night from the huge hotel bar. We strolled along the promenade and looked at crazy art displayed there, took the Star Ferry everywhere, had lunch at the Royal Hong Kong Yacht Club, which is as homely as any British yacht club, and took a sampan ride around Aberdeen Harbour after an old biddy with an umbrella lured us out of the crowd to her sampan. Towering over Aberdeen Harbour were high-rises with millions of people crammed together on a few square kilometres, so much humanity, hard to digest. From the Peak we gazed down onto the skyscrapers that were partly disguised by a smoggy haze.

When I visited Hong Kong in the 1980s, it still had felt very European. How quickly it had changed. Now even in the Interconti Hotel we as non-Asians were a small minority, and the breakfast buffet with its Asian-European mix fascinated the kids endlessly, especially the marinated snails and other Chinese delicacies for breakfast. The huge lobby at night filled up with hip, young Chinese for a drink and a snack to enjoy the light show on the high-rises above the harbour. We didn't feel adventurous and stuck to old-fashioned rum and Cokes and fish and chips, beautifully presented.

The Temple Street Night Market was fun despite the fact that the goods on offer were as touristy as it gets. Lizzie landed a silk sarong and Finn looked at Buddha statues. John ate some prawns at a stall, number one on the guidebook's list of what not to do, and some lemon chicken that tasted of chemicals. He survived. Lizzie with her blond hair and straw hat was asked to take centre between smiling Chinese women all the time to pose in holidays photos, though she soon got tired of the attention. The kids had new cameras, and Finn took uncountable photos of buildings and building details.

Art on the promenade

"We have to watch that," Finn yelled out when he saw a poster of the fourth part of *Pirates of the Caribbean*. Why not? Here nobody cared whether our children were the right age to watch Jack Sparrow and enemies, and we were the only ones in the cinema.

In the afternoon the hotel pool was just the relaxation the kids needed while we slurped cocktails on sun lounges; it was even the right sort of rum. The only thing we didn't like about Hong Kong: taxi and bus drivers tried to kill us on frequent occasions, completely mad driving.

Practical Tips: City tours are great for a family and always a highlight of our travels. The kids have their own digital cameras and happily snap away. We choose a central hotel with the main sights in walking distance or a short taxi ride away. We get a good, small travel guide that has lists of ten things to do with kids, sights to see, best restaurants. We take a tourist bus tour for an overview first, ideally hop on, hop off. Or a boat trip as in Hong Kong or Istanbul. We sightsee in the morning and hang around the hotel pool, or room, in the afternoon. We often eat in the hotel if tired or have a big lunch on the go and don't eat in the evening. Choose museums wisely according to your kids' ages (e.g., natural history museum in Paris instead of the Louvre. The Uffizi in Florence or Doge's Palace in Venice is torture for children. They do not have to see everything on this trip, they likely will be back).

CHAPTER 5.

EUROPEAN JOLLY AT FIRST

"Travel is nothing if not a roller coaster of emotions, especially travel with your family in the confines of a small boat." Mike Litzow[2]

John and I had met sailing, at a yachting event in Sardinia in the year 2000, and sailing was our passion. We read sailing magazines from cover to cover, look at boats on the web, and discuss boat innovations. Our current boat, Swan 46 *Senta*, was John's sixth boat and my second. We had bought it in December 2006 with this sole purpose in mind: a family sabbatical. A year or more away on this boat.

We were Swan people, and the Swan 46 was spacious, fast, and solid. Our dream boat! We bravely bought her with a mouse click on the Internet after two years of searching for the right Swan 46. *Senta* could accommodate up to ten people, handy when we took my parents and some friends, and had a nice galley with a fridge-freezer and two toilets, but only an outside shower. She was not an easy to handle boat, built in 1983 as a cruiser-racer designed for plenty of

---

2 Mike Litzow, *South from Alaska*, Sydney 2011

crew. In the first few years when the children were small and kept me busy we had professional help during our holidays on *Senta*.

Now we were by ourselves. The children were older now and we had more experience in sailing the boat, but there could be problems in putting her into some marina berths. She weighed almost twenty tons and did not go well backwards like many boats of that vintage. It would be a challenge!

After our arrival in my hometown Stade in Northern Germany that June, the usual mayhem of shopping and organising began. Kids and grandparents were happy to spend time together while John and I hired a truck, loaded half a garage full of boat stuff and holiday clothes, and raced up to Rendsburg where the boat was in a shed waiting to be trucked to Slovenia. We unloaded all the gear in half a day, slept at the marina, did some more work, and drove back; amazing how fast an Iveco truck can go. The amount of time it took us to pack up the house and unpack our belongings into the boat was substantial. It was really hard yards.

A TASTE OF COPENHAGEN

In early June, the German-Danish school in Copenhagen wanted to meet the children before they started school in August. Fair enough! So on a Sunday afternoon we boarded the train to Hamburg and then on to Copenhagen, a seven-hour journey. We also wanted to meet our landlords and see our new flat.

The whole family had a cold by then, as so often happens after a plane trip, some kind of virus which miraculously turned into gastro. We only noticed the extent of the lurgy when Finn threw up in a café in Hamburg Central station waiting for a train. We got through the school interview without incident as Finn had used the flowerpot in front of the hotel before. I wiped down train station floors, ferry stairs, and a lot more. The kids had the gastro and John moved to bronchitis. I left the hotel alone to meet Heiko and Tina, the lovely people whose flat we were renting. Everybody else stayed in bed. The train trip back to Stade was a challenge. But there was no stopping us now.

SLOVENIA

At 5:00 am, the taxi drove the six of us, grandparents included (Einar, 77, Edith, 77, John, 58, Karen, 49, Finn, almost 9, Lizzie, 6), to Hamburg airport to fly to Koper, Slovenia. The boat was on the motorway down south already, as it could only travel by night due to the trailer's width, and John wanted to be there for the unloading. In Koper we checked into the one and only hotel, a leftover from the communist era, and organised the boat to be lifted into the water, mast stepped and rig put back together.

When necessary my family can be very German, so every morning we took the challenge and battled for prime position around the breakfast buffet with an Austrian skittles club. You could call the Hotel Koper two-and-a-half stars. One of the funny moments was when John and I were still in bed early in the morning looking out over the harbour when two blokes stood themselves in front of our open window on the roof ledge to have a smoke, chatting animatedly.

Senta **arriving in Koper**

Slovenia has a short coastline, squeezed in between Italy and Croatia. There are several large marinas like Isola, but Koper was known as a commissioning marina for boats trucked in from Northern Europe. The tradesmen worked well enough under John's supervision while I stocked up the fridge and the kids played on the pebble beach. The market near the harbour offered amazing raspberries and cheap capsicums, and the town also had a good supermarket. People did not speak English or German, but I got by with sign language.

Slovenia split from Yugoslavia in 1991 and was the first former communist country to join the European Union, in 2007. Slovenia has a developed economy and is per capita the richest of Slavic states.

Great relief when we finally moved onto the boat. John had developed pneumonia by that stage but didn't stop working on the boat (no further comment, things were tense). Finn had the odd vomit, but the kids, grandparents, and I went shopping, to the playground and pebble beach, keeping things halfway normal. Boats are ongoing projects—too many moving parts. John found cooling fluid under the floorboards in the bilge after some engine gismos sounded alarm, so it took two more days to fix a leaking hose and top the engine up with coolant. Finally we felt ready to go. Where to? To Venice.

Koper Beach

CHAPTER 6.

VENICE

"All of Venice is built on a bed of huge wooden nails." Francesco da Mosto

We left for Venice at 6:00 am in brilliant sunshine, fifty-five nautical miles to go, and despite a forecast for decent wind ended up motoring almost all the way, the Adriatic shiny and smooth.

One of the greatest movie scenes featuring yachts ever: James Bond and the love of his life sail into Venice in a breathtaking yacht. The stunning yacht set against the Campanile and San Marco square, glistening sunshine, who wouldn't want to be there? The film was inspiration—if James Bond could do it, so could we.

Venice is undoubtedly one of the most beautiful cities in the world, almost a romantic cliché. For centuries its strategic position at the top of the Adriatic ensured its dominance as a centre of commerce and arts, and the golden-red flag with the winged lion is still flying proudly over the rooftops today. We would come across the Venetian lion all across Croatia in our travels.

Venice canal

The City of Bridges stretches across 117 small islands in the swampy Venetian Lagoon. La Serenissima is full of contrasts and enigmas; it is mysterious and frivolous, glittering and dark, opulent and decaying, prosperous and poor, smelly, doomed, sinking into the water, but alive and buzzing. It has attracted writers, poets, film makers, not to mention the 15 million tourists a year amongst the few thousand remaining Venetians. But surprisingly few yachties, likely due to the lack of berths.

World cruising legend Jimmy Cornell has been here, but where hasn't he been? Incredibly the Cornells explored the over-crowded canals teeming with crafts of all manner and form in their own dinghy. "Forget the gondolas," they said. With two children and two senior citizens in tow we didn't follow that advice. He also called Venice "the most attractive of all Mediterranean destinations." I couldn't agree more. Sailing into Venice on a yacht is an unbelievable thrill.

ARE WE THERE YET?

Senta still had several miles to go when biggish cities started popping up along the coast between Venice and Trieste. Somehow I hadn't expected it to be so built up, had thought of Venice in solitude, calmly in its lagoon. Our navigation was spot on; after we sighted the big marker at the entrance there were port and starboard marks standing out before the low-lying land. No sign of grandeur yet but lots of cranes and big waterworks that remained a mystery, was this land reclamation? Having read up about it I believe it is part of the MOSE project of building a lock system that is hopefully going to protect Venice from high waters in the future.

From a friend we had heard about the little marina under the Palladio church tower on the island San Giorgio Maggiore right opposite San Marco square. It belongs to a yacht club, private and exclusive, and has very few berths for visitors. I started inquiring about a berth via e-mail half a year before our arrival, no reply. We had an Italian-speaking friend phone the yacht club, to no avail. We tried phoning ourselves, no answer. We just had to take our chances it seemed. Plan B was the equally private marina Sant'Elena a bit further north.

The channel wound on. In the distance the Campanile's top came into view while more and more beautiful buildings started to appear. It was already mayhem, boats everywhere, barges, sailing dinghies, speedboats, ferries. Slightly shell shocked we needed the chart plotter to find our way. Lots of markers, plenty of shallow water, but even cruise liners got in here.

In the end the marina was easy to spot, marked by two big white stone towers on either side. But how to get a berth now? John had tried to raise the harbour master on the VHF on approach; he heard a lot of Italian but no answer. The skipper looked frustrated, but when we slowly motored along the marina wall a white-clad portly figure came out of a tower and started gesticulating. He didn't speak English, of course, but after a bit of to-ing and fro-ing it was established that he had a berth for us for one night, close to the entrance, bow to the quay. We were in!

Maybe five visiting yachts were moored near the entrance, the deepest part of the marina. We were next to an English X 50 and soon were sipping some wine with Julie and Richard. The harbour master was a different guy every day and nobody bothered us again, so there was no problem staying four days. At ninety-five euros a night we had a great deal. Only the neighbours on the other side were a worry. An Italian girl in her twenties, Claudia, on her Jeanneau 52 with about twelve of her nonsailing friends equally entertained and stressed us over the next few days. She spectacularly T-boned the boat on the other side, left the marina the next morning in an incredibly odd and dangerous fashion, and then, oh no, came back later that day minus most of the crew.

Senta in San Giorgio Maggiore

15 Million Tourists and US

But we had to stop worrying about the boat, we had things to do, sights to see. Venice with two children and two oldies—there had to be something for everybody. Our allergic kids had been attacked by mozzies on night one and Lizzie had to be carried for a day (forty bites), while my father usually wants to sit down after walking for only fifty metres. Unlike the Cornells, we decided that our own dinghy with six people wasn't tempting. We tried out a variety of water transport in Venice starting with the ferry that brought us from the island to San Marco, a good taste of how busy and water oriented this city was.

For two hours we hired one of the stunning wooden powerboats that zoom around the canals as they do in *The Tourist*. We had also been keen viewers of the BBC program *Francesco's Mediterranean Voyage*. The charming presenter, Francesco da

Mosto, lives in a Venetian palace. "I wonder which palace is Francesco's," I mused as we charged up and down the Grand Canal and its side waterways. Then we heard some loud horns, music, and six-year-old Lizzie cried out in delight, a Venetian wedding. The bridal party sat in the suitably decorated little boat at the front with an armada of little powerboats around it, and somebody was playing the guitar, just beautiful. We followed alongside through the picturesque maze of lanes and canals for half an hour until we all got spewed out into the open water at the big San Marco square.

Lizzie's Diary

"In the holidays I went to Venice. On the first day we went to look at the souvenir shop. Finn liked the weapons and I liked the masks. When we went Finn was sad. After that we had dinner. I had a whole chicken and it was great. The next day my dad got me a mask, it is pink and golden with glitter. Then we went back to the souvenir shop and Finn loved it and I got a glass dolphin. I had a great time in Venice."

On day two, thoroughly refreshed after a cold shower under the hose on the quay (surprise, surprise, no shower facilities in the marina), we joined the hundreds of thousands of tourists and did what had to be done, the incredible basilica, the Rialto Bridge, the fruit and vegetable markets, left out the Doge's Palace, and almost had our heads blown off by the six o'clock bells on top of the Campanile when we were just taking in the view. All those tourists, the same as us, didn't matter a bit; they could not distract from the immense beauty of the place. One felt it was only just that everybody wanted to see it.

San Marco square

And we didn't feel ripped off considering this was one of the top tourist destinations of the world, had two great pizza meals in prime tourist locations, and did pay the six euros each just for the privilege to sit in the Café Florian on the square and listen to the band, on top of the thirty euros for a glass of prosecco and a beer. The best meal, though, was up some tiny back street after following two *gondoliere* during their lunch break.

And finally, on the last day of our stay, we gave in to the children's nagging and hired a gondola for an hour. It went under the Bridge of Sighs and through the narrow side canals. Just magical. We slowly floated past ancient houses with cast iron gates to the water, sunlight reflecting on mosaic windows, peeling paint, and falling render, a tranquil, serene, and beautiful scene, magnificent in its decay.

Gondola ride

From our young helmsman we learned a lot about the *gondo-liere*. He knew every other boatman, greeted and yelled out at them, and knew how to steer his gondola within a centimetre of a wall or obstacle, never hitting once. Venice's 450 gondolas are all privately owned; they are family businesses. Our man's gondola belonged to his father who owned a second one named after his sister.

John and I spoiled ourselves with a late afternoon visit to the Guggenheim Museum without the kids and oldies. The sun was already setting when we got on the ferry, beautiful evening light. The ferry headed toward San Georgio island when John suddenly said, "And here comes Francesco." Indeed, there he was, motoring toward us in his little blue powerboat he had used in the TV show, really close. John leant out of the ferry window and yelled a greeting to Francesco who waved to us, shouted "hello," and smiled his boyish smile. What had been the chances of that happening, amongst all these people?

San Giorgio Maggiore from the Campanile

John's top three Venice experiences were
1. getting a berth in the marina
2. the basilica, where he was even able to take communion in passing
3. the view from the bell tower over Venice

Karen's
1. seeing Francesco da Mosto
2. the amazing architecture on the Grand Canal
3. seeing the city from the water from all angles on ferries, taxis, gondolas, and from the boat and even watching a wedding procession on the water from a ferry

CHAPTER 7.

CROATIA

After our short sojourn to Venice our three-generation family sailed from the top of the Adriatic across to Croatia and down the Croatian coast. We left the boat in Split to have it sailed to Dubrovnik where it was going to winter on the hard stand. Then we were finally off to Denmark.

Croatia is a cruiser's dream. Parallel to its longitudinal Adriatic coastline of almost 1,100 miles lie thousands of beautiful islands. Mainland and islands offer crystal clear water, ancient history, a stable summer climate, industrious, honest people, good food and wine, and excellent yachting facilities and so make the Adriatic country a perfect sailing destination for that middle time of the year when it is raining in Australia—or Northern Europe, for that matter.

Senta **at sea**

ISTRIAN WINE IS UNDRINKABLE

Our first Croatian port was Rovinj, which the guidebook describes as Istria's "star attraction." Approaching from the west we could see the Cathedral of Saint Euphemia towering over the old city from miles away. Rovinj was first mentioned in the seventh century, and it is believed that the town could even have emerged between the third and fifth centuries. Now *that* is old. Present-day Rovinj is a summer destination for lots of tourists but still has maintained its fishing port charm.

Rovinj

As we were entering Croatian waters for the first time we moored alongside the customs pier to go through some formalities with the harbour police and customs—mainly pay for a vignette valid all year and get an official crew list approved.

The large marina opposite the old town is home to many Austrian and German boats as it is one of the most northern Adriatic ports in easy reach by car from landlocked European areas. Hence the standard was high. A harbour master on watch on the jetty showed us to our berth and helped with the lines, necessary with the Med way of mooring stern to with ground ropes. A chandlery, restaurants, a small supermarket, and the ancient town close by made it a comfortable place to stay for a few days. The saltwater pool near the marina proved very popular with the kids.

The Rovinj restaurants on the waterfront were a bit touristy, but only a short walk away and one could get decent meat or fish and the local cured ham and feta cheese entrees. However much we tried, though, the Istrian wine seemed undrinkable to our soft

Australian palates, and pretty soon everybody gave up and changed to beer or water.

The new shower block at the marina was still getting the finishing touches, so it was ladies and gentlemen together, which in the morning rush hour had its comic moments. For Lizzie and me that went like this: 7:30 am with towels and wash bag on the way to the shower following the trail of other people with similar items. Through a door that I had seen two women disappear into. Inside, though, numerous men with towels around their waists, with shaving cream on their faces, some wet, some dry, hmmm. We bravely walked down the middle corridor and found a door with what looked like a lady. Inside, though, Lizzie took one look and said, "This looks like for men"—a row of brand-new urinals. So back through the crowd of men, and outside I asked a builder where the "Ladies" was. Back in where we had been before; we clearly had been on the right track, past the guys, through the door, past the urinals, finally the showers. In the cubicle we listened to men left and right having a chat while showering, interesting insights.

ISLANDS

Having left Rovinj in blazing sunlight and with a nice ten-knot sailing breeze, conditions got suddenly unfriendly when we turned around a headland into the head wind. So we abandoned the plan to sail up to the island of Cres. Beam reaching in twenty-five knots, we headed for Mali Lošinj instead—a picturesque town with a lovely promenade, popular even in the late eighteen hundreds as a health spa for the Austrian aristocracy. To our surprise mooring alongside the town jetty didn't cost anything, but there was no electricity or showers.

Our new Italian friends Ugo and Rosy from a Hallberg Rassy 40 who we had met in Rovinj recommended a swimming bay around the corner, Luka Čikat, where local entrepreneur Igor was running a small marina. We could swim from the boat because the water was so clean, they said. It was an idyllic spot worth a longer stop. Snorkelling, watching the very popular water polo, sipping cocktails in deck chairs near the beach, a holiday feel started to emerge.

Finn snorkelling

To keep the superb quality of the water around us Igor was very strict with his water regime. No boat toilets were to be used and the washing up had to be done in the shower block. The latter being in theory only as I am sure everybody washed up on the boat after darkness without using detergent. We kept to the toilet rules, though, slightly restricted by the one key we were allocated for six people. The shower block had one door, a basin, and a shower plus a toilet to the left and to the right, but no dividing door. The more prudish ladies (like my six-year-old Lizzie) dressed and undressed behind the shower curtain with the additional difficulty that there were no clothes hooks, while the more hardy just stood around in the nude towelling off with strange men present. Also Lizzie noted with annoyance that since Igor himself used the ladies toilet all the time, it might have been cleaner.

Igor's jetty

As Croatia is so popular with boating tourists, marina prices had been steadily rising over the past ten years until regulars from Germany and Austria stopped coming in protest. Now prices have levelled out a bit, but it is still not cheap here. However, the Adriatic spoils yachties not only with stunning scenery but with mainly stable sailing conditions in summer. We never saw the famous Bora with its thirty-knot northeasterly; in six weeks we enjoyed only flat seas and light to moderate winds.

At Iloka we picked up a mooring buoy close to a deserted island and decided not to go ashore but have a swim and relax in the cockpit. "What sort of animal is that, Mama?" Lizzie asked, pointing to the shore.

"That is a sheep, darling, just a bit thinner than the ones we know, because they can't find enough to eat." Never seen sheep so scraggy.

Road rage is not restricted to dry land. We witnessed unbelievably bad behaviour on the water there in Iloka. A large German yacht with a crowd of men on it was heading slowly toward a mooring buoy close to the town quay. One guy was standing on the bow, boat hook ready; they were almost there. At the entrance to the channel we saw a smaller Italian boat approach the bay at top speed, still far away, inappropriately fast within the crowd of moored boats.

"I don't believe it, he is heading for the same buoy as the Germans," I said.

The German boat was now almost on the buoy; the Italian screeched to a halt exactly there, almost ran over the buoy, and secured the spot. Later Lizzie and I swam over to the Germans now moored somewhere else and commiserated with the skipper, who was, like his mates, stark naked, to Lizzie's absolute horror. After our little swimming party and salad dinner we watched the huge bonfire ashore with some drinks in the cockpit.

Zadar is not on the main cruising trail, but we wanted to pick up some German friends, so we headed for the ACI marina there. Government-owned ACI runs most major marinas in Croatia. Zadar, the main city of Northern Dalmatia, is described in the guidebook as having the "look and feel of an ancient Mediterranean city," which is certainly true for the old city with its marble streets and great sixteenth-century fortifications. The main sight is the circular Church of Saint Donat from the ninth century built over the Roman forum and the big fortress wall of the old city. From the marina a ferryman rowed us across to the old town in a punt; the kids just loved it.

Zadar, Church of Saint Donat

The area around the marina, however, reminded of the not so distant history of former Yugoslavia. Looking for a laundry we walked through a modern suburb where many walls still showed multiple holes from machine gun fire. In 1991 the city was under siege for three months.

In Zadar we spotted a familiar boat and—small world that sailing is—soon had several drinks with our Australian friend Basil Diethelm, who was sailing with his son Shane. By sheer coincidence our laundry got mixed up with theirs in the town laundry, which led to hilarious scenes the next morning after laundry pickup. "Whose boxer shorts are these, what about this towel, etc."

The next day with our German friends Bummi, Helgart, and Nico safely on board, we were now a crew of nine, almost the maximum for the boat in terms of bunks and space. We headed out into the archipelago again for the long-stretched island of Dugi Otok. Through a narrow channel we sailed for the popular bay Mir where we picked up a mooring buoy. The vast salt lake five minutes' walk from the bay had good swimming. The kids, however, were more fascinated by the wild donkeys hanging out near the footpath.

FRESH FISH AT GORAN'S

From Dugi Otok onward we followed the recommendations of a yachting article describing the best *konobas* (restaurants) in this part of Dalmatia. Without the article we would never have short-tacked up the big bay to Telašćica, practising manoeuvring with the big genoa and our two forestays. We had rung ahead to secure one of the few mooring buoys with Goran, who had taken the restaurant over from his father, Toni. Goran's son was driving around Toni's supermarket in a small open boat full of supplies. He also took orders for fresh bread and donuts for the next morning, great.

Goran grilling fish

Goran, who would be in his sixties, had the look of a true eccentric, and his place was a match. In the entrance there was an enclosure with tortoises. Soon we saw him get the live fish out of a cage in the water; it doesn't get any fresher. The bream-like fish was expertly prepared on an outside wood fired grill, served with salad and potatoes, a simple but delicious meal. A few glasses of Goran's clear spirit finished off a fun evening.

Telašćica

KORNATI ISLANDS

Our next stop was the famous Kornati islands, those barren moulds of limestone well known from Croatia postcards. Vrulje is the biggest town in the Kornatis with ten houses and a few restaurants built on reclaimed land. My godson Nico got the Opti rigged and went sailing with Finn, we swam, went briefly ashore, but ate on the boat. Although the Kornatis are a national park, the land here is privately owned by around four hundred Croatians, who maintain second homes on them and breed shaggy sheep. The lunar landscape was very calm and soothing to look at.

Kornatis

With poled-out genoa and main next morning we drifted along miles of rugged cliffs toward Opat, a small inlet between high hills. The Opat Restaurant proprietor took our lines himself from his small jetty, a privilege granted if you eat at his place, which we wanted to do. Opat was only a few houses, the restaurant, the shop, unfortunately closed, and a new bar where the boys enjoyed a cool beer. A brave contingent including the children climbed the hill above the harbour, a steep path on spiky rocks, rewarded by an amazing view over the Kornati islands. The evening meal in the Opat Restaurant was also a great success, especially the selection of fish and squid-based starters followed by a big fish in a pan with potatoes, beautifully cooked. In this part of the Med meat is cheap and fish comes at a premium, but it is money worth spending.

A feast in Opat

DALMATIA

In Murter we had to say good-bye to our friends. Passing through the very shallow entrance to the harbour bay we could see the rocky bottom, but the channel opened to reveal a huge marina with tightly packed boats. It was hot, thirty-five degrees, so the brand-new shower block was very welcome after four days in the wilderness.

The town was slightly uninspiring and didn't endear itself further when Lizzie started to scream in the main street that she had been stung by something. I pulled out a huge spike under her arm where she had squashed a bee or a hornet while a waiter from a nearby café came racing with some ice. Lizzie was still screaming when a sympathetic grandma stopped and offered some soothing cream, which I quickly dabbed on.

That last evening with our friends my mother decided we needed to go out to enjoy spit roast pork and music at the marina restaurant. We even danced after the proprietor had provided us with a free bottle of the local spirit, Slivowitz.

Dancing

Skradin was next, home to the famous waterfalls. Everybody had recommended them, but should we spend an hour motoring up the Krka River for a crowded tourist attraction? We didn't regret it, stayed a day, and went by tourist boat to the falls. It was hot, hot, hot. The falls are terraced, impressive, unlike any falls I had ever seen. They are the site of the first hydroelectric power plant in the world. The local mayor masterminded the various construction challenges. Unfortunately, despite being conceived and commenced first in the world, a similar plant was quickly opened in the United States to claim the glory for the first such power plant.

But the main attraction was you could swim in them. No health and safety, just a line separating the swimmable rock pool from the actual falls. The crowds changed into swimmers between tree roots, dogs splashing, the current sweeping oldies and toddlers along, utter mayhem. After the very salty Adriatic, swimming in fresh water was heaven, topped by a shower under a waterfall.

Skradin waterfalls

In Skradin we had to go to the doctor with Lizzie's beesting, as her arm was really swollen and she was in pain. We were old hands at Croatian doctors; Finn had been in Dubrovnik hospital in 2006 and John had already twice visited a hospital on this trip with pneumonia. The health service is great. The waiting room etiquette initially was difficult—this language is super tricky—but we eventually understood how it worked. A very competent female doctor prescribed antibiotics and antihistamines, all good.

In the classical seaside resort Primosten we put the anchor out first, but then spotted abandoned mooring blocks without ropes underneath the hull, so John dove down and put a rope through one. The medieval town with narrow streets is dominated by a gothic church on a hill and is crawling with tourists, but you can get a good meal anywhere you try. No Croatian evening is complete without live music; all communities seem to invest heavily in the entertainment of their guests. But it is no folk music; there is usually a band or a DJ blasting rock favourites or house music at top watts in a central location. In Primosten it was a Bruce Springsteen impersonator; it could have been worse.

Together

When we sailed to the island of Vis five years ago the little village of Kut in the entrance was a well kept secret, but not any longer. We were early and had no problems finding a spot on the stone quay, but the places filled up quickly and soon crews were lingering in the new fancy bars on the waterfront. We made our way into the back streets again and booked a table at fish restaurant Pojoda. The waiter showed us the biggest snapper we had ever seen. The fillet alone weighed two kilos. We had to have it! All of it.

Pojoda snapper

Only a week to go, we revisited another favourite. Hvar is Croatia's Saint Tropez, and the very bumpy town quay hosted an impressive selection of super yachts from all over the world. Our choice again was the ACI marina Palmizana on the Pakleni islands, a short water taxi ride from Hvar. A few new dresses for the girls, a pizza on the town square, our sort of luxury.

Its sister island, Brac, was our last destination before heading for Split at the end of this part of our journey. The incredible mountain landscape served as backdrop to our visit of the idyllic village Pučišća where we joined the locals in a busy public harbour pool and played ball.

Pučišča

Pučišča is known as "Stone City" where the famous "white gold of Brac" is broken here, a very pure limestone which has even been used for the White House in Washington, DC.

Split had seemed grotty and unpleasant when we were last there. It couldn't have been more different this time. The marina building had been renovated, and the little water taxi chugged into town every half hour. The fruit and vegetable market was as colourful as ever, but the highlight was the terrace restaurant above the marina, overlooking the Adriatic, that served excellent food at affordable prices. On that terrace we felt a million dollars, on holiday, just good.

Split restaurant

Chapter 8.
Arriving in Copenhagen

A tight fit

August 3, the car was packed, not even a biscuit would fit. The kids were barely visible amongst the bags, cushions, and bedding on the back seat. They had something to read and snacks on their laps. I had left plenty of time from Stade, Germany, up to Puttgarden near Lübeck and on to the ferry across to Rødby in Denmark. But due to road works on the German motorway we missed the ferry and had to take one later; no problem about the reservation, though. On the Danish side torrential rain; after seven hours we finally arrived. I found a close-by parking spot in the quiet street, and the kids helped unpack the car; they were very excited. We collected the house key from the supermarket cashier on the corner and almost collapsed. Within a few hours everything was put away, what a relief.

Brobergsgade 3

Having moved countries twice before and therefore knowing what it's like, Copenhagen made it easy for us to love it. The flat in Brobergsgade 3 was even nicer than I remembered, very close to a Christianshavn canal full of sailing boats. Our landlady, Tina, and baby Perry were already in the States, but we had pizza with Heiko and daughter Maibritt at the canal before they left, and Finn and Maibritt really clicked. Soon they were both hanging out on her bunk bed reading books. He does get on well with clever girls, not a bad thing.

Finn & Maibritt

Our new home occupied the two lowest stories of a house with twelve parties, part of a big rectangular art deco block of flats. The inner yard was huge, enclosed, and had its own playground that the kids could reach through a back door in the flat. Our flat had three bedrooms, a study, living room, one bathroom, and a huge kitchen in the basement. The kids felt at home at once and started playing with Maibritt's Playmobil, and Maibritt soon joined in. She and her dad, Heiko, were staying with neighbours before flying to the States. So he could tell me all there was to know about the flat.

Copenhagen living room

The location of Brobergsgade in Christianshavn had seemed far away from the school on the map, but actually couldn't have been more convenient. The huge bakery near the Metro had an amazing range of bread, rolls, and cake, and the supermarket on the main square was close by and with not a bad selection. Apart from supermarkets, most shops had a number system similar to the Australian Road Traffic Authority's, where you pull a number out of a machine at the entrance and then know exactly when your turn is. Quite clever.

Our first dinner was fried fish on salad. The children already felt very comfortable, but Lizzie soon stormed into the study shouting excitedly, "I can hear the people above us." I was only glad there was nobody below us, so they couldn't hear our children stomping, only yelling. Living in a house like this with numerous other parties reminded me of my student days in Hamburg. It was completely different from our life in Hunters Hill, especially for the children.

Kitchen idyll

From the cosy kitchen in the basement we could see the people walk by and from the curtainless study and living room windows observe the action on the street just below us. There was a little supermarket right next to our house and uncountable bicycles on the pavement in front of the house; everybody cycles everywhere here. I thought, "If I can't get a resident parking permit I will drive the car back to Germany as I won't be needing it during the week. Only for excursions at the weekend."

Despite the fact that the free state "Christiania" was only one street away, our landlord assured me that the area was really safe. Theft is really uncommon. Christiania is a big area that has been occupied by squatters since the 1970s with lots of stalls and shops offering hippie stuff, marihuana, or other greenie things. It is now also a major tourist attraction. I had to buy my wood blocks there for the heating in winter.

I had taken my parents' German-registered car to Copenhagen for the move, not realizing what a problem that would be. We live in the European Union, don't we? No big deal. After the first parking ticket of 750 Danish crowns, I realized that it was resident parking almost everywhere in Christianshavn where we were living, and so I parked the car far away at a sports ground. To get a resident parking ticket you had to fill in some council forms, pretty straight-forward, unless you had a foreign car. Then you had a problem. Foreign cars had to be registered in Denmark and possibly a luxury tax paid on them something like two weeks after your arrival. You could apply with the tax office for a permit to drive a foreign car in Denmark (what did they have to do with it?), but chances were slim that it would be granted. I applied for that permit and never heard anything. The car was still at the sports ground months later and I checked every few weeks that it hadn't been nicked. Two months later a rear window was smashed.

CHAPTER 9.

COPENHAGEN HISTORY AND DANISH QUIRKS

In my completely biased opinion, Copenhagen is the most charming of Scandinavian capitals, easily discovered on foot or by boat. A low silhouette of ancient buildings in warm colors dominates the centre. The several-kilometres-long pedestrian shopping street Strøget gives easy access to shopping, palaces, museums, churches, the fun park Tivoli, and the restaurant quarter Nyhavn.

Old Stock Exchange

Copenhagen is the capital of Denmark with an urban population of 1.2 million people; overall there are only 5.6 million Danes. The city is seen as one of the most livable cities in the world. And Copenhagen is also considered one of the world's most environmentally friendly cities. The water in the inner harbour is clean and safe for swimming. Thirty-six percent of all citizens commute to work by bicycle. Every day, they cycle a combined 1.2 million km. In the last decade or so Copenhagen has added an opera house, new theatre, and huge library to its urban landscape and has even been described as a boom town. Not only due to the massive investments in cultural facilities and infrastructure but because of a new wave of successful designers, chefs, and architects. The world's best restaurant, Noma, is located in Christianshavn, just around the corner from our flat.

Copenhagen's founding has traditionally been dated to Bishop Absalon's construction of a castle on the small island of Slotsholmen in 1167 where Christiansborg Palace stands today. Recent archaeological finds indicate that by the eleventh century, Copenhagen had already grown into a small town with a large estate, a church, a market, at least two wells, and many smaller habitations spread over a fairly wide area.

Many historians believe that the town dates to the late Viking age and was possibly founded by Sweyn I Forkbeard. From the middle of the twelfth century it grew in importance after coming into Absalon's possession, who fortified it in 1167, the year traditionally marking the foundation of Copenhagen. The excellent harbour encouraged Copenhagen's growth until it became an important centre of commerce. However, it did not become the nation's capital until the middle of the fifteenth century, and the archbishop still has a residence in Roskilde.

The city's origin as a harbour and a place of commerce is reflected in its name. Its original designation, from which the contemporary Danish name is derived, was Køpmannæhafn, meaning "merchants' harbour" or "buyer's haven" (German "Kaufmannshafen"). The English name for the city is derived from its Low German name, Kopenhagen. As the town rose in prominence, it was repeatedly attacked by the Hanseatic League. In 1254 it received its charter as a city. During 1658 and '59 it withstood a siege by the Swedes and successfully repelled major assault. In 1711 the plague reduced Copenhagen's population of about 65,000 by one-third.

CHRISTIAN IV

Denmark is the oldest monarchy in the world, not a well-known fact. Living in Copenhagen you can't avoid learning something about King Christian IV, the architect king, as he is known. Most famous old buildings in Copenhagen were built by him, and he almost bankrupted the country with his projects. "Christian IV (12 April 1577–28 February 1648) was the king of Denmark-Norway from 1588 until his death. With a reign of more than 59 years, he is the longest-reigning monarch of Denmark, and he is frequently remembered as one of the most popular, ambitious, and proactive Danish kings, having initiated many reforms and projects."[3]

Young Christian, the six-year-old future king of Denmark, started his school life as Lizzie did in mid-August at his local primary school near the royal palace. The photos show him fidgeting between his parents like any lively six-year-old—trouble ahead.

I did get a few gossip mags with photos of "our Australian" Mary, Fredrik, and the kids and eventually bought a book about Queen Margrethe's forty years on the Danish throne. The Danes love their royal family. And lots of elderly women on the street look just like the queen.

3 Wikipedia

THE DANES, FROM THE *XENOPHOBES GUIDE TO THE DANES*

"The Danes are seen as the epitome of good order and good sense. They are not very excitable or romantic, they have neat painted houses in neat countryside and wear sensible shoes – a bit like the Swiss but without the mountains. Their language is unlearnable, and once their lack of tact is forgiven, everyone likes the Danes. They have a huge sense of social responsibility, the touchstone of any activity or point of view is whether it is socially useful.

"The Danes have confidently liberated themselves from the petty forms of etiquette and the residue of subservience which still passes for manners in other societies. They are not hamstrung by politeness. When confronted with obnoxious lunatics [of which there seem to be a lot on the streets, observation by Karen], epilepsy or the victims of street violence the average Englishman will purse his lips like a prune and scurry across to the other side of the street. A Dane will steam in and clean up the mess.

"The Danes do not appreciate lateness. When they are invited somewhere they turn up strictly at the specified time if not before.

"Queuing is disliked. Nothing makes a Dane happier than if an additional checkout opens and he can beat other contenders to the conveyor belt. No one bats an eye lid.

"However, Danish society is consensual rather than adversarial. Danes cooperate.

"Danes are Olympic drinkers – it even says so in 'Hamlet.' It is possible to buy drink without difficulty 24 hours a day. You see people drinking beer at 6 am on the street or any other time of the day. The launch of Tuborg's snow beer in November causes national celebration.

"Children don't wear school uniforms but they don't need to as from the age of six months they are dressed alike anyway. Clothing is index-linked to the weather forecast. By the time children start school the parents are fully aware of the advantages of practical, washable, 100% waterproof, thermal, wool-lined garments that fasten with Velcro."[4]

Those are quotes from this entertaining book. What I can add is that the Danes are extremely family minded and kid friendly. They ooze relaxedness and are not as uptight as the Germans. I haven't seen any obese people, maybe because everybody is on their bikes.

In terms of the ethnic mix on the street, obviously the majority is Danes; you see very few Asians, but there are more African people than in Australia. We noticed a lot of homeless, drunk, or deranged people. Lizzie was always pointing at crazies while I dragged her on, but this was the inner city.

To my surprise my Danish was sufficient to get me by in all everyday situations. People understood what I wanted, and I could even have a Danish conversation with my massage therapist, who did not speak English. The kids learned Danish phrases and songs, but the time in Copenhagen was too short for them to really learn the language.

SHOPPING

Copenhagen is no. 4 in one of the top ten lists of most expensive cities in the world. Just going to the bakery is outrageously expensive. We collected the bakery receipts, and when one thousand Danish crowns had been spent we got a free cake. We got quite a few of those during our stay. So I wasn't too tempted by the usual brand name stores on the Strøget. We still managed to spend a truckload of money on not that much: a new raincoat, winter boots for the kids, Christmas presents for all. I could, however, not resist my favourite Copenhagen store Illums Bolighus that has design wares for the home and was right next to porcelain legend Royal Copenhagen. Most of the products are "Made in Denmark": there are very few poor-quality Chinese goods.

---

4 *Xenophobe's Guide to the Danes*, London 2011

Bakery display

Transport

Did we love the Metro? You bet. Only a recent addition to Copenhagen's public transport net, it was our daily mode of transport to school and elsewhere. It is deep below the ground with long, very steep escalators. You need to clip a ticket, and ticket controls are frequent. There would be fifteen strong guys with black bomber jackets at the top of the escalators checking your ticket, and the many offenders were lined up and fined on the spot, very efficient. We rarely took a bus, but sometimes we rode the S-tog train to the central station and to Tivoli. I walked and walked, did something for my fitness, and enjoyed the architecture and water views of my walk from Christianshavn across the bridge toward Christiansborg castle and the Strøget.

BICYCLING

Initially our experience with cycling was limited to not getting killed by a bicycle in this city of two-wheelers. As we were waiting for Lizzie's bicycle seat to arrive from Germany I constantly pulled my children back from the pavement edge where commuters whizzed by at breakneck speed. The sheer quantity of people cycling to work was astounding and their speed scary. Fortunately there were dedicated traffic lights for them, but one-way streets and pedestrian zones were full of traffic-law-breaking bikes. I was nervous, as I would soon be guiding my nine-year-old through the bicycle rush hour to school and didn't know the unwritten rules yet.

Instead of the seat, wheel, pedals, and bar that would convert Tina's bicycle into a sort of tandem for Lizzie and me, I could have invested in a Christiania bike that has a wooden box at the front and takes two children, comes with a rain hood, and looks fabulous. Lots of people with children had them, despite the fact that you could buy a car for the price of one. The hippies of Christiania charge outrageous prices, so I abandoned that idea.

CHAPTER 10.

SCHOOL – THE BIG ISSUE

"He who opens a school door, closes a prison."
Victor Hugo

After having worked our way through a mountain of books on Asperger, we are still of two minds as to where on the autism spectrum Finn is. His condition is quite light, we believe, and are adamant that his Aspergers should not become an excuse for unacceptable behaviour. His confirmed high intelligence has and will help him compensate for social insecurities. Also our very busy household with friends coming and going at all times has conditioned him from an early age to accept a lot of different people around him. In contrast to usual Aspergers behaviour he will look strangers and friends in the eye and greet them properly. He enjoys his friends' company and is not a loner. He tries not to dominate play, and in team sports he does his best. He does not seem to be very sound sensitive and doesn't often show unusual repetitive behaviour.

Things are not that bad at all, we know now. He will just need more explaining and patience, we believe. The school in

Copenhagen, however, didn't accommodate our special boy with what we hoped would be an open mind and helpful attitude.

Sankt Petri Skole school yard

"What do you mean he is going to be in year 4?" My husband, John, looked at me reading from a school letter, incredulous. When it had sunk in that Finn was going to be put a grade higher than his age and abilities, I immediately contacted the school. Talking to the principal was not as easy as in Australia where you could speak to her on the school ground every day or be put through from the office. Here I had to explain my issues to the receptionist, and then the principal would call me back on my mobile, likely when I was shopping or at other inconvenient times.

The headmistress told me firmly that year 3 was full, and as we were only going to be here a few months (eight, actually), year 4 it would be. Notwithstanding the fact that we had visited the school in early June and she had happily agreed on the years 3 and kindergarten for the kids. She conceded the situation would be reviewed after a few weeks.

First school day

A typical school day

I get the kids up around 6:00 and we leave at 7:15, walk past the bakery to get their morning tea, same two white rolls for Finn and different Danish pastries for Lizzie, and by Metro get to the school at 7:45. The kids go straight to their classrooms; there is no line up, no announcements, no teachers. Interestingly most kids get dropped off by their fathers on their way to work in the morning. At 8:00 lessons start that each last forty-five minutes; for German, Danish, sport, and English there is a double lesson once a week. Today Finn has mathematics, religion, German, Danish, and sport. In the two big breaks the boys play soccer in the churchyard against the big boys—the school goes up to year 10. Lizzie finishes at 1:00, Finn at 2:00, so in between Lizzie and I do some shopping as the pedestrian shopping street is only five minutes from the school. Almost all children go into after-school care, which you have to sign up for, for the whole year, which I didn't do. Finn's teacher I never see; you communicate through a contact book. Lizzie's year gets delivered to the classroom by the parents as it is their first year, so I can talk to the teacher.

Only a few weeks after our arrival in Copenhagen I vented my frustrations in our blog. *Naturally not all things could run smoothly here as they wouldn't with such a drastic move. The German school did not do the right thing by Finn. The headmistress is arrogant and unapproachable, you don't get appointments and you get lucky if she phones back at some stage. So after I had talked to all of Finn's teachers and got the clear impression that year 4 is not the right thing for him, she has decided that that's where he is going to stay. He has been frequently bullied by classmates and older boys in the first few weeks, which with his Asperger will be the story everywhere, but it still is very hard as he so wants to fit in and make friends. The decision if Lizzie can move up one class has also been made, it's a firm no. Very disappointing all in all, and it would be very upsetting for Finn if I had to pull him back one year once we get back, and with Lizzie I am unsure now which year she should rejoin Hunters Hill in.*

On school day two I cornered Finn's teacher on the stairs and asked if she had gotten the school reports and other material I had sent in for her information. "No," she said, astonished.

"You do realize he has Aspergers," I wanted to know. Another surprised no. We made an appointment for the next day to talk through his issues. I also copied again all the information I had submitted. The school office turned out not to be very organised.

Finn had two class teachers, Naomi and Pia, the latter being hostile from the start. But despite Naomi's friendliness she did not discipline the bullies in her class after major incidents. The tone was set within the first few weeks.

Aspergians get bullied; they are odd and attract teasing and pushing around, and are easy to wind up as they take everything literally. Finn soon had distressing situations at the school in Copenhagen, such as being held down by some boys while he was filmed with a mobile phone after he refused to kiss another boy. His head was crashed into a wall. Or he was chased into the toilets, the toilet door then broken down. And much more.

Finn's class room

No sympathy from the authorities, though. After Finn had given a little speech in front of his class explaining about his Aspergers, it seems some parents called the school to inquire/complain about this special needs kid in their child's class. So the school suggested an explanatory letter about Finn by me should be sent to all parents.

Soon I realized the school tolerated bullying. In the year above Finn's, half of the class had left the year before because of bullying. And dealing with the headmistress, I soon understood why.

During another stressful chat with the headmistress she suggested that Finn shouldn't participate in the school sport week. So I took the children to my parents instead. That woman was a bully!

My parents' house

After the drama at the school, a whole September week in my hometown of Stade was bliss and relaxation for everybody. I went to Hamburg just for the day and caught up with my friend Axel at the magazine *Der Spiegel*, where I used to work, a few days before the offices moved buildings and the 1970s canteen was transferred to the design museum. Great to have lunch there before that happened.

I also caught up with several members of my yacht club commodore Fifi Schaper's family. I had been great friends with his daughters Undine and Cathrin but hadn't seen them for twenty-five years. They still live on the harbour front in Oevelgönne, Hamburg. It was like travelling back in time for me. On Saturday I met up with Hans Martin, just returned from his Atlantic circuit, and my oldest friend, Antje. Just as thirty years ago, Antje and I went to the harbour festival in Wedel, talked to lots of people only slightly aged, sang along to the 1970s band Sailor, and had a good time.

Antje and I

CHAPTER 11.

EVERYDAY LIFE

At the end of September, almost two months into our stay, life was ticking along fairly normally, with school five days a week and often visitors at the weekend.

Due to the fact that in most families both parents work, Danish children have to be more independent. Most children in Finn's year 4 arrived at school by themselves after having taken a bus or the Metro. For a play date on Saturday, Finn's friend Philip arrived after a long Metro trip and watched the time himself to get back home for dinner. Soon I did not collect Finn from school after guitar lessons in the afternoon but let him take the metro by himself. He was really proud of being able to make this journey alone, looked after his ticket, and was back by the time I expected him.

One of the most positive aspects of our stay in Copenhagen was our season ticket for the fun park Tivoli. I had enjoyed its attractions numerous times as a child, and my kids quickly got addicted to its fairy tale ambience too. Tivoli occupies a big parkland area next to the central station Hovedbanegården. It is a world famous amusement park and pleasure garden and very old, having opened on August 15, 1843. It is nothing like Disneyland, but has more old-fashioned entertainment like an enchanting pantomime, the oldest roller coaster in the world, made out of wood, but also some modern rides. Danes of all ages flock to the park on balmy summer evenings, eat, drink, and dance. Lanterns illuminate the little lakes where kids steer Chinese junks in circles. We went whenever we could, summer and also in winter, when it opened for just four weeks and hosted a Christmas market with real reindeer.

Horse racing in Tivoli

"It is a curious story, really." So titled the introduction of a book about Christiania. When visitors from Germany or Australia arrived we did Copenhagen's main sights, differing ones depending on our guests' interests. But we always went to Christiania, a five minutes' walk from our flat. It calls itself a free state within Copenhagen, an alternative community that in 2011 was celebrating its 40th birthday and went public with a share offering. Christiania covers an area of about 34 ha only five minutes from the bustling centre of Copenhagen. The first thing you see when entering Christiania is Pusherstreet. It is the most famous street in the free town and has had a turbulent history. Foreigners can't believe their eyes but in this street cannabis is openly sold from little tables, although hard drugs were banned in 2004. For years the free-spirited enclave attracted many poorly socialised individuals, for instance homeless Inuit from Greenland. It all began in the late 1960s when a bunch of hippies moved into the area of abandoned army barracks under the bemused eyes of Copenhagen's bourgeois citizens. After a number of years and great efforts to renovate the buildings and develop the area, the Christianians felt they had the right to use the area, now bursting with colours and culture. And after many conflicts and street fights with police and four decades of illegal squatting, a "normalisation process" was announced. Today there are still jugglers, artists, vendors, dealers, and theatres, music and dope but also community meetings, a school and kindergarten for kids born in Christiania, and the share offering in 2011.

Since the shares have been offered, more than a million have been sold, and the proceeds go toward buying the land from the government.

When visiting Christiania, where taking photos is forbidden, you expect rasta locks and hippie attire. But the majority of Danes seem to wear black, jackets, coats, etc., maybe to be better seen in the forthcoming snow? The hashish dealers have shaved heads and black jackets and do look slightly menacing. Lots of big dogs run around, and fires burn in oil drums. But today the free town is a really safe place and one of Copenhagen's major tourist attractions.

My diary says in October: *"One has to say though that it rains virtually every day, yesterday, when I was just getting on my bicycle to collect the kids from school, this morning for the last five minutes before getting to school. We stayed halfway dry but a lot of the kids cycling to school got drenched and would be sitting in their classrooms with wet trousers all day. No wonder they don't get colds as easy as we get in Australia, they toughen up every day. Yesterday was a day of great successes in my small world. We cycled to school and back, I was very nervous and it wasn't easy to cycle straight with Lizzie on the back, as well as her backpack, Finn's sports bag and my handbag. If you don't cycle straight and keep to the right an over-taker will likely mow you down. Finn also kept up well behind me and Lizzie when she wasn't talking was the designated spotter to turn around and see where Finn was. We got there and back in one piece and didn't get wet. No cycling today as we have swimming after school. The second major success was getting a trolley load of wood bricks from Christiania. While I was load-ing the wood there was an English guided tour in the shed, the tourists looked at me wide eyed likely picturing me dragging my load into my ramshackle communal house share. I felt very hippie. In the afternoon Lizzie's parent teacher interview went very well, no problem there. Interestingly on the list to put your names down for the interviews it was 80% fathers attending the interviews by themselves. A recent birthday party for a boy in Lizzie's class was also organised and hosted by the father though the mother attended."*

Cycling – an adventure

By early October autumn really had arrived with wind, cold, and flying leaves. Everybody was looking forward to John's arrival. At school Lizzie did crafts with chestnuts, making little animals, and sang autumn songs. Finn and I practised multiplication and division, hopeful for some good results. Maths is really hard as he is a year behind.

SWIMMING

What would we have done without Marlene? The kids needed to continue swimming lessons if they didn't want to fall irreparably behind in Australia. But in this country surrounded by water formal swimming lessons are hard to come by, and the kids start to swim much later than in Australia. Without success I contacted the main public pool, tried this and that, and then mailed the Australian embassy for help. They gave me a list of Copenhagen swim schools. Marlene ran the one in Frederiksberg, but she couldn't give me much hope initially. I got us onto a list and waited. A few weeks later she phoned to say we were in, slightly spaced out on a Thursday afternoon so that we had to splash in the pool between lessons for an hour. It was a done deal. John later had the times adjusted so that Lizzie, the Australian freestyler, was in a more advanced group and the wait between classes wasn't so long.

HOW DO THEY LIVE?

Every Danish woman I met said to me: "You don't work? So what are you going to do with yourself all day?"

Little did they know that I don't work back home either and most of my girl friends don't. Danish women have to work because housing is so expensive and taxes are sky high. Their men share the housework and the kids in equal parts, and cycling to work and having all the shopping at your doorstep makes logistics easier than driving all day between Australian suburbs Gladesville, Lane Cove, and Chatswood. Also the after-school care in Denmark is outstanding, and a lot of the children go to the "Fritidshjem" (direct translation "free time's home") all afternoon. Taxes have to be so high to pay for the welfare system, including child care, a vicious circle.

Another observation: Danish design is legendary, and people are well dressed, or look like real eccentrics. There is no apparent cheap culture. However, everybody wearing wellies is not out of necessity but a fashion craze from Paris that has also washed over to Germany and here. I am glad I didn't buy some.

SIGHTSEEING

Nyhavn

We only visited Copenhagen's major attractions when we had visitors. But that happened frequently, and we saw what we considered important and returned to the favourites. One of the "must do's" in our Copenhagen sightseeing program was a one-hour harbour trip on a canal boat from Nyhavn that went past our house, the royal Danish yacht *Dannebrog*, and the Little Mermaid.

Royal yacht *Dannebrog*

The kids loved to run up and down the ramp of the Rundetårn, the Round Tower, from 1642. From the top one has a great view of the city.

Rundetårn

In our immediate Christianshavn neighbourhood the spiralling tower of the Vor Frelsers Kirke just had to be climbed, Finn decided. Lizzie and I aborted the attempt halfway up due to vertigo whereas Finn made it to the top, even climbing the outside staircase.

Vor Frelsers Kirke

Another worthwhile destination for visitors was Rosenborg Slot, built as a summer house for Christian IV from 1606–34. Today the Renaissance castle houses the crown jewels and well preserved ancient royal apartments.

Hans Christian Andersen's Little Mermaid is a small statue near Langelinie harbour. To avoid the tourist masses we visited her early in the morning on a grey winter's day.

Little Mermaid

IMMIGRATION

Danish politics are complicated, and there are often different large coalitions in government. I did not get a daily newspaper and enjoyed my news free bubble. But I did know that the Danes elected a new prime minister while we were in Copenhagen, the first female leader, and there was the general expectation that the antiforeigner stance of the previous government would be softened.

John had not been able to be with us due to tough immigration laws and kept working in Sydney, which was hard on us all. We telephoned as often as we could, almost daily, but Skype was unreliable and didn't work with the camera at all. And with the big time difference it was hard to find a time when we were both chirpy and upbeat and not tired and grumpy. Long-distance relationships are not for us, we knew that before. But John earned good money while we were away and laid the financial base for our ten months on the boat.

My visits to the Borgerservice, the all-powerful administration that deals with passports, foreigners, and more, were relatively successful. To get our new passports I had to go to the big building on H. C. Andersens Boulevard four times, once with the kids. In my almost fluent Danish I could make myself understood, and although we as overseas born Danes were a special case, there was no doubt we would get the all-important CPR number that we frequently had to show in shops, administrations, and elsewhere, and also our passports. On top of that I would get some child benefit, which was very welcome. The first lot of passports arrived and showed the place of birth for the children as Germany instead of Australia. That was clearly wrong, so back I went. The new passports came by mail, and I breathed a sigh of relief—a major goal of this trip had been achieved.

NORTHERN AUTUMN

There are a few nice things about Northern European autumns, and German schools make the most of them nowadays, the same as they did forty-five years ago when I went to primary school. There are leaves and chestnuts. Then and now school children collect leaves from various trees, press them between book pages, and learn what they are. Lizzie and her class also collected vast numbers of chestnuts and with matches made little animals out of them.

Autumn

Another positive thing about autumn is the occasional fog that creates a mysterious atmosphere. And also one can fly kites, which doesn't work as well in an inner Copenhagen school yard as it did on the hill behind my parents' house. The flip side to autumn is the chilling cold and growing darkness.

Chapter 12.

The Eating Problem

Finn

Finn's diet is catastrophic, has been for the last seven years. No dietician, psychologist or hypnotherapist has made a difference in changing his eating behaviour. And all my attempts to make him try something new have also been in vain. He eats no meat, no fish, no pasta, no rice, no vegetables, no fruit, no yogurt, no cheese, nothing with grains. Just plain bread and hot chips.

While still in Sydney I had signed Finn up with the online consulting website of a clinic in Graz, Austria, specializing in small children's eating disorders, mainly tube weaning. Finn's gastro specialist had recommended we see somebody there, and after months and months of e-mailing without any new ideas on how to change his restricted diet we decided to bite the bullet and spend the money on a three-week intensive course there at the beginning of the new year. Later we abandoned the plan as we were not sure that the therapy would be successful.

The appointment at the Rigshospital, Copenhagen's biggest hospital, with a paediatrician about Finn's eating and sending him to Graz was interesting. Finding the clinic in that vast hospital was difficult, as there were no receptionists, so we wandered aimlessly about for a while. The paediatrician gave us no hope of getting public funds to go to Graz as the doctors there had not published anything about how they help children like Finn in any scientific journals. We wouldn't pay more than ten thousand euros ourselves on a faint hope, so that chapter closed.

The Danish specialist, however, helped me a lot: "You won't make him eat, not at this age. You have to try to use more supplements." We have a new big Lego box and star chart to try to get some supplements down. He lives now on three plain bread rolls, two croissants, and a portion of chips per day. So be it.

Reading Aspergers help books has made me learn and discover a lot of things about myself and come to the conclusion that I have a light form of Aspergers as well, but like so many of my generation, I was never diagnosed.

I have always seemed to be a bit different, and as a friend once described my relationship to others, "People either love you or hate you." I used to be very picky about food, but this got much better in adulthood. Had the same paranoia about bits, pips, and fish bones that Finn has. Am terrible at auditory processing, can't learn and understand by listening, have to see the information in front of me. Can't take part in discussions with several people, am much better one to one. And have a surprising ability to guess what people will say next, eg in movies or discussions. John might offer me to a circus soon. The things you learn about yourself late in life.

CHAPTER 13.

ITALY – AN INTERLUDE WITH DAD

"Italy, and the spring and first love all together should suffice to make the gloomiest person happy." Bertrand Russell

John came over for the October school holidays and we decided to escape the chill and take the kids to Italy. On a Friday in mid-October we got up in the middle of the night, drove my parents' car, now christened "Luna," in a fast two hours to the ferry to Germany, watched the red dawn break while having breakfast in the ferry cafeteria, and drove on to Hamburg-Altona. Here John put "Luna" onto a car train, drove past pedestrians, shops, and bakeries in a real Blues Brothers moment while we stood by and watched.

Hamburg-Altona station

We found our comfortable compartment that would be home for the next twenty-four hours. Leaving at lunchtime we read books, watched the scenery, drew pictures, and napped. I ate in the dining car by myself as nobody else wanted to (all those snacks), and we soon got the compartment ready for sleeping.

"I want to be on top, I want to be on top." Five bunks could be folded out. A great adventure for the kids. No problem sleeping for any of us to the chug, chug, chug of the wheels. The Alps in the morning looked majestic, and the fresh bread rolls and jam for breakfast were delicious. We left the train at around eleven to pick up the car from a different platform in Verona.

Sylvia, our trusty GPS navigator, soon led us into the maze of Verona's old town, where we with some difficulty found the Hotel Accademia. Our two interconnecting rooms overlooked a beautiful sunny courtyard, and the beds looked inviting. But no resting here; off to see the amphitheatre, Verona's main attraction apart from Romeo and Juliet's balcony, which we gave a miss. The arena was impressive, well preserved and good fun to run around in.

Finn had his picture taken with two Roman legionaries (soldiers in the ancient Roman army) before we had a pizza on the main square. This is the life—Italy, sunshine, good food. Due to fantastic kids TV in the room, John and I sneaked away in the evening and sampled some glasses of the local Valpolicella in a very authentic wine bar.

The next morning it dawned on John that Australia would play New Zealand in the Rugby World Cup, and how could he watch it? So I moved heaven and earth to find a pub with live coverage and sat him amongst a small expat crowd. He got back at noon, really pissed off as the Wallabies had lost, and he continued to be grumpy all day, great result. Arrivederci, Verona!

After a two-and-a-half-hour drive we reached Florence, through hills and tunnels, difficult driving but lovely countryside. We got lost a bit but finally found the Hotel Kraft, old-fashioned and nicer than expected, the kids in one bed head to feet in our room. The hotel had a great roof terrace with an icy pool and a great view of the surrounding hills in the famous soft light.

I had avoided travelling to Florence in my younger days; the tales of tourists en masse had put me off. John, however, had enjoyed his lengthy stay here in the year 2000. With the kids we were there for just three days of sightseeing, which seemed much harder than Venice in June, maybe because of a lack of water views. Or because of the crowds. It was a ten-minute walk to the centre, and on our first stroll along the Arno River a young guy walked toward us with a big, black pig on a red leash. Hilarious!

Pig in Florence

Ponte Vecchio was full of jewelers and the displays a bit over-whelming; on day two I managed to find a pair of green quartz ear-rings. We discovered an old-fashioned horse carousel on the Piazza de la Republica and had plenty of gelato. We didn't buy anything in the Armani shop but both John and I got new belts near the cathedral. John was disappointed that we didn't see any Florentine beavers (huge water rats) as he had on his previous visit.

The horse carriage ride through the old city, like the gondola in Venice, was worth the money. The Duomo, however, is splen-did outside but disappointing inside, after all that waiting. The queues were horrific, I had prebooked tickets for most sites, and we still waited for over an hour. Uffizi and Accademia could only be called hard work with children (not another Madonna!). And finally, sambuca in an unobtrusive local bar still tasted as nice as I remember.

It is hard to find acceptable food in a touristy town like Florence, but to our surprise the Gilli restaurant on the main square served good enough Italian food and a lovely rose wine to calm our nerves. Also the view from the hotel terrace in the evening was beautiful and the pool freezing, but not cold enough to stop the Australian children from hopping in, although very briefly. Our new little DVD player didn't do *Lord of the Rings* justice on the small screen, but we all watched it in bed together anyway.

Off to see some friends. We drove to Croce di Poggibonsi, Colle Val d' Elsa, near Siena where Joe and Frances Vescio were renting a house for nine months with their children. They were doing the same as we were, connecting to their roots for the kids' sake. By coincidence our friends Greg and Sigrid were also in Italy, and the Vescios organized for us all to stay with them. The Vescios lived in a hilltop wine resort closed for the winter. They had one flat, we another (two beds, two baths, one kitchen), and the Patches were next door in a third.

The view over to San Gimignano was picture postcard. Tuscany with its wine and delicacies is rightly a popular travel destination. We stayed for two days; while the three guys started to work on Hunters Hill council affairs, we mothers chatted nonstop and the kids got on like fire. We drove to San Gimignano for the day, bought wine and wild boar salami, and admired the stuffed pigs in the displays.

Pig in San Gimignano

We had lovely meals out and at the ranch, culminating in a feast at the house where the chef produced a multicourse meal with wine tasting.

On the road again I decided driving holidays were not for me as the street manners in Italy were bad and the Italians overtook in any situation—preferably when there was oncoming traffic and no room on the very narrow streets and motorways. The drive to Imperia took four hours—great mountain scenery—past Carrara's marble, through numerous tunnels, up the hill above Imperia to Diano Marina where my friend Nuschi lives with her partner, Otto. They produced a fantastic pasta and barbecue lunch for us and we caught up with a few glasses of wine on their balcony with a panoramic view. Nuschi is an artist, and I viewed her latest paintings while Otto showed Finn how to shoot with a real crossbow. We drove to Imperia for ice cream, Nuschi and I in her little convertible feeling thirty years younger.

But we wouldn't stay overnight; unpacking the car again seemed too much. On to Nice for two hours, into the darkness, not a good drive. Too many lights, tunnels, cars. We managed to find Heather and Milen's flat and collapsed there. I hadn't seen their beautiful daughter Siena, my goddaughter, now two, since she was a baby. And Heather and I put the world to right until three o'clock in the morning, only stopped by Siena waking up. Did I have a monster hangover the next morning, a reminder of the golden days of Dow Jones, where Heather and I would party and then go to work at 7:00 am the next day.

John and I had our first date in Antibes in 2000; I flew into Nice that September. We had forgotten how beautiful the Cote d'Azur was. The water, the food, and the old towns. It felt so good to be back. After breakfasting on thirty little croissants, our group drove to Villefranche and visited the Villa Ephrussi de Rothschild that towers on a cliff top in amazing gardens. Located on a peninsula with panoramic views to bays on either side, the house is spectacular with its fountains synchronized to classical music. Water features, Japanese gardens, antique furniture, and a story to the house that was left to the French public by its owner, Baroness Beatrice, who took seven years to build the villa. In the Nautor Swan marina nearby we looked at some boats and finished the afternoon on the beach in Villefranche where the kids dug sand castles, Milen swam, and the rest of us just relaxed.

By car train we reached Hamburg. A short visit at my parents' seemed appropriate, then another six-hour drive to Copenhagen, and our car holiday was over. It was great fun seeing all the friends. But the driving scared me, and the packing and unpacking was annoying.

CHAPTER 14.

GOOD-BYE TO COPENHAGEN

"Wonderful, wonderful Copenhagen
Friendly old girl of a town
'Neath her tavern light
On this merry night
Let us clink and drink one down
To wonderful, wonderful Copenhagen
Salty old queen of the sea...." Danny Kaye

A second update interview with the teachers and the principal had been scheduled for after the autumn break. John was still in Copenhagen, and we all amiably sat around a table when the principal opened the meeting.

"We will speak German and you will translate for your husband." The principal set the tone for what was to come. Her English was perfect, but she had sidelined John with one stroke.

Then the teachers reported on Finn's progress. One started with, "Obviously maths is a catastrophe; he can't keep up there."

I answered, "But he had top marks in his first test. Did you not speak to the maths teacher?"

They were a bit embarrassed. Then out of the blue the principal suggested that I take Finn for walks outside the school grounds to avoid conflicts twice a day at recess and lunch. What conflicts? He was playing soccer with his friends during the breaks, and he would have told me about recent incidents. What was this all about, what was she intending by asking me for an impossible task, going walking twice a day with him for half an hour in the middle of winter? Completely mad! I said to John, "We are leaving," and to the enemies' surprise we marched out of the meeting.

Consulting a lawyer John found out the German-Danish school operated outside Danish school law, so there was very little we could do against this bullying by the principal. Reluctantly we decided to cut our stay short and leave at Christmas. The sole reason being that Finn continued to be bullied and pestered, while the school made huge efforts to get rid of us as we were turning out to be difficult.

After Finn's experiences at the German school in Copenhagen we certainly said good-bye to the idea that we could school the kids at different locations in Germany, Istanbul, or elsewhere on our travels and that the transition would be easy. There would likely be no more foreign schools for Finn and certainly no German school if this was their attitude toward students with handicaps. The survival of the fittest attitude of the boys doesn't gel with Aspergers.

Friday, November 4

Thank god it's Friday. It has been a long week of spilled raspberries, lost swim bags and other everyday dramas with kids. Also we had to get used to being without John again who flew home last Friday. It's just so much nicer to have him around and be a complete family again. He had a busy three weeks here, ten days in Copenhagen and ten days on holiday in Italy and the South of France. Here in Copenhagen our general mood is a bit bleak. It is autumn now, quite cold already, the leaves are off and it is often foggy. No rain yet, though, very lucky.

John and I had left the principal's office under protest and very angry the week before. I have bumped into the headmistress twice in one week, she came over for small talk, gushed over Lizzie. And all that after her bullying has made us take the decision to leave the school and move to Germany. She doesn't know that yet, and I won't have a conversation with her again, I am not going to be pushed in a corner again. Apart from that, the week went ok until Thursday, when we had swimming. I had a lot of bags to carry, so let Finn carry his swim bag himself. And he leaves it in the Metro. I can't help myself and tell him off on the way home from the tube, and he starts to scream and defend himself and make a scene on the street. I am too tired to care. Phone the Metro lost and found office twice without result. So on Friday after school I take two fighting children first to the Dubliner Pub for lunch – that calms them down a bit – and then to the toy departments of the two main department stores. We buy a new towel. Back home completely knackered I unpack and can't find the towel, more yelling and screaming. We determine that Finn must have left the towel at the slot car track of department store Magasin du Nord. So on Saturday after the movies we go to the department store, fight our way to customer service and voila, there is the bag with the towel. Sounds easier than it was. What stress! Do I let him take responsibility for his things again? After numerous phone calls I travel to Vestamager two weeks later and collect his swim bag from the Metro lost and found office. All this in a foreign country where I don't speak the language properly.

Monday, November 14

Temperatures really dropped during the weekend, car windows were frozen over and the wind was biting. The sun was out, however, and Copenhagen looked beautiful. My friend Claudia from Düsseldorf was here, and after some shopping Saturday, on Sunday we dragged the hermit kids out of their room and made our way to the famous Little Mermaid. As it was cold and a bit grey there were no crowds in Langelinie, so I managed to take good pictures. We were all tired from walking so we hopped onto a sightseeing bus and did a lengthy tour on which we learned a bit more about Copenhagen while warming up. The Christmas market at Nyhavn was very atmospheric and Lizzie got another hat, this one looked like a racoon. We had Gloeckk, a mulled wine, and a typical Danish meal with rye bread and herring in a pub at Nyhavn. The afternoon: Harry Potter part 7 for all at home.

When I was watching Harry Potter part 2 one night last week, the one with the snake for those in the know, and everything resolved in a somewhat positive way in the end, I was thinking how hard middle age seems to be. During my relaxed 20s and pretty wild 30s my main aim in life was to become a wife to a loving man, mother of two children and carer of a Golden Retriever by the millennium. I missed that mark by two years and Pauli didn't get to retriever size but otherwise it all worked out great. Now other worries have surfaced that seem no less important than the big picture questions before. One thing is apart from the rapidly decaying looks the deteriorating middle-aged female bodies and its ailments, that are increasing and mainly incurable.

Tuesday, November 22

I'm a bit down today as they have switched off analog TV here in Denmark yesterday so my landlord's telly doesn't have any German TV any longer and only a few obscure Danish channels. As I have been by myself I have watched quite a bit of TV and really enjoyed the German series. Now I have to entertain myself solely with reading.

Finn was at the dentist Monday, traumatic, two major fillings, another appointment Friday. Dentistry and doctor services are for free here in Denmark. Lizzie is about to lose one of her front teeth so will never look the same again, gaps first, then rabbit teeth.

I gave notice to the school today, without a problem, and informed the teachers. Three weeks to go. I will drive to Stade with the first load of stuff this weekend. The Christmas decorations are out in the pedestrian zone, it gets dark at 4.30 now, so a lovely atmosphere. I have worn my red duffle coat for the second time only, first was once in Thredbo, an Australian ski town. It was just the right thing for the damp cold yesterday.

ADVENT TIME IN COPENHAGEN

The Christmas decorations in the Strøget were a bit different to the unschooled eye: big, red plastic hearts over the pedestrian zone. Illums Bolighus had beautiful Christmas items, but I only bought rotating reindeer. The department store Illums next door was copying Harrods with its window display of stuffed toys. The toy goats singing a Spanish song while waving a red lace bra and knickers must have been the Scandinavian touch. The kids also thought two girls standing naked in a fountain holding protest notes against fur totally crazy.

Lizzie in her winter outfit

After our visit to Stade on the first Advent Sunday at the end of November, my parents came back with us to Copenhagen. It was a shocking drive, very windy, the ferry was lively, and on the motorway from Rødby to Copenhagen it was hard to drive the car straight. It was raining so hard on arrival that unpacking seemed impossible and just getting to the front door left us completely soaked. Horrendous!

My parents settled into their routine of TV and reading, with Inspector Barnaby on DVD. Unfortunately my father's hearing aid didn't work again. We had a lovely meal in Skipperkroen, Nyhavn, where we had been together many times before. An attempt on Friday to go to Tivoli had to be aborted due to whinging children. We managed a meal at a steak house, but the lemonade made Finn so giddy that afterwards a woman said to him, "You must have taken drugs." Man...

I had to recover from all of that over the weekend after my parents left, and the next weekend the kids didn't even leave the house. Finn had been very difficult, sensitive, tetchy, aggressive, unreasonable, blowing up on the slightest excuse, the poor muppet. He does sleep better, though, after taking a melatonin tablet at night.

Now that we were almost gone, eight school days to go, we got lots of invites, and I finally had friendly chats with other parents from Lizzie's class. Everybody makes an effort in this first year of their child's schooling to form a good base of friendships, I have heard. We would have found some nice friends here eventually, I was sure. Germans mainly, through the school. Still my knowledge of how the Danes lived came from observations on the street. No personal contact, a shame.

When my parents were here we went to a typical Danish corner wine bar, Stærkodder or so, dark wood, hundreds of years of drinking. At lunchtime a happy crowd of pensioners hung out here, some very lubricated. My mother ventured to the bar and had to kiss a guy on the way back, which she did without flinching. He shouted us an ancient rum later. Very jolly atmosphere.

The kids still listen to Harry Potter in the afternoons while I have started to use the iPad as a book source, reading crappy novels, now that I have to rely on live stream on the computer for TV. The evenings are certainly less entertaining for me. The cold seems biting, wet and chilly. No problem keeping the house warm with the wood, though, easier than expected. I will have to go to Christiania again to get some more.

Travel plans for next year are almost in place, after numerous phone calls to Air France about changes to the March booking. When I started yelling I ended up with the supervisor who got the changes done. I have also booked the flights to Dubrovnik and hotel accommodation in Istanbul with Glenn. Lots of different places next year, exciting.

FREQUENTLY ASKED QUESTION: HOW HAS FINN BEEN?

I could be seen as a tough mother dragging my poor children, one handicapped, to a foreign, cold country for theoretical good in the future. But I do believe this sort of experience widens the horizon, and all in all Finn coped astonishingly well with the school nightmare. Very rarely did he say he didn't want to go. He made some friends and tried to keep out of trouble. He excelled academically and learned how to play the guitar. He relaxed in the afternoon and didn't have to do extracurricular activities. He slept better due to melatonin. He and his sister formed a stronger bond. The daily routine worked well. The Lego shop became his mecca and Tivoli also was fun.

Did he suffer from the bullying and unfair treatment? For sure. Was it maybe too early to learn how to deal with such situations? I don't think so. He will be bullied again, and again. The German boys gave him a real taster. Unfortunately. But he learned how to be cool, fell in love, took the Metro and bus frequently by himself, and got much more independent than any Australian boy his age would be allowed to. I am really proud of him.

Lego shop

ELIZABETH

Lizzie missed her Hunters Hill friends Liv and Jenny a lot. Fortunately she made heaps of new friends and really enjoyed playing with them. She quickly became one of the queen bees in her class and charmingly bossed everybody around. She was underchallenged in her class, effectively repeating kindergarten, and should have been one year up, but we have been writing these five months off as an experience, nothing more.

JOHN

John was stressed and busy at work, and stressed and annoyed with running his private life himself, cooking, washing, shopping, paperwork, etc. He missed us and family life a lot. On the positive side, he got invited out regularly, and our family and friends looked after him really well.

KAREN

I enjoyed being in this beautiful city that I have always loved. It was a great chance to get to know it better. Christiania was a hoot and the Strøget lovely. The daily walking was refreshing and good for my physical health. I had time for writing, reading, and my photo books. But I am still battling health issues. Also being with the kids so much wore me out They just never shut up. I needed a break from them.

COLD WEATHER

We were so lucky in that it must have been one of the driest Novembers in Danish history. Temperatures till we left Denmark at Christmas rarely went near zero. It still felt cold to us Australians but was OK with the right clothing. The twenty pairs of socks of all materials and thickness went unused in a bag as I wore woolly tights ever since the cold arrived. Both kids did the same. I had forgotten how pale one gets in a European winter, and for the first time in over a decade I had to use a tinted face cream that made me look halfway human.

Tuesday, Dec. 6

It is Nikolaustag, a day that has a sweet tradition in Germany. The children in the morning were very happy to find some gifts and sweets in their wellies left overnight outside, St. Nikolaus got just the right things. Also there would be cake at the school today to celebrate. So no complaints about the freezing cold walking to school this morning, around zero degrees I would think. Finn is still not wearing gloves, while my hands are cold even with them.

We have begun a series of goodbyes, play dates, invites, we are sorry to go now. However, the one person who has guaranteed peace, sibling cooperation, endless entertainment at home in the kids' room has been: Harry Potter. The seven audio books on maybe 100 CDs have run every afternoon and evening nonstop while Finn played Lego or read and Lizzie was drawing. At the weekends then the accompanying Harry Potter films. Lizzie is an expert now too. Five month in Denmark would have been impossible without Harry Potter.

Finn and his class are busy preparing the Christmas play that they are going to perform next Wednesday in front of the whole school. He is a banjo playing street bum, we built a banjo out of a frying pan. Eight school days to go.

Thursday, Dec. 8

When I got home from school drop off this morning I saw the big yellow graffiti on our front door, and on all the gates and houses opposite, joining other less bright sprayings from before. There are graffiti removal vans everywhere, clearly a business to be in. I do wonder about the place looking like a tip, broken bottles, human turds, rats on the street (one sighting, might have been a pet, very tame) and the graffiti. Clearly a lot is alcohol fuelled and Christianshavn is that sort of area. But I do wonder whether the kids being looked after in public institutions from an early age because the parents are both working maybe don't get told enough that you don't litter the streets and spray houses etc.

Lizzie is going on a play date with twin girls of her class this afternoon, very exciting. For just an hour she will go to after school care with them and has been quite worried what is happening there. I am sure she will have a ball. No swimming for them, our routine is dissolving.

Tuesday, Dec. 13

Our last week in Denmark is in full swing, fairly organised but with some hectic days ahead. My biggest worry is how to fit everything into the car on Friday, there is little boxes with Lego and CDs everywhere apart from all the clothes. But before I can tackle the car project we have Finn's class's Christmas play on Wednesday, one more time swimming Thursday and a few goodbyes that involve baking. It is raining, no white Christmas for us, but hopefully the Alps have snow so we can go skiing after Christmas. Have followed the current ARC rally across the Atlantic on the internet, next year it will be us, and I am looking for pointers on food and boat routine.

At the big church service on the last day of school the impertinent headmistress was heading for me again, what is it with this woman, guilt, cruelty, I just looked away. I am done with this school. A few weeks later I wrote a five page complaint letter to the foreign school authority, but she defended herself well, as expected, and nothing came off it.

Chapter 15.

Living in Stade

"There is no place like home." L. Frank Baum, *The Wonderful Wizard of Oz*

The kids and I left Copenhagen December 18 very early in the morning. The car was so full that I could not see Finn behind me and could not see or hear Lizzie at all, unless we both yelled. Our belongings were loaded up to the roof in the passenger seat and the boot, and it was clearly not safe. I decided not to buy two loaves of the delicious rye bread as it wouldn't have fit. At least I got everything out of the flat so we didn't have to come back. The drive was good in rare sunshine, but I got nicked for speeding close to Stade.

One core ingredient of a sabbatical and living overseas is the constant packing. We got used to it and quite good at it, but we always had more things than space; it's your life packed into a few bags (and boxes).

The relief to be back home was immense at this time, although later on I viewed the time in Copenhagen as a great experience. It was sad to part from new friends. Still, it was Christmas, we were in Stade, John was almost on the way. The week before Christmas was as hectic as it would be anywhere: buy and decorate tree, wrap presents, buy booze, etc. John touched down on Dec. 23 and was a bit weary after lots of work and partying.

SNOW

We got through the festive days all right (apart from the crisis around John's missing snow boots, left in Sydney) and flew to Mayrhofen, Austria, on Boxing Day to go skiing. I had been there with my parents years ago, and the hotel was as nice as I remembered it—very traditional Austrian, which seemed to be popular with the multitude of Russian guests. We hired gear, put the kids down for ski school, and the next day hit the slopes.

To get to the kids' training area you had to take a big cable cabin for 160 people. John was delighted at the height of the mountains, the snow, and the scenery. The kids got put into the same group, which Finn swallowed without a word, and we were off. John and I had two good days of skiing with only one major fall by me but no broken bones this time. I took it easy as my legs were still not the same since my accident year before last.

Then it started to snow, so goggles and neck warmers came out, and did it snow! The ski school closed, you couldn't see a thing, the usual whiteout stuff. We had that for three days and skied every day, and then another sunny day in the fresh snow. The village looked like a winter wonderland. We met up with my cousin and her husband from Holland that we hadn't seen since our wedding. New Year's Eve celebrations were lively with a load of Russians and Germans in the hotel, and the kids stayed up until 1:30 am while we were dozing on their beds. Finn fired off multiple rockets into the then rainy sky. It was a great party for all.

Back in Stade, after quick unpacking, John and I turned around and flew to London for our tenth wedding anniversary. The Dean

Street Townhouse Hotel in Soho was the right choice for a romantic break; we had nice meals, shopped till we dropped at the Harvey Nichols' sale, and saw Suzanne and her new family and our good friends Yasmin and Derek. John then had another few day sorting through our gear at Stade before he had to fly back to Oz. He didn't even have two months before he would be back in Europe and we would be off on our long trip.

Chapter 16.

Homeschooling

"There is no school equal to a decent home and no teacher equal to a virtuous parent." Mahatma Gandhi

The kids have had their first week of home schooling, the tutoring being mastered by an old school mate of mine, Peter Hansel (a maths teacher) and me, five hours a day roughly, one child each with a teacher, really hard work and very challenging. They have been relatively good so far as there is a prize each looming, the old bribery trick. The Sydney Distance Education material is very detailed, but has lots of "soft" projects that I don't care about and find hard to get through with the kids.

I have also started to tidy up our family home, as my mum is a compulsive hoarder, and I can't live in those surroundings for months. So I have been to the paper tip every day so far and hope to progress further.

The weather is typically North German, wet and grey. We have had two days with frozen car windows, otherwise it has been a really mild winter at around 5 degrees with heaps of mist and rain, and the flowers have started to shoot through. John couldn't believe how dismal Stade looked in contrast to when he has been here in summer. The kids avoid to go out, there is nothing to do there. I have been completely unfazed by the weather and darkness, which surprised me after such a long time in the subtropical Southern hemisphere. Pauli, our dog, is very settled with my parents but, still hates the rain and won't go out if it is unpleasant.

Finn has been really happy since we have left Denmark, a completely different child, chirpy, no tummy aches etc. So it was the right decision to cut this Denmark stay short. Lizzie is very stroppy, which seems part of her nature, and obviously misses her friends. They have to make do with each other here as there are no other children we know.

The further plan is to keep home schooling and stay here until April 1 when we are flying to Dubrovnik. John and I will meet for a short romantic break in early March in Paris and he will then fly to Croatia to sort the boat out. From Dubrovnik in mid-April we will sail to Montenegro and then Corfu. But a lot of homework before.

Saturday, Jan. 21

It is an interesting experience to live in my home town again, in the house I left aged 18. I grew up in this house next to my grandparents' home, my parents have never lived anywhere else, and most of the people in the street have been there since I was a child. It seems like a time warp. But it feels much quieter, maybe because it is winter and only dog owners venture out, or because there are less children and more old people. What did we do in winter as children? I do remember lots of TV. My generation, the people born in the early 1960s, were the strongest birth years ever in Germany. Our parents had struggled their way up after the war and come to moderate welfare, lots of children were born. But the parents were all working really hard, and the freshly invented TV must have substituted for babysitters. And in the dampness of a North German winter even hardy kids would struggle to find a game to play outside. When I wander past the very familiar houses to the new bakery every morning I remember the children in those houses that I played with, or didn't play with, and wonder how and why these groupings developed. Our parents never had any influence on what we did in the afternoon, we were very free. Our house is on a hill overlooking the fields and I still find it very idyllic, others would think the landscape very flat and now in winter quite forlorn.

Sunday, January 29

It finally has snowed and the temperature is minus 6 and will move to minus 9 at the end of the week. The snow came as a complete surprise, it was there in the morning when I went to the bakery in pitch darkness. Great feeling of stepping onto the pristine, crunching snow, childhood memories. Pauli was pretty surprised too, having never been in the snow before. There was enough snow for a good snowball fight, the kids were thrilled. I have to get the new snow off the footpath with a broom in the morning, as we are legally obliged to do, so nobody has a fall.

Sled riding in Stade

All in all things are in a sort of routine, but the homeschooling is a nightmare, the kids are so not interested. Also there is a lot of material to get through. I will try it out for a few months and see whether that program makes sense for the boat. The tutor does three hours of maths every day.

John has only got four weeks of work left, busy as always, and then has a few days of sorting boat, car and his belongings before he heads for Paris where we will meet up without children. He will visit the Spencers in Kiwiland first weekend of February.

I don't know why everything is always so hard with our children, I don't really blame it on Finn's Aspergers. But just getting them dressed and their teeth brushed in the morning takes most of my enthusiasm for the day away. Also the discontent and constant whinging and non-stop bickering are very disappointing. No respect either. Need a break.

Now off to the garage to do more packing of boxes to go home to Oz and to the boat.

Tuesday, Jan. 31

Temperatures are now between 5 and 9 degrees minus in bright sunshine, and with the icy easterly wind it feels like minus 20. That didn't stop my Australian kids to want to go swimming like every Tuesday, in the heated indoor pool obviously. But you can swim out through a corridor to an outdoor pool, where the head gets very cold when not completely submerged. After the swim the kids wanted to have another go with our new sled, half an hour before darkness. There is no snow on the hill left but ice and fast grass so the speed is quite impressive. After a few fun runs my wet hair had frozen and I was scared it would break off and leave me with a sort of fuzzy look. So inside for hot cocoa. If the minus temperatures continue for another few weeks lakes will be frozen and I could try my new ice skates, break a bone here and there and introduce the kids to skating.

Hohenwedel roundabout

Tuesday, Feb. 7

Yesterday was the coldest night so far with minus 12, it is slightly warmer today during the day with minus 8. But in Eastern Germany and Eastern Europe they have up to minus 30 and lots of snow. So there is a state of emergency in several countries and people freeze to death. We looked at the massive ice on the river Elbe at the weekend, had another sled ride, and this coming weekend will travel to Hamburg where the huge inner lake has frozen, and there will be a street party on the ice for the first time in 15 years. I will also go to a yacht club ball and see lots of people from the Hamburg sailing scene.

I am pleased that the kids have been able to experience a real German winter after the mild weather in Denmark before Christmas. It would just be better if there was more snow and slightly warmer temperatures. Could still change.

Finn's new Kindle packed up last night which caused a major tantrum and will keep me busy for a while. I am a real grumpy old woman in relation to modern technology. The Kindle had to be an American one, to be able to upload English-language books that Finn likes (mostly Rick Riordan). So now I will have to send it to the US to have it repaired. I wanted to buy a German Kindle anyway, but you can't upload most English books on that. To buy an English language one in the UK means having it sent to a friend in London as they won't send it to Germany. I assume we will end up with three different ones to be covered. We can't take many books onto the boat due to lack of space.

The planning for our time on the boat is in full swing. People flying in and out, flights to be organized, marinas booked. I am rereading books and articles about the ARC rally across the Atlantic in November, and now it is much more real as we will be doing it in only ten months.

Happy Valentine's Day to you all!

The mood here has improved slightly as we had a fun weekend in Hamburg with my friend Hans Martin and my godson Lasse. Finn, Lizzie and I went by train and met the others near the Alster, Hamburg's inner city lake. It was frozen enough (20 cm) that the city allowed people onto the ice, while stalls with food and Glühwein lined the foreshore. In my years in Hamburg I have only been on the ice once before, and the last time it happened was 15 years ago. More than a million people went on the ice this time for a walk or skate. We went early, good idea, and just took a sled to pull a tired child. I really enjoyed it, while Finn got quite frustrated, because he fell over a lot trying to slide like Lasse. The kids will remember it I hope, a once in a lifetime experience for them. In the evening Hans Martin and I put black tie gear on and went to the Süllberg hotel, where five of Hamburg's yacht clubs had their annual ball. Lots of friends, dancing, prosecco, to bed at 3 am. Kids left alone in Hans Martin's flat, never stirred once, I love that about Germany, no legal ramifications. On Sunday, back home, the kids watched TV all day and I lay on the sofa. The snow is melting now, and it is foggy and wet, three degrees plus.

Ice on the Elbe River

Sunday, Feb. 19

Snowflakes and rain this morning, but spring is definitely on its way. Birds are tweeting and some spring flowers are poking through the ground. Clearly there could be more snow to come, and ice, in the eight weeks until spring really starts. But I am optimistic and hope it will get warmer soon. The kids haven't been outside in days, and as I have done something to my knee swimming we won't go to the public pool this week. For the enforced inside activity I bought two puzzles. My parents have been visiting my aunt for a few days, while the kids and I enjoyed a quiet house. The six of us in this small house (including Pauli) works quite well, but a little break was nice.

John is slowly packing up his things in Sydney and getting ready for his departure early March. I am organizing more flights, in my next life I will become a travel agent or freighter, down into the garage now, to weigh some boxes.

More grumpy old woman ranting about technology. Brand new camera back in its box to be repaired, new internet gismo for iPad back at the shop to wait for a technician that can make it work.

Tuesday, March 6

The kids and I went to Hamburg for a final time and looked at the amazing new building of "Der Spiegel." A former colleague showed us around, and afterwards we spent some time in the Lego shop. The whole family drove to Cuxhaven on Sunday, walked along the water and had lunch in the local sailing club where we have been uncountable times during our sailing time on the Elbe. And now I am sitting on packed bags to fly to Paris tomorrow and meet up with John, who is already in Singapore now. The sun is out here with 8 degrees warmth.

The luggage issue and all those boxes being sent around the world are super stressful. I am fretting about the usual scenes at the airport, when they will possibly weigh our hand luggage and we get hit with a huge fee. I believe DHL's annual profit will be mainly supported by the Cole family. Today a box sent to Croatia ten days ago came back. Off it goes again tomorrow. There will be no space on the boat to store our belongings. The logistics of this dream trip are just huge and I've just about had it.

CHAPTER 17.

CARIBBEAN BIRTHDAY CRUISE

Paris was utterly charming, as only Paris can be. John flew in from Australia and I from Hamburg, and by some miracle we found each other in the maze of Charles de Gaulle airport on a sunny day in early March. We wanted to spend two nights in the French capital. As always we stayed in the Hotel de Lutece on the Isle Saint Louis and walked everywhere. By chance we stumbled into a real interesting art exhibition with some crazy displays. We hadn't seen our good friend Götz in ages, so he had us over for a meal, and we met his son Felix, aged two. Years ago he had given us a restaurant tip, so again we had a superb lunch overlooking the Louvre courtyard the next day, after admiring impressionist paintings in the Musée d'Orsay. A great start to our relaxing holiday.

After eight comfortable hours of flight we landed in Saint Martin in the Caribbean where it was almost thirty degrees. The hotel transfer turned out to be a small problem, so we ended up in a taxi trying to beat the rush hour in Saint Martin—interesting street life. The hotel was acceptable, a crazy big room, the restaurant Molasses, however, had a great selection of Caribbean food. In the morning we strolled down the high street of Philipsburg lined with shops for expensive watches. How many watches does one need? We also found a Star Wars museum and got some memorabilia for Finn. Lunch in the Sint Maarten Yacht Club was delicious, and we looked at boats and watched a little boy sailing his Optimist.

Check-in on the *Star Clipper* in contrast to big cruise ships turned out easy—leave passports and drag bags up the gangway. Our cabin No. 331 was a pleasant surprise, very maritime feel with wood and brass, heaps of storage, a big enough bathroom, and a good location near the dining room and stairs.

The boat had 170 guests, more than eighty Americans, fifty Germans, Swiss, and Austrians, and the rest from anywhere. The staff was from the Philippines and Indonesia, the management and officers from Sweden and the Ukraine.

This was our route in the Leeward Islands, eight nights: Saint Martin–Nevis–Isle de Saints–Dominica–Guadeloupe–Antigua–Saint Barth–Saint Martin.

Star Clipper

The *Star Clipper* is a four-masted sailing vessel, and the captain really tries to sail whenever possible. The furling sails came out on the yardarms straight after leaving port mainly in the evening, with most of the guests up on deck watching. The motion at night was soothing; she didn't heel so much as to roll us out of the bunk, but you had to watch keeping your balance having a shower. The boat had two little pools mainly used by the four kids on the boat and sun loungers everywhere. We mainly hung out in the huge bar area where there was also Wi-Fi reception (John still had work to finalize), and they served excellent rum punch.

Star Clipper **dining**

Within a few days and with free seating in the dining room we had met lots of lovely people, our main dinner companions being Bruce and Margot from Florida, who sailed a fifty-footer and gave us invaluable tips about harbours and anchorages. In the evening we had a few big nights with karaoke and a talent show. As our friends can imagine, karaoke is no problem for John, who was accompanied by our new lady friends. The boat, its intimate atmosphere, fun fellow passengers, and super friendly crew exceeded our expectations by far and we can strongly recommend a cruise on the *Star Clipper* or its sister, *Star Flyer* (more than 65 percent repeaters on both).

We had chosen the Caribbean route because we wanted to see what it was like before our Atlantic crossing on *Senta* in November. After our horror trip to Vanuatu on a cruise liner a few years ago we were positively surprised about the cheerful and confident Caribbean people who eke out a living from tourism and farming. We felt safe at all times and enjoyed some great excursions. Just a brief summary here:

On Dominica, which is known for its lush vegetation, we went river tubing, which meant sitting on a big swim ring and trying to manoeuver through rocks and rapids with a little paddle, super fun. The river wound not through a tropical jungle but through a lunar sandy landscape because a dam had broken a few years earlier and had washed tons of grey sand down the river and wiped out forests.

On the beautiful Isle de Saints, our favorite, we wandered up a steep hill in the heat to look at the great Fort Napoleon and its museum. Goats at the wayside, tourists on scooters, and amazing views. The rose wine and salade Niçoise at the waterfront restaurant were well deserved; we were surrounded by lots of our crew connecting with their loved ones on the restaurant's free Wi-Fi.

Isle de Saints

In Guadeloupe two guides took us and four more couples on kayaks for a few hours through the mangroves, a real nature experience.

Exploring the mangrove forest

After an interesting taxi ride across Antigua and a view across English Harbour from Shirley Heights, we met up with Jane, Micah, and Jacob from Mount Desert Island who spend a few months here with Jane's family every year. We had met them in 2008 when we stayed in their marina in northern Maine, in Southwest Harbor, on *Senta* where Finn and Jacob had become friends. The sailing world is small; over a rum and Coke we exchanged news of friends we had in common and chatted about sailing and life.

Saint Barth is super yacht country, and we had a look at a few big boats before a lengthy lunch in a French restaurant. Clearly the French islands are preferable to the English due to food and streetscape. We left the *Star Clipper* in Saint Martin very relaxed. Eight days went by too quickly, and we surely will sail on *Star Clipper* again.

Chapter 18.

Preparations for The Big Sail

Friday, March 23

John and our student help Dom left Stade this morning to fly to Dubrovnik to get the boat ready for our cruise. We will follow him next week Sunday. Bags are halfway packed, a lot of stuff to go on the boat.

Tuesday, March 26

John and Dom are working hard to get the boat packed, cleaned and in the water before our arrival Sunday, while I am still posting boxes and packing up stuff. We will as always have too much luggage at the airport, I always admire those families that travel with hand luggage only. For us 20 kg each is never enough. My mother is in the middle of packing for eight weeks, the main weight will be in all the tablets. Lizzie and my father have a bad cold and my mum and I are fighting it, but really can't afford it just before our trip. Only Finn who lives vitamin and iron free never gets anything. He has gained some weight here in Stade, which is great, as often on the boat he will lose some. He is off all his reflux and other medication and is very happy. No wonder, no school and no stress. His schoolwork for the last two weeks didn't arrive, so he has had a lazy time.

Here in Stade the spring flowers are out and the sun is shining with temperatures around 12 degrees during midday. I feel much more positive about this place now that winter is over. But we are off South now.

PRACTICAL TIPS FOR PLANNING A SABBATICAL

Start planning eighteen months to two years ahead; you will need the time.

Job: First talk to your group or potential relief and prepare them for the sabbatical. Have answers and structures ready for the crucial talk to your boss. Have a financial plan.

Home: Renting out your house for the period could be a big contributor to the sabbatical finances. House swaps are usually only for up to six weeks, for holidays rather than living in a place. We rented out our house for eighteen months to a local family planning to build a house. I advertised in the school newsletter and spread word of mouth. We would have used a real estate agent if necessary, but it was not. People did not want to rent the house furnished or partly furnished; they all had their own furniture. We just left some pictures on the wall and our books in the shelves. All our other belongings went into storage space under the house, which saved us a lot of money. We put in lots of rat poison. Using storage companies can be expensive for a longer period, so do your research.

Sabbaticalhomes.com is a website used by professors teaching stints at overseas universities. We found our fantastic Copenhagen flat through that. Be careful: Flats in foreign cities are often rented unfurnished without a dishwasher or washing machine. You do not want the cost of fully furnishing a place. Serviced apartments often cater to the business environment and are very expensive. Do a lot of Internet research.

Schooling: The Sydney Distance Education School has a fool-proof program that you can enrol in. They follow the NSW curriculum and will keep your children up to where their peers are. Material gets posted every two weeks; the kids have a class teacher.

Flipside: You are the teacher and it is a lot of work. There is similar programs in the US and UK.

If you want to enrol the kids in a foreign school that is non-English consider language courses beforehand to give them a soft landing. There are a lot of international and English-language schools abroad; choose the school wisely and get as much information as possible.

Insurance: Good health insurance for overseas is vital, as our student help Dom had to learn the hard way. Most travel insurance policies have a maximum stay of six or so weeks on them. Our private health fund was happy to suspend the home policy for the time away but would not cover anything overseas. We were insured with public health funds in Denmark, and for the boat we got a special cruising policy that was very expensive. Start doing the homework on that topic early.

Cars, etc.: You will be back, don't sell everything, you don't get much for it, and things cost a fortune to replace. We let friends use two of our cars and pay for rego and upkeep during the period, but not major repairs. One of our cars by accident was out of rego by our return and it was a real hassle to reregister it. We did not consider selling them. They were good family cars, and twelve months are over quickly.

PART TWO

CRUISING THE MEDITERRANEAN

CHAPTER 1.

ONE MAN'S DREAM TURNS INTO ONE FAMILY'S ADVENTURE

"Happy are those who dream dreams and are prepared to pay the price to make them come true." John

My husband decided to marry me after a difficult sail from Gibraltar to Vilamoura in Portugal in the autumn of 2000, shortly after we met. Despite battling with seasickness I seemed to have passed a test and qualified as his partner not only for life but also for his lifelong dream of setting sail for a longer period.

Twelve years and two children later we were off. Leon Schulz in his book *The Missing Centimetre* described cruising in four stages: dreaming, planning, sailing, and readjusting. We had done a lot of dreaming, got through the agony of planning, and were now sailing.

Senta's crew for the first few months of our sailing adventure was: skipper John, 59, Karen, almost 50, Dom, 19, Finn, 9, Lizzie 7, and the grandparents Einar, 78 ("Opa") and Edith, 78 ("Oma"). Dom, our student help from Sydney, wanted to see Europe while helping with the kids' tutoring and the boat.

We had picked our time window carefully. Although our children had been sailing since they were newborns, we experienced the toddler years as too difficult on the boat. Safety and life on board only got less problematic when the kids were around five years old and easier to entertain and more sensible. We also did not want to interrupt the high school years when the teenage kids want to be with their friends more than being away from home. Obviously lots of long-distance families sail with their teenagers, but we believe boat life and schooling is more enjoyable for all with the children aged five to twelve.

Cruising families choose destinations differently, taking into account the kids' desire for swimming, playgrounds, historical sites, or other interests. Having children aboard amplifies the pleasures and discomforts of cruising. On passage, even when the parents are exhausted, someone has to take care of the kids, who might be seasick or need a meal and someone to play cards with. There is no after-school care, babysitting, or other way out. We were in this together!

The Coles are off!

John and I were no novices to what lay ahead; between us we had plenty of sailing experience. He started sailing while at university and had owned several cruiser-racers before *Senta*, while I had sailed with my parents from the age of ten and had owned my own yacht. John and I had met racing in Sardinia in 2000. But being on a boat 24/7 for almost a year would be a challenge for both of us.

We knew that in reality living on a boat with limited creature comforts meant work and effort, endless repairs and maintenance. A life led by lists; as soon as one job gets crossed off another one gets added. Also relationships can be tested even among the most harmonious of couples. In the hothouse atmosphere of a small boat it can easily extend to how you close the fridge door.

John and I are Swan owners with all our hearts. *Senta* is John's third Swan and my second. The instant I saw the 1972 Swan 40 that German friends of mine had bought in the 1980s I fell in love with it and subsequently bought a sister ship. The beauty, quality, and seaworthiness of *Bella Gioia* got me hooked; there was no going back to the Toyotas of the boating world. German friends of mine and I were racing that boat, a temperamental, slightly aged Italian lady in Porto Cervo, Sardinia, in the year I met John.

It all started, where else, but in the Clipper Bar, Porto Cervo. The only place to be during the Swan Cup. It was September 2000, Wednesday night. I was harmlessly chatting to Mark from *Sotto Voce* when our little group was accosted by an arm-waving Australian, energetically jumping from a wall and proclaiming how easy the Italian language was: "You just put an 'o' onto every word, Marko— and by the way, who are you?" The encounter lasted about five minutes, and then we were all swept away by different currents into the turbulence of the bar.

I might have mentioned there and then that I was to attend the owners' dinner the next day. What was his name? John, I was glad to remember, when he determinedly steered toward me on the crowded terrace of the Yacht Club Costa Smeralda, where I was admiring the view with my best friend Hans Martin.

John and I ended up sitting next to each other at dinner, and being naïve, I thought it a coincidence. Later it emerged that John and his friend Chris had gained entrance in borrowed jackets as Mr. and Mrs. Robinson on the tickets of the *Assuage* owners Terry and Sue. It was an impressive effort and a very nice evening.

The next day John and Chris came around to inspect my boat, Swan 40 *Bella Gioia*. She was a bit of a project, to say the least, but John had the ideal solution for my knackered primary winches. In his shed at home in Australia there were several brand-new winches the correct size that I could buy off him. Telephone numbers were exchanged. I was a bit sceptical about the practicalities of shipping gear from the other end of the world, but who knew, something might come of it.

I went along to look at *Loki*, the brand-new Australian Swan 48 that John was sailing on. He had been joint owner of the previous *Loki*, a Swan 44 Mark II, but his co-owner Stephen Ainsworth had wanted to upsize, and having just gone through a costly divorce, John decided not to take a share in this new racer.

And that could have been it. One couldn't speak of blossoming romance after these brief meetings, but as I was sitting at my office desk in rainy London the following Friday I listened to my phone messages. "John Cole, ring me back." I picked up the phone, slightly nervous. "Where are you?" I asked.

"In Antibes, the owner's cabin of (Swan 65) *Desperado*. Why don't you come down for the weekend?" John had joined *Desperado*'s delivery crew from Sardinia to France. So I booked a flight and landed in Nice that night. We did recognize each other at the airport and had a fabulous time.

The next weekend John flew into Hamburg to go sailing with me and my parents on the river Elbe, and that also went well. John was now travelling Europe by car for the rest of his sabbatical, and we met every second weekend in a succession of romantic European cities—Rome, Milan, Madrid, Paris, London, Gibraltar... and Vilamoura, Portugal, where John took over the management of my extensive *Bella Gioia* renovation project.

By Christmas I had quit my job and by April 2001 we were engaged. Things were moving fast; it just felt right. We have been married for more than ten years now and live in Sydney with Finn and Elizabeth. We did go back to Porto Cervo in 2002, where John raced on *Loki* again, and I stayed ashore with baby Finn. And we did have a sentimental drink in the Clipper Bar.

CHAPTER 2.

RETURN TO DUBROVNIK

"There is no ideal age, but I know that if at all possible the best time is now, as tomorrow may be too late." Jimmy Cornell[5]

The preparations had started as early as 2005 when we began looking for a boat for this faraway dream of a sailing sabbatical. We knew we wouldn't be gone forever. Our young kids would need educating ashore afterwards and John needed to keep his job for our life after the break.

Cruising is an affair of the heart. "For most of us, our commitment to cruising is not something that is lightly done—it is something that we work hard to undertake and just as hard to continue."[6]

Sun and leisure, limitless time for relaxation, and the in-depth experience of other cultures represent the positive side of long-distance cruising, and seventy-five percent of boat owners confirm that yachting keeps them healthy. But any boat owner struggles to

5 Jimmy Cornell, *A passion for the Sea*, London 2007
6 Frank Virgintino, "Cruising: That Magic Moment," *Caribbean Compass* 12/12

justify the money and efforts spent on his boat. We had bought our Swan 46 *Senta* for this particular trip six years earlier. She had been underused and a big financial commitment in the planning stages but also a huge step forward in our long-term goal to go away for a longer period.

Swan 46 *Senta*

Many travellers are forever looking for places that nobody has ever been to, the remote anchorages and isolated islands where one can get down with the natives, hike around the jungle, climb mountains. We were not that type of adventurers. Instead we enjoyed the buzz of foreign towns, historical sites, were moored in comfortable marinas as often as anchoring in nature. Sometimes we only went as far as finding the closest ice cream parlour. As a family on the move we had a lot on: the schooling, the boat, provisioning, and other mundane tasks. We did not make our life harder by roughing it any more than we were doing already. Nevertheless we did see a lot. And although we did not seek to meet the locals, John with his unique people skills always found a harbour worker, taxi driver, shop keeper, or mechanic that would give us an insight into their life.

April 2

Breakfast at pool café, no shower possible, no time, boat like a bomb site, unpacking, mad day, dinner at restaurant.

Church opposite ACI Marina Dubrovnik

Wednesday, April 4

The whole family has safely arrived in Dubrovnik, the boat is in the water and the major chaos has been tidied away. We still have four boxes to arrive and have no space left. Imagine a 20 sqm room with a few small cupboards and the belongings of seven people for ten months. But the stress levels are down a bit and even I can smile occasionally. The kids will start school soon, and a new routine has to be found. Lizzie and I sleep in one bunk in the stern cabin at the back of the boat, Finn next to us in a single bunk, John and Dom in the middle of the boat and my parents in the front cabin. The oldies have been having a great time so far, sitting in the cockpit watching everyone while the sun is out. We had drinks yesterday with a lovely Australian couple, Jill and David Henry from Sydney, who know many friends of ours, small world as it is in sailing. We are scheduled to have drinks with them on our boat this afternoon, have to try and relax.

We will leave here as soon as all the tradesmen are off the boat, likely after Easter. In Montenegro we will hopefully visit the ports of Porto Montenegro and Kotor. Then an overnight sail past Albania to Gouvia in Corfu. It will be cold at night!

The shelling of the ancient walled city of Dubrovnik in 1991 during the terrible war that ended in the collapse of the Yugoslav state shocked the world. But the UNESCO World Heritage Site was quickly rebuilt to its former glory thanks to the massive inflow of foreign funds. Like Venice, Dubrovnik in summer is a tourist circus, but like La Serenissima, manages to maintain its unique cultural heritage and atmosphere.

Dubrovnik offers visiting yachts the noisy roadside berth at Gruz, or a space in the large ACI marina out of town. Our *Senta* had wintered on the hard stand in the ACI marina, and due to the harsh snowy weather local tradesman Boris and his marine specialists were still busy recommissioning the boat and finishing minor upgrades.

We had been in Dubrovnik before, in 2005, for ten endless days with a sick four-year-old and a one-year-old starting to walk. We had to take Finn to hospital in Dubrovnik that time and they diagnosed tonsillitis. But it actually was foot and mouth disease and he had a bad time with it. In 2011 we spent five relaxing weeks cruising down the Croatian coast and couldn't speak more highly of the country, its beautiful landscape, remote bays between uncountable islands, ancient towns, and good food. The people, however, were plainly unfriendly. I joked, "That's what fifty years of German tourism does to a country."

But as I was not immediately recognizable as a German and John was English speaking, it still did not explain the frosty waitresses and stone-faced vegetable salesmen. In another cruising book I read that the occupation during World War II had crushed the spirit of the people, but since then they had won another war in the 1990s, and to us they seemed a very proud people. Industrious and honest, but certainly not friendly.

On this, our third visit to Croatia, with most boxes unpacked, we boarded the bus into Dubrovnik town and climbed the ancient city wall. The staircase to the walls is immediately to the left of Pile Gate at the entrance to the city. The first set of those walls that Dubrovnik is famous for were built in the thirteenth century and continuously strengthened in the centuries thereafter. A walk around the two-kilometre-long wall that is up to twenty-five metres high is a true tourist highlight, as the views over the old town and the sea are magnificent. A sharp eye will be able to tell the difference between the old roof tiles and the ones that had to be replaced after the war. From the wall we made an excursion to the Maritime Museum in Saint John Fort that showed the history of navigation in the area with models, charts, and paintings. A round of gelato crowned a good day out.

JOHN'S INSIGHTS INTO CROATIA

By talking to tradespeople and marina staff John often found out how the people thought and what it was like to live in that particular country.

"Previously the region got money (aid) from Russia and the United States, and as people were mainly employed by the state they did not have to work that hard. Living by the motto 'If sick on Friday so what.' Nowadays jobs are hard work, e.g., the mechanic at the private operator in the Dubrovnik yard lived in the capital hundreds of miles away. He had been made redundant in the shrinking post-GFC market and it was the only job he could get. He went home every now and again, sometimes weekends. So even though for some entrepreneurial types capitalism offered opportunities, the majority felt they were worse off than under the socialist regime of Tito, which surprised us. But all felt the dominance of the state negatively, and favouritism (corruption) was rampant. The marina was state owned and the new general manager was a political appointment, not merit based. Inefficiencies in state-operated businesses were apparent.

"One local we met said his father had left him and his brother a number of properties. He lived in Switzerland, had a French mother. But he came back to Croatia to try and develop the land. He refused to bribe the officials for a fast track approval; hence he was relegated into the very slow track (three to five years). 'I don't mind if people are prepared to pay bribes to jump the queue, but it is wrong to be penalised for not paying. I just wanted to be in the normal queue,' he voiced his disillusion.

"Entry into the European Union in 2013 was viewed by many Croatians with mixed feelings. The VAT, or goods and services tax, which was raised fairly recently, was needed for the EU entry but had a negative impact on many businesses. It also encouraged a black economy, no surprise in that. Workers in private enterprise were diligent, focussed, and competent and stayed till the job was done. These were the people we dealt with, though apparently they are in the minority."

Sunday, April 8 Easter Sunday

It is raining, and after an exciting Easter egg hunt on the boat we manage to get some schoolwork done. Jill and David in their dinghy collect us for the 11 am Easter mass in the big church opposite the marina. We are early, so get seats on some benches along the side. Within a short time the church is packed, a lot of people are standing. The church service in Croatian is quite long, but we have time to think, meditate, observe the people and listen to the strong hymns. The kids are patient but only too happy to finally get out into the sunshine. Their reward is to explore the creek up to an old weir in the Henrys' dinghy. The afternoon flies by with me preparing the Easter feast, a huge leg of lamb with all the trimmings. The Henrys don't mind that my oven doesn't manage to cook it through completely, we gnaw on the edges. The evening is cheerful and cosy.

Jill Henry, Lizzie, David Henry

Tuesday, April 10

Very cold! Maybe 8 degrees. Kids in the shower, schoolwork, John deals with stainless man, carpenter, almost ready. At 12.30 we are finally away, covered in streamers from David and Jill, a lovely farewell in warm, bright sunshine.

Chapter 3.

Montenegro – A New Home?

"... The most beautiful encounter between land and sea." Lord Byron

Maybe it was due to the very harsh European winter, but the weather in Croatia was unseasonable cold, and we felt it. It took almost a week of boat preparations and waiting for a weather window before we made the thirty-five-mile hop southeast to Montenegro. It turned out to be a pleasant, sunny motor sail, and when we rounded the fort at the entrance to the Bay of Kotor we were overwhelmed by the spectacular mountains towering above the glassy waters. The Venetian name *Montenegro* means "black mountain," and black they are and almost two thousand metres high.

Lizzie raises the courtesy flag

"I'll do it. No, it's my turn, you did it last time. I still want to do it. Papa, he did it last time, he always gets to do it, it's not fair!" Lizzie won the usual competition between the kids and proudly hoisted the Montenegro courtesy flag under the starboard spreader. Past the former Yugoslav submarine bunkers we motored six miles down the bay to Tivat, home of the new marina development Porto Montenegro where we tied off at 7:00 pm. A friendly marinero raced John to customs and immigration, and without much bureaucracy we were in.

Montenegro lies east of Italy across the Adriatic Sea and is bordered by Serbia, Albania, Croatia, and Bosnia and Herzegovina. A sleeping beauty for the last forty years, the Adriatic country of unspoilt natural beauty had been a haven for film stars such as Sophia Loren, Elizabeth Taylor, and Kirk Douglas in the 1950s and '60s. Montenegro has only recently again experienced an upsurge in popularity due to its focused government and investment from five-star resort operators. The small country is a candidate for membership in the European Union and run by an enthusiastic young president. After the dissolution of Yugoslavia, Montenegro adopted the deutsche mark as its currency, and now uses the euro despite it not being a member of the European Currency Union.

In this little country of 650,000 people that only cast off from Serbia in 2006, a Canadian gold magnate with a super yacht based in the Med saw the potential and with Porto Montenegro has created a super yacht haven without comparison in the Med's east. Built on a former Austro-Hungarian naval base within the coastal town of Tivat, it is close to the beautiful Bay of Kotor, another UNESCO World Heritage Site, and the deepest natural harbour in Southern Europe.

Porto Montenegro, Tivat

The first marina stage opened in 2009, and so far over one hundred million euros has been invested, with investors like Lord Jacob Rothschild and LVMH Chairman Bernard Arnault supporting the project. Apart from the state-of-the art marina there are waterfront and village promenade houses and apartments for sale. The next phase will see the completion of a Regent hotel and the takeover of the major ship yard on the opposite side of the bay, which has been used as a naval base since the days of the Roman Empire. The bay existed for centuries as the boundary between Christianity and Islam.

Wednesday, April 11

Porto Montenegro is very clean, the staff gurney off the pavement and park the tradesmen's white vans on plastic sheets to keep the dock clean. We are the smallest mast in our row. Schoolwork is hard-going, Finn throws a tantrum most mornings. The weather is grey. But spirits lift, at lunchtime. "Do you want to join Opa and me for lunch at this nice restaurant up there," my mother asks around noon. Great steak with chips. The marina is trying to be the biggest super yacht marina in the world with 860 berths.

Friday, April 13 (Orthodox Good Friday)

We have been in Porto Montenegro/Tivat in Montenegro now for a few days and really like it. The whole family has enjoyed the good restaurants, shops, and efficient laundry service. The Sydney born development manager here, Oliver Colette, generously organised a speedboat and a driver today, and we all zoomed to the medieval town of Kotor, a Unesco Heritage Site like Dubrovnik, only without the tourists. We climbed up the fortress wall of Sveti Ivan following some donkeys on a rugged path to enjoy fantastic views over this most dramatic medieval town. With a Venetian lion at its gate, Kotor's unbroken line of five kilometres of defence walls snakes up the rugged mountain behind Kotor and back down at the other end of town. There is a little market with high prices for e.g. honey, I don't buy anything. But there is also a stall with cheap plastic toys. Lizzie does not even try to convince me. "Dad, Dad, can I get that box, a Barbie with clothes, look, Dad, Dad, I will do my homework really well tomorrow, Dad, Dad, please." After a few days of enthusiastic play this cardboard box with a copy Barbie and too many shoes annoyed me month after month flying around the back cabin, and eventually got stuffed behind the bathroom door.

After a town square drink and chat to our knowledgeable driver Jellco we speeded to the Church of our Lady of the Crag. In 1452 locals piled up rocks to form the island the church is on. The church is full of marine paintings and maritime items. Seafarers leave tokens at the church's altar to ask for safe passage. John had something ready to hang up next to the altar. Next Jellco stopped at the little town of Perast for a grilled fish lunch. When the waiter filleted the whole fish at the outside table it started to rain, so we all rushed in. The weather is unstable, yesterday it was brilliantly sunny, today grey and cold. Nevertheless the speedboat tour was great fun.

We love the whole place. In the marina there are lots of big boats to look at, the property development is outstanding and of great interest to John, who is a property lawyer. We will stay here for another few days before the big hike south, 180 miles overnight to Corfu, Greece.

Speedboats are fun!

Sunday, April 15

Since our fantastic speedboat trip Friday it hasn't stopped raining, and apart from the boss we have all coped well squeezed in the boat together doing homework or listening to "The Chronicles of Narnia" on audio CDs. The Oldies are watching Inspector Barnaby in their cabin, happy as. The rain is heavy, and no outdoor activity is possible. Also our departure is uncertain in this weather. But we had a very interesting coffee afternoon with the manager of the Porto Montenegro development and his wife, Sydney born Oliver and Pia. They also kindly offered their shower, as the harbour showers run out of hot water after a few punters, and John has been very grumpy due to the lack of a hot shower in the morning. The town of Tivat has a former socialist feel to it in its architecture, but prides a great fish monger, huge butcher and fruit market. Everything is super cheap. The boat's freezer is full, and I have relearned the forgotten skill of gutting fish, urgh.

By now I was a veteran at grocery shopping in countries where I didn't speak the language and they didn't speak mine. I tried to learn "good morning," "hello," and "thank you" straight away and then used hand signs and other tricks. Mooing or baaing to find out which animal the meat is off was one method, or buying what the lady in front of me chose. The butchers in Tivat's main meat shop were not friendly, but I got what I needed for very reasonable money.

A typical day on the boat began at 6:30, walked to shower, made breakfast for us seven, and started school at 9:00 am. We often didn't last past 11:00 or 11:30 with the schoolwork, but it was school holidays in Sydney so the pressure was off. We mostly had a light lunch of sandwiches or soup and the kids entertained themselves in the afternoon while we shopped, got laundry organised, or did other work around the boat. Dinner around 6:00 pm and most of us were in bed by 8:30.

Last night we went to the Australian run harbour bar where a hostess from a super yacht celebrated her 30. birthday with an Abba party. Some of the dress ups were hilarious, and we talked to a wigged Balmain guy who had attended Hunters Hill High, a bright Kiwi and an Englishman who knew lots of people we knew. Small world as always. John only did not dance on top of the bar because I didn't have my camera with me. We went home early, though, not a wild night.

Wednesday, April 18

Thick fog! Later sun out.

Yesterday cabin fever really hit the Australian contingent on the boat due to the torrential rain, day five of it. The boat is cold inside and the kids' schooling was very trying for Dom and John. I wrote an article and was out of it for once. Also to us Northern Germans or assimilated kids the weather was just like my hometown Stade in summer. The positives of the day were another great pizza meal out plus Finn and Lizzie soaking in Oliver and Pia's bath tub, very generous. In the morning or evening the boat is so cold that getting up is a challenge, and in the evening my face cream is so cold I do without. Instead of an overnighter in these temperatures we will likely stop in Albania after all. Seems the mines are cleared out of the fairways, and the former communist country welcomes visiting sailors. We might see some of the 750,000 individual bunkers the dictator Hoxha built to protect his people. Finding a weather window that satisfies the skipper has not been easy, it is 15 hours to Durres in Albania, maybe tomorrow crack of dawn. Today John will try and organize a speedboat to look at the Yugoslav submarine bunkers.

Man fishing

Thanks to our new benefactor Oliver, John, I and the kids hopped onto a marina RIB and in glistening sunshine zoomed toward the old submarine bunkers. It is hard to say what is so fascinating about old bunkers, but we were all thrilled to be able to tie the boat at the bunker entrance and then walk on the narrow ledge into the bunker, where Yugoslav submarines had been waiting to defend their country. We then sat on the dinghy and ate fresh croissants. It doesn't get any better than this.

Bunker adventure

Not too fast, Dad!

Thursday, April 19

A big Mercedes bus with a friendly driver took us around the gulf of Kotor up a serpentine road to a plateau high up in the mountains. The drive in rain and fog up the winding road was scary, but the views and the alpine highland were worth it; the landscape looked like the Black Forest in poorer times. Our driver knew a local rustic restaurant where in front of an open fire we enjoyed the specialities of roast lamb, hard cheese, ham, and salami. Drive back down through the low clouds, back on the boat at 17:00, very tired. Great day!

Montenegrin specialities

Our driver noticed John's interest in the local property market and took us to look at his late grandmother's property in the hills behind the marina. John got all fired up; we took photos, paced the size—would this not be a perfect European base for later generations? The land was not cheap, though, and we were worried about the dominance of Russian investors in Montenegro.

Almost our new land

We did not see nearly enough of this stunning country. Possible activities would have been white water rafting down the Tara River, Europe's deepest canyon second to the Grand Canyon in Arizona, winter skiing in two major resorts, paragliding with eagles in the mountains, or windsurfing amongst the pelicans on the vast Skadar lake, home to the biggest bird reserve in Europe.

John's Insight into Montenegro

"Montenegro has a small population and a well-run government. They cashed in their currency into deutschmarks years ago and then converted to the euro. The country is very open to foreign investment, e.g., converting the Tivat naval base into a super yacht marina and resort. They have invested in infrastructure, e.g., the freeway into the mountains for skiing. People are genuine and hardworking, but a lot of them were seduced by the products of capitalism and sold their land to see the proceeds disappear into cars, phones, and other consumer goods. The Russians bought into the country in big style and have pushed prices up. That has led to unrealistic expectations and will lead to problems in the future, as the Russian presence will deter some Europeans from investing. Housing stock on the Gulf of Kotor is solid, but newer developments are stagnating following the GFC. Montenegro has an interesting planning approval system. If you have a house on the block already you can pull it down and build whatever new house you want. Not very bureaucratic.

"The country has the ability to do big things in a European sense. It combines physical beauty, mountains, the Gulf of Kotor, and the medieval city of Kotor—of similar standing as Dubrovnik—good climate, and an innovative government. We did not hear anybody complain about corruption. The Christian majority is secular and accepting of the Muslim minority; no apparent racial tensions.

"An example of how hard life was only fifty years ago are the farmers on the plateau above Kotor. They would walk their donkeys for eight hours down the serpentine road with their produce of hard cheese and ham to offer it on the market in Kotor. They then walked back up during the night."

After eleven nights in Porto Montenegro and seven days of pouring rain we decided to depart, whatever the weather, at the end of April. So we headed out into the Adriatic at 6:00 am in full wet weather gear. The sea was confused and bumpy, and although there were barely fifteen knots of breeze, part of the crew had to lie down. What looked like seasickness at first turned out to be a nasty stomach bug that affected everybody in our seven-head crew eventually. Stopping in Albania seemed a good idea to recover some strength. We did not see any mines; they are a myth, but coming closer to the shore we were surprised how built up with high-rises the coast was. We honestly did not know a thing about Albania.

CHAPTER 4.

THE LAST FRONTIER OF ALBANIA

"Albania? You can't possibly go there, it's not safe, there are still mines in the water." A friend.

A sip of port against the cold

"Hello, hello, is that Llambi?" John yelled into his mobile phone. We were approaching Durrës in Albania, and he wanted to be sure our agent was expecting us. The contrast could not have been any bigger. From the cushy dock of a Montenegrin super yacht marina with Australian pub, pizza restaurant, electricity, water, and all amenities to a grain dock in a corner between freighters in Albania. An article in *Yachting World* about sailing to Albania had mentioned the name of an agent and fortunately included his e-mail address. After an introductory e-mail and a few phone calls former merchant ship captain Llambi Papa was waiting on the dock in Durrës to show us our berth and help with the lines. We were almost too close to the mooring rope of grain freighter *Chelsea I* from Valetta behind us.

Senta **in Durrës, Albania**

Durrës has been inhabited for the last 2,700 years and was once a hub between East and West and controlled by every ancient power at some stage. Julius Caesar's rival Pompey made a stand here in 48

BC. In the Middle Ages it was under Byzantine, Bulgarian, Sicilian, Serbian, and Norman rule. Two Irish pilgrims who visited Albania on their way to Jerusalem in 1322 reported that Durrës was "inhabited by Latins, Greeks, (...) Jews and barbaric Albanians."[7] We can't agree; we only met very friendly Albanians.

Modern Durrës harbour was as commercial as it gets. We were jammed between grain freighters that were being loaded by big cranes next to a harbour building site. Soon the boat was covered in grain and concrete dust. But the harbour atmosphere was great, and the people friendly. The formalities turned out very low key.

"What do we have to do for registering, harbour master, customs, immigration?" John asked Llambi. Turned out we were registered as a visiting ship like a freighter and hence did not have to deal with any immigration officials, just had to pay the harbour master a small mooring fee. Llambi was a gem.

"Mum, where can we get an ice cream?" We were ready to explore!

Due to the extreme isolationist policy of its former leader, Albania is a blank page to most European travellers. Few know that the former member of the Eastern bloc turned itself into the Republic of Albania as early as 1991 and has been a parliamentary democracy with a transition economy for more than two decades. It has applied to become a member of the European Union, and the country's transition from communist to free market capitalism is seen as largely successful.

"Awaking Sleeping Beauty–like in the 1990s from her hard line communist isolation, Albania was a stranger from another time. Her cities weren't choked by car fumes, her beaches were unspoilt by mass tourism, her long-suffering people were a little dazed and confused. While things have changed a lot since then, this ancient land still offers something increasingly rare in Europe these days – a glance into a culture that is all its own. Raised on a diet of separation and hardship, Albania is distinctly Albanian." Lonely Planet describes the Balkan country.[8]

---

7 Wikipedia
8 Lonely Planet website

Durrës promenade

Its recent history is dominated by one man and his bizarre policies: "From the end of World War II to his death in April 1985, Enver Hoxha pursued a style of politics informed by hard-line Stalinism as well as elements of Maoism. He broke with the Soviet Union when Nikita Khrushchev embarked on his reformist thaw, withdrew Albania from the Warsaw Pact in 1968 in protest of the invasion of Czechoslovakia and broke with the People's Republic of China after US President Richard Nixon's 1972 visit to China. His regime was also hostile toward the country's immediate neighbors. Albania did not end its state of war with Greece, left over from the Second World War, until as late as 1987 – two years after Hoxha's death – due to suspicions about Greek territorial ambitions in southern Albania.

Streetscape in Tirana, Albania

"Hoxha was as unfriendly toward the more moderate Communist government of Tito in Yugoslavia, accusing Tito's government of maintaining 'an anti-Marxist and chauvinistic attitude toward our Party, our State, and our people.' He asserted that Tito intended to take over Albania and make it into the seventh republic of Yugoslavia, and castigated the Yugoslav government's treatment of ethnic Albanians in Kosovo, claiming that 'Yugoslav leaders are pursuing a policy of extermination there.'

"Albania still maintained some links with the outside world at this time, trading with neutral countries, such as Austria and Sweden, and establishing links across the Adriatic Sea with its former colonial power Italy. However, a modest relaxation of domestic controls was curtailed by Hoxha in 1973 with a renewed wave of repression and purges directed against individuals, the young and the military, whom he feared might threaten his hold on the country. A new constitution was introduced in 1976 that increased the Communist Party's control of the country, limited private property and forbade foreign loans. The country sank into a decade of paranoid isolation and economic stagnation, virtually cut off from the outside world."[9]

Sunday, April 22

After a bit of school we go on an excursion along the Durrës promenade. Very interesting. Shocking brown beach. Uncountable Mercedes cars, stolen in Germany? Possibly. "Mum, look a horse cart." Finn points at two guys in a little cart. Lots of well-dressed people on the promenade that seems to try to attract tourists. High rises new and old, a lot of decay. Communist monuments. Amazing seafood lunch at "Riazza" restaurant, o our surprise starters and desserts are for free. A German Kosovo Albanian talks to us, calls the place a "gold mine." Two other yachts arrive, an English Jenneau 39 and an older Polish yacht.

Lizzie's Diary, April 23

"Yesterday my family, an English couple and me took two taxis to Tirana. There was one driver that could speak English and the other couldn't. There were cows eating green grass on the side of the road. Mum asked why there were so many Mercedes. He said because the roads are so bad. We saw lots of hub cap shops, we don't have them in Australia. I drove a toy motor scooter and Finn drove a small racing car. Dad and I climbed a high tower and Dad looked out over the city. Oma and Opa had a drink in a park, and my dad and I looked at a water fountain. Today we are next to a crane."

The taxi ride from Durrës to Albania's capital, Tirana, took forty-five minutes, Lizzie on my lap, and we were astounded by the many commercial buildings, factories, and car dealerships along the four-lane highway. Remnants of a former time were the single cows on a rope, guarded by old ladies or men patiently sitting by the roadside, waiting for the animals to feed on the highway's juicy green strip.

---

9 Wikipedia

Tirana, a city of four hundred thousand inhabitants, is the centre of the country's political, cultural, and business life. Its wide, big streets are filled with Mercedes cars of any age. The architecture is a mix of the socialist and fascist influences the country has been through. Tirana's former Old Bazaar and the Orthodox cathedral were razed to the ground for the erection of the Soviet-styled Albanian Museum that we unfortunately couldn't see from the inside.

Museum in Tirana, Albania

There were ice cream stalls and popcorn machines on the street as everywhere else in the developed world. We were, however, puzzled about all the people leisurely strolling around. Didn't they work on a Monday?

The kids climbed on one of dictator Enver Hoxha's famous 750,000 four-man bunkers that dot the Albanian landscape, left over from the cold war as relics of the paranoia and skewed priorities of the former dictator. Individual bunkers to protect the population from the world, what a crazy idea! Now the Albanians wonder what to do with the sturdy concrete manholes.

Hoxha bunker

Back at the port Llambi told us we would have to move berths as a NATO troupe carrier with eight hundred soldiers was expected for the night to protect the northern border, unstable as part of the Kosovo conflict. With Llambi's and some harbor workers' help we moved to the other side of the pier in pitch darkness, not as big a deal as we feared.

The next day John and I took Lizzie on a shopping expedition. It was a long walk to find some little shops and finally a good supermarket with a great selection but almost no meat. In the evening we watched freighters and fishing boats enter and leave the port.

JOHN'S INSIGHTS INTO ALBANIA

"Mercedes everywhere. Corruption pervasive. The docks have no facilities for cruising yachts; we were alongside a commercial freighter dock and later had to move for a NATO ship to berth behind a Russian grain ship. The quay was concrete with steel reinforcing bars protruding out. We asked our commercial shipping agent how tacky was the dock like this; it couldn't cost that much to fix it. Certainly less than knocking down completely workable warehouses on the dock and building new ones. We heard the public official in charge of the docks gets a political appointment for five years and has to make as much money personally out of this as he can in that time. It hasn't got anything to do with best economics or public interest. Big contract, big bribes; small contract, small bribes.

"In Tirana we see the very interesting combination of Italian fascist and communist architecture. There has been a big influx of European investment, and property prices, particularly for commercial and industrial buildings, have risen, lots of money to be made. But the GFC has had an impact here too, and half-finished shells of buildings are apparent. A political/military presence is still noticeable. Armed guards interfered with Lizzie's attempt at taking a photo of a public building. Numerous second hand hub cap stalls along the streets (stolen or from the roads?). In the supermarket we buy the cheapest Italian sambuca of the trip. On a Sunday stroll on the promenade we notice the waterfront is full of thick black seaweed, very unattractive, and the community is building a shell-shaped concert hall into the water there. A bit like the Sydney opera house one might hope."

Fascinated by this country of contrasts we considered a visit to the Albanian Marina di Orikum or the harbor of Florres, but would have had to get another agent and decided we wanted to press on toward Greece and warmer weather.

CHAPTER 5.

FINALLY SPRING – THE IONIAN ISLANDS

"There is something so exhilarating about the elements, the sea & the wind & the sun, and one feels far away from the horrors of modern civilization with its noise and its eternal hurry." Queen Elizabeth the Queen Mother, 1934[10]

It was now late April, and spring was starting to arrive. Leaving from Durrës later in the morning than planned due to the strong winds, we arrived at an island anchorage north of Corfu at 11:30 pm after a good motor sail along the Albanian coast, completing 105 miles. Nobody was sick for once. However, the anchorage was so unsettled the whole family did not sleep at all that night. Another motor to Gouvia in the morning in sunshine and glassy seas, four dolphins greeted us really close, a thrill for all.

---

10 William Shawcross, *Queen Elizabeth The Queen Mother: The Official Biography*, London 2009

Approaching Corfu

Lizzie's Diary, April 28

"On Thursday afternoon we arrived in Gouvia Marina in Greece. Before we arrived in Gouvia, just outside the harbor, we saw dolphins putting their fins up out of the water. This morning my mum and I had breakfast at a café. I had an orange juice and a ham and cheese toastie, and my mum had a peppermint tea. Yesterday we went to a lovely bay and there went swimming. The water was cold at the start. Finn was freezing. I swam around the boat three times. Later on we saw turtles at the front of the boat. They were on the sea bed. For dinner we had two dishes, pasta and tortellini. I liked the pasta more."

April 26–31

We are in Marina Gouvia, Corfu where I kept my previous boat "Bella Gioia" for a winter in 1999. It is a huge marina now with 1200 boats, a lot of them English. We got a good berth and found the showers, blissful after a week without. Longest that Dom would have been without a shower ever

I would think. Over 20 degrees, we could have enjoyed it if John, Finn and I hadn't gotten the gastro bug that Dom had a few days ago. Three days later, Opa got it too. Nevertheless we resumed school yesterday as we had lost so much time with Albania, the sailing and illness. It is always hard to start again.

John and I had to taxi into Corfu town to customs and the police to check in, and afterwards looked for a telephone shop for a Greek sim card. It seemed a beautiful old place with lots of small streets, hopefully we will take the bus in tomorrow and have a closer look. We enjoyed one Greek meal yesterday when all stomachs were halfway settled, with tsatsiki, grilled eggplant, haloumi and moussaka. Quite expensive here, and no comparison to our amazing seafood restaurant in Albania, where starters and desserts were for free and they did great seafood, very rare in the Med now, almost no fish left.

Saturday, April 28

Normal breakfast, kids ratty, school goes ok, John trouble at work, super irritable.

Only in retrospect and having read the illuminating cruising book by Mike Litzow[11] do I understand a bit better why John seemed stressed a lot of the time on the boat. The ongoing responsibilities for his work at home and the difficulties solving problems remotely, combined with looking after the thirty-year-old very complex boat was a huge responsibility and a full-time job. The family, me included, didn't always understand that.

Corfu had a special atmosphere. In ancient times the island had been occupied by Corinthians, Romans, and the Byzantine Empire. The Venetians ruled it for hundreds of years in the Middle Ages, and in more modern times the British took it over from the French and ruled until 1864, when Corfu was given back to the Greeks. Despite the hordes of tourists mainly from cruise liners at this time

11 Mike Litzow, *South from Alaska*, London 2011

of the year, the capital, Kerkyra, or Corfu Town, breathes history and is elegant and attractive. Two massive forts dominate the town silhouette, and it is easy to get lost in the labyrinth of the old streets.

We climbed up to the Neo Frourio built by the Venetians that has magnificent views over the harbour. The kids explored battlements, cellars, and dungeons, and we enjoyed the coolness of the old building. The old town is a maze, and we fought our way through to a waterside restaurant, on the way picking up a wooden honey twirler.

Corfu Town

Tuesday, May 1

From Gouvia we went to Paxos, the beautiful bay of Lakka where the boys got the Optimist dinghy out on the water and everybody had a sail. Extremely peaceful in beautiful surroundings, so we stayed a day. Then on to Levkas, up at 5 am. We made it by 12 o'clock for the Levkas bridge, which actually was a ferry put in the gap between the island and mainland, with trucks driving over it, very inventive. Levkas marina was huge and empty. We went for an early meal in a taverna near the water and had a feast there of typical Greek fare, great. We got the laundry done, found post office and optician and got loads of fresh food. The only pain were the showers again, Lizzie and I showered in 20 seconds, for me then to run after John, dripping and in a towel, so he could manage to shower Finn in the remaining few seconds on the charge card that should have been full according to the marina officials. John had to take deep breaths in the marina office not to explode.

Friday, May 4

The fuelling up at the fuel dock was difficult, both were foaming, John and the diesel. We motored down the Levkas canal, beautiful landscape before high mountains, built around 7th century BC. We drove past Onassis island Skorpios and could see some buildings. I had just read the Greek shipping magnate's biography which was a thrilling read with most of it sounding like a mafia crime story.

Levkas Canal entrance

Senta stayed the night in a little place called Spartochori on Meganisi, allegedly lots of Australian-Greeks have houses here. We had to anchor backwards onto the quay for the first time which did not go as well as hoped. The boat hit the back of the jetty and some gelcoat came off. John very unhappy! Pretty, tidy town with lots of summer houses of expat Greeks. We walked up many steps to the quaint village with a lovely church. The kids fished to no avail, we had steak and salad for dinner.

Then on to Odysseus's home island Ithaca in windy 25 knots on the ear, a great sail with the sink flooding the boat a bit. We arrived in a harbour called Kioni.

Sunday, May 6

Greece votes for a new parliament today, the first one after the financial crisis. It feels way more sophisticated here than Montenegro, Croatia and naturally Albania. The average yearly income here is $29,000 in contrast to $14,000 in Croatia and $6,500 in Montenegro.

Vathi, Ithaca

No school today, yippeeeh.

Finn managed to catch a fish today but fishing is over for him for the time being as John and I spent hours untangling the line. Lizzie is setting up Polly Pocket scenes on her bunk. Short motor to Vathi, Ithaca, we berth Senta along the quay which is not legal but so far so good. The town is very quiet, kids do puzzles, computer games, we take an ice cream walk.

Monday, May 7

The Greek elections result in no government, the extreme parties gain and the two main parties lose 45%. Business owners and waiters we meet on the islands say that the election results are bad for them, Athens is a world of its own. There are no German boats to be seen, only English or Dutch charters.

"Rugged Ithaki, Odysseus' legendary homeland, has yielded no substantial archaeological discoveries, but it fits Homer's description to perfection: 'There are no tracks, no grasslands...it is a rocky, severe island, unsuited for homes, but not so wretched, despite its small size. It is good for goats.'"[12]

May 8–11

Fiskardo, Kephalonia

We set out in more than 30 knots, later there is less wind. An English photographer takes photos of Senta sailing into the bay. The back anchor manoeuver turns into a disaster, but we find a good spot eventually. Three flotillas gather in this lovely harbor with its many restaurants. We meet Kevin, the photographer, a former London police man married to a Greek from Kephalonia, and agree to do another sailing photo shoot when we leave.

---

12 *The Rough Guide to the Greek Islands*, 2007

In Kephalonia we hired a small red car for the day, and the four of us drove around the severe, mountainous landscape of the largest of the Ionian Islands for a day. All of Kephalonia's towns and villages were destroyed in the 1953 earthquake. The Kephalonians also have a legendary reputation for being eccentric with an insular pride and stubbornness. Unfortunately we did not get to know anybody well enough to experience those quirks.

After a few kilometres' drive we turned off to see the small village of Assos and its ruined fort out on an isthmus. The walking ramp up to the old fort was wide and smooth—the things European money can do—but the climb was endless and we gave up before we got to the top.

From Assos John had to concentrate to drive steady on the steep, winding road up and down the mountain's edge. We looked down onto turquoise water and the long, sandy Myrtos beach that is considered one of the most dramatic beaches in the world. There was nobody else there, and John and the kids braved the cold surf. The beach was made of small white pebbles and sanded their skin off. Soon we drove toward the Melissani Cave, which was unlike any cave we had been in before. Partly submerged in water and with a broken roof, the cave collects the sunlight, and reflections from the dark water create a mysterious atmosphere. We boarded a little wooden boat rowed by a guide and spotted bats, stalagmites, and other tourists. The goat herd near the parking lot of the Drogarati Cave was a huge attraction, but the cave looked more normal with its chambers of stalagmites and damp paths downhill.

Melissani Cave

Back in the afternoon we felt we had seen a lot. The dinner at Vasso's restaurant cost seventy-three euros for the seven of us, which seemed to be the amount we paid everywhere when we ate out including drinks, very reasonable.

The next day was an admin day in Fiskardo with cleaning, computer work, and clothes sorting. The kids played a board game with Oma and Opa and listened to audio tapes. Later after a lengthy walk we found a bay, swam, played ball, and rock climbed.

Friday, May 11

We have school for the first time outside, in the cockpit. Lizzie says she is not well again. I believe that has something to do with the tedious school tasks, as she quickly recovers as soon as it is play time. We leave at 1pm for the photo shoot in little wind. Kevin takes the kids to some caves in his speedboat, they come back glowing and happy from the experience. The photo shoot is not easy in not even 10 knots of wind. Kevin later sends us a photo CD and there are several nice shots, especially of Oma with a champagne bottle at the helm.

Chapter 6.

Toward the Corinth Canal

Thinking naught of woe or grief. Dancing, prancing, like a leaf. Caring not for cliff or reef." "Song of the Wave," Robert Frost

Saturday, May 12

Leave at 6.40, motor sail 65 miles, cloudy, cold.

Trizonia marina sounded good in the guidebook, which also mentioned a welcoming Australian B&B host. The book needed an update; the B&B had burned down, the nice Australian had died. The whole place turned out a bizarre experience. A fine marina in theory, but it had never been completed. The docks were almost derelict with broken glass and loose electrical wires on the walkway. At least nobody charged us to moor there. The marina had many abandoned boats, one ketch sunk right in the middle of the inner basin. It would be a good place to start if one wanted to pick up an interesting project boat.

Des from Western Australia helped us tie our ropes; later the kids went swimming with a gang of older German boys. We had a late dinner at a fish restaurant with our table surrounded by stray cats. The meal came to an astounding eighty-one euros, eight more than usual in this remote place.

With another flotilla on our heels and no wind we put the gear-stick down and raced to Galaxidi, from where we wanted to visit Delphi. Des and Liz and their friends on *Abrolhos* joined us on the dock, and a while later the flotilla arrived. The flotilla's young Kiwi supervisor, a hero of patience, didn't blink an eyelid when one of his boats managed to motor in backwards perfectly, but the man at the bow had not deployed the anchor. "We'll just row it out on the dinghy," he said stoically.

Monday, May 14 Galaxidi

Admin day, Lizzie not keen on schoolwork, gets sent to her bunk. Cleaning, shopping. Drinks with Australians Carolyn and Paddy from "Kristiane." Dinner is pasta carbonara.

Tuesday, May 15

We had hired a car and the five of us minus Oma and Opa drove through miles and miles of olive groves to Delphi to look at the ancient ruins. It was a great drive up the mountain with flowers blooming along the road. The ancient Greeks were not stupid, Delphi is located high right under Mount Parnass, and overlooks a vast valley. The gods had a fantastic view from here. The museum amongst the many sculptures and artefacts displayed the huge statues of Kleobis and Biton. The kids were surprisingly interested and liked the museum. We managed a steep climb in the heat through the ruins, and looked at the amphitheatre and the well-preserved stadium, but by that time the children had lost interest. We had a great lunch looking down onto Itea and Galaxidi from a cliff-top restaurant, just starters, very nicely prepared. Back early afternoon. Dinner with 13 people, another two Australian boats, "Abrolhos" and "Kristiane."

Delphi

Wednesday, May 16

Galaxidi to Korfos 45 miles

We left at 7 am with Western Australian boat "Abrolhos" with Des, Liz, Tania and Clive who we had dinner with the night before. We had agreed on a photo shoot first thing, and despite the lack of wind the cameras clicked non-stop. However, when we left the sheltered bay we saw white horses (white foamed waves) and "Abrolhos" soon rounded up. "Senta" was also a handful under No 3 jib and full main, so we put in a reef and furled the jib a few metres. John got completely soaked getting the reef in, the waves were huge. We still were going very fast, sometimes over 10 knots, and had to hand steer which was hard work, so John and I swapped every ten minutes. But the sun was shining, nobody was sick, and we made fast progress toward the entrance of the Corinth canal.

Rough conditions

We were allowed into the waiting area with A. and an Italian boat and started motoring circles for 45 minutes. The Italians were annoying as they motored too slow, there was very little space and still over 30 knots of breeze. John handled it really well. The highest gusts had been 35 knots on the way. We were the first yacht to be let into the canal behind a tourist boat. The canal was amazing, high sand walls, often crumbling, a few high bridges, green water. The transit takes 15 minutes. The canal cuts the journey by around 150 miles and costs an outrageous 250 Euros, they are mad, the Greeks.

Corinth Canal

After a short stop for the formalities at the canal exit we motored to Korfos, another 10 miles downwind that went quickly. Opa thought he was in Denmark and kept saying that the Cuxhaven sailors also would take this way, wouldn't they. We also talked a lot about his friends the Rincks and he found it hard to believe that Peter Rinck is dead. It was a long trip and he is worse than normal, stressful for us all.

A restaurant owner waved us to his dock and we took the easy lines. The filled peppers went into the fridge and we had a meal there. Des and Co also ended up in front of a restaurant nearby. We were tired after a hard day on the water, Dom had his first real sailing day and admitted it has been exciting and a bit scary.

Lizzie's Diary

"I was still sleeping when we left Galaxidi early in the morning. When I woke up there were big waves and the wind was strong and I wished I was still asleep. We finally arrived at the Corinth Canal, it was amazing. The walls were up high above us. Grandma asked are all these people going to pay. Then Grandma said, oh, I was dumb, they must be on their way to the toilets, that's what they normally do. It was dinner time, we ate at a nice restaurant, I shared a chicken dish with Dad."

Thursday, May 17

Stay in Korfos, school, difficult, cold. I haven't been able to upload many photos as our internet connections everywhere are slow and fragile.

Friday, May 18

Rain, wind, cold, long trousers, socks, who wants this. We decided to stay in Korfos and just batten down the hatches. Lots of school and some lazing around. In the afternoon a walk through the tiny village with lots of cul de sacs. We had dinner again at our quay host George's restaurant who had been a merchant seaman and made Oma giggle with his German. Lovely fish for 10 Euros each. We tend to spend the same amount everywhere for a meal for us 7 with four mains and a few starters and drinks.

Dom has been quiet, his back is hurting, he says, he has a bad back from rowing. Also Lizzie has been a bit aggressive so he has schooled Finn lately. He finds the schooling quite stressful, and who would blame him, so do I. Our children are just something else. John has a talk with him and we are trying to work out a plan to make him happier.

Saturday, May 19

After the schoolwork we left George and his wife to their cleaning of fish on the dock and left Korfos for Poros. We got both sails up and sailed leisurely for a while, before the speed dropped to under three knots and we motored the rest of the way. Dom spotted a dolphin on the way in, while I concentrated on two high-speed ferries, likely to Athens. We motored past the picturesque Poros town promenade, and headed back to Russia bay where we were going to spend the afternoon and next day. The anchorage was peaceful, only a few other boats there, and the kids, Dom and I went swimming straight away. The water had warmed up to maybe 20 degrees, and Lizzie and I swam into a bay to watch a flock of goats hopping around the foreshore, very cute. We had fried fish, lemon, capers, roast potatoes and peas for dinner and then watched Harry Potter the second last. To bed way too late.

Sunday, May 20

Godson Lasse's birthday, I left a message. The German crew contingent had a bread and boiled egg Sunday breakfast and then no mercy, straight into school. The kids were lucky, at 10.30 our friends from "Abrolhas" Des and Liz with their Canadian friends Clive and Tanya brought some delicious honey, sesame and almond Greek pastries for our tea and coffee and we had a good chat before we parted ways. We have met some great Australian people so far and will be busy catching up with everyone once we get back to Oz. After they left we had a big swimming session and then big lunch so dinner will be light and not slow us down for the last part of Harry Potter. We watch DVDs at weekends on the computer and that time is sacrosanct to the kids.

Chapter 7.

Piraeus is Nice

"So much I've tried
I've never found a port
To captivate my heart
As Piraeus does."

Song "Children of Piraeus," Manos Hadjidakis

Monday, May 21

We are in Zea Marina, Piraeus, near Athens

The Greece pilot book guru Rod Heikell warns about Zea's noisiness, but also praises its facilities. Being urban, not nature, people by heart the buzz here has not bothered us, it is merely interesting to watch Greeks of all ages promenade past our boat as we are on Piraeus fitness parcour. People power walk past our boat on the jetty or the concrete road one metre above the jetty all evening. One can note that most women are too round, and that young men come in herds and wear beards. Lots of Greeks of all ages drive by on scooters, as traffic seems horrendous. We have experienced a few exciting taxi rides.

Piraeus

Piraeus reminds of San Francisco with its steep hills, but without the convenient cable cars. The buildings are mostly six-story apartment blocks in light colours with sun awnings on the balconies, a quite pleasant city scape. Off putting, however, is the graffiti on all surfaces and crumbling decay everywhere. Also the lack of town planning with the chance for a decent town promenade lost in concrete. Piraeus still would be calling itself a substantial super yacht centre, there are around fifty of the big buggers here, but Porto Montenegro would be a huge competition now, as Zea marina has really nothing much to offer to visiting yachtsmen. They are expanding, though. The harbour café is badly run and overpriced and the population walking through the place at all times is not the privacy super yacht owners nowadays prefer. However, we are enjoying the ok showers, excellent Carrefour supermarket in walking distance and plenty of boats and street action to look at. The safety concerns have so far been unfounded.

Initially we were quite happy to eat Greek food, but after four weeks it lost some appeal. We always started with tsatziki, which the girls of the crew loved, a yogurt, garlic, cucumber dip. We often had fried calamari or anchovies and a Greek salad. For mains, however, the choice was very limited. It was moussaka, chicken souvlaki, or, rarely, fish. They served chips with everything, and that was that. Greek wine, however—and more importantly—had been a very positive surprise, and we drank the open wine of any colour at restaurants without any problem, light and nice. The rose we bought from the supermarket in 1.5-litre bottles cost around four euros and was perfectly drinkable chilled.

Australian and German friends alike have asked about what it was like in Greece, in the ongoing crisis, what we can tell about the country. For a German like me it looked like this country with a barren, moonlike landscape and no industry to speak of apart from tourism and some foods has lived on borrowed money for a lengthy period and through that has elevated its society to a good standard of happy consumerism and welfare. Now, that reality has hit, nobody wants to get back to goat herding and olive oil making, and they blame their likely corrupt politicians that have been in power far too long. So they have voted for communists, socialist, and fascists with all their empty promises. On election night people in the bars were watching football, not results. So another election had to be called. They all want to keep the euro, and hate the Germans, who want them to start saving, which hurts. The cafés are full of Greek men of all ages drinking coffee at any time of the day. Unemployment must be huge. The admin and bureaucracy for yachties is horrendous, but you can see missed opportunities in harbours for businesses and for making money everywhere. On the positive side, people are really friendly, not uptight about anything, and helpful.

The Zea marina office provided a multipage address leaflet for marine services around Piraeus that was extremely useful. The girls in the office were particularly helpful and let me use the lobby computer and copy machine for some of John's work. Nobody could read a map, though, so directions were often somewhat patchy.

John took advantage of the good marine facilities and spent hours in the chandleries. Electrician George tried for a whole day to get our new Wi-Fi booster antenna working, to no avail. He was only the second of numerous electronics and computer experts that had a go and failed with this task that should have been easy.

A call to the laundry service on the marina's information sheet was comical as the laundry person did not speak English, but within an hour two small, old people arrived in their little rusty car and lobbed big bags of our laundry away, likely to their washing machine at home. The clothes came back as clean as no other laundry service on this trip had managed so far.

In Piraeus, before we left the boat to travel to Germany, John and I had a big fight. It started with something trivial—the height of the fenders above the water—and ended in endless shouting and the "d" word mentioned. Completely out of proportion in retrospect. But try to imagine staying together in one of the smallest rooms in your house day and night, a space so small that you are constantly touching as you move around doing the chores. Throw in a fussy ten-year-old, an emotional eight-year-old, and two octogenarians, one with dementia. Then clutter the space with all the stuff you have in your house deemed necessary to live. Add to it the constant worry about repairs and maintenance of this thirty-year-old mobile home and whether you will find a suitable space to park it. Then see how the petty discomfort of being crowded together ignites tempers.

Chapter 8.

Turning Fifty on Helgoland

"Fifty, but still a kid inside." Karen

Thursday, May 24

Travel from Athens to Hamburg via Copenhagen

I turned fifty in the year 2012, as did Tom Cruise, Jodie Foster, and Sheryl Crow, mixed company. My birthday has always been important to me, time spent with my family, time for a party, time for reflection, appreciation by friends. My birth year prided itself on being the second year to see more than one million babies born in Germany. Clearly there were lots of us, born in the early 1960s. The TV kids, we were called, the first generation to be brought up in front of the box.

My fiftieth birthday fell on the same day as my mother's seventy-eighth birthday on May 26, and I felt strongly that I did not want to celebrate in Athens. My parents were due to leave the boat and return to Germany to get out of the heat. So my mum and I decided we would, in keeping with tradition, celebrate our

195

birthday on the island of Helgoland in the North Sea. Dom wanted to see Prague and Venice by himself, fair enough. Off to the airport and go!

For almost thirty years my parents and I, with numerous friends on board, would take part in the Nordseewoche, the North Sea racing week over the long Whitsun weekend either in May or June heading to the North Sea island of Helgoland thirty miles off the German coast. It was one of the highlights of the North German racing calendar, a huge meeting of hundreds of yachts and many familiar faces. Helgoland therefore has a special place in my heart. The fun we have had there over the years! It also is a unique place. A red island rising high from the North Sea, owned by England for seventy-six years before Germany exchanged it for the island of Zanzibar in 1890. Completely rubbled in World War II, it is now a well-preserved example of 1950s architecture.

We travelled from Athens via Copenhagen to Hamburg and on by taxi to my hometown Stade on the Elbe River. After half a day of shopping, doctors, and hairdressers we crammed everybody into my parents' car and drove to Cuxhaven, the town on the mouth of the river. We caught up and stayed with old friends there, and on our birthday took the catamaran ferry to Helgoland.

Lizzie's Diary

"On Friday we drove to Frank's holiday house at Cuxhaven. The next morning we took the ferry to Helgoland, then we went to our hotel. The hotel was very nice. When we went to bed Grandma put on the TV. On the next day Grandma and I went to a shop and I got lip gloss and perfume. The lip gloss was gold. On the next morning we went to the Oberland, we saw some birds on the way around the island. Then we went to see the seals, then went down to the hotel. On the next morning we went swimming, then we played mini golf. Finn won, Dad came second, I came last. Then we ate an ice cream."

Helgoland, only one square kilometre in size, is an extremely interesting place for mariners, soldiers, historians, and ornithologists. During World War II the civilian population remained on the main island and was protected from Allied bombing in rock shelters. The area around Helgoland was the setting of the aerial Battle of the Heligoland Bight in 1939, a result of British bombing attempts on German navy vessels in that area. The area was frequently mined by British aircraft. Following the island's penultimate air raid, on 18 April 1945, using 969 Allied aircraft, the island was evacuated. The bombing raids were conducted with Lancaster and Halifax bombers from the UK, where John's dad was stationed as a navigator in the Lancaster RAF 465/466 Squadron. I bet he was flying on Helgoland during the raids from 1944 onwards.

Helgoland for us was sunny, as is the tradition at Whitsun, and the harbour was full of racing boats. When the ferry pulled in, my oldest friend Antje and her husband stood on the wharf to greet us, a beautiful surprise.

Helgoland harbour

The first time in a hotel on Helgoland, not on a boat, and the Strandhotel on the promenade could not have been nicer. John and I had the water view front room while the grandparents shared with the kids at the back. Immediately we set out to the harbour bar to meet old friends for a drink in the typical North German beach baskets.

For the evening and again in line with tradition we booked a table at the Hamburger restaurant, named after the city, not the fast food, and Antje joined us, to my delight. The following race week prize-giving party at the convention hall with heaps of dancing and too many planters punches led to the most shocking hangover. John and I spent most of Sunday morning recovering while the older and younger generations watched German TV, sorely missed during the long months on the boat.

When all I had had in mind through my teenage and twen years was parties and racing, exploring the island had not been high on the agenda. And in thirty years I had never walked around the Oberland, the plateau on top of the island. This was the year for it. The stairs to the Oberland seemed endless, but eventually the children whizzed off on their scooters while we slowly walked around the cliffs, taking in the fantastic views over the island and the North Sea.

The island is a geological oddity; the main island's red rock in the middle of the German Bight is unusual and is the only formation of cliffs like it along the North Sea coast. Uncountable sea birds like gannets, sea gulls, terns, and the common guillemot nest in the red cliffs. We had a good view onto the Lange Anna, a forty-seven-metre-high stack of sandstone standing by itself. The kids decided to shorten the trip and go cross-country; we hoped that venture was relatively safe and that they wouldn't fall off some cliff. Soon we found them lying on a meadow waiting for us. An ice cream was in order after our safe return to the shopping street in the Unterland.

Red cliffs

We also for the first time took the small boat across to the sandy island Düne to see the seals. The Düne is smaller than the main island at 0.7 km², lower, and surrounded by sandy beaches. It is not permanently inhabited, but it is the location of Helgoland's airstrip. After a mega-ice cream and a short dip into the cold North Sea (the children) we started hunting the famous Helgoland seals. The beach where they were supposed to rest in big numbers was empty, so we walked around the whole island until we spotted some dark, sausage-like shapes on the beach. The sleepy seals were not scared or in any way perturbed by our presence.

Helgoland seal

Close to the ferry jetty now we noticed a bank of fog descending on the island. Soon we couldn't see a thing. The little boat took us back to the main harbour in very bad visibility. After some duty free shopping for our favourite rum costing only eight euros a bottle, tired and happy, we climbed onto the catamaran ferry heading toward the river Elbe. After a day of errands in Stade we were back on the plane to Athens. The whole family was sad to leave the grandparents in Germany, but it turned out to be a wise decision, as the summer's temperatures rose to record heights around the whole Med.

DOM'S MEDICAL DISASTER

We arrived back at the Zea marina from Germany on the last day of May after lunch, and as nobody had really checked with Dom when he would be back that day, we did not worry about him until the next morning when I tried to text him about his whereabouts. We went supermarket shopping, and in the meantime Finn took a call from a

200

hospital somewhere and wrote down a telephone number. It was about Dom, he said. The number didn't work, and we didn't even know which country the hospital was in. He had been in Italy last, as far as we knew. My mother phoned from Germany and said she had received a phone call from a hospital about Dom but hadn't taken down the number.

We only had to wait another fifteen minutes when the hospital called again. It was located in Patras on the Peloponnese, and Dom had collapsed on his way from Venice on a ferry. From what we could figure out he had had a sort of seizure on the ferry and had been given shots by a medic there. He sufficiently recovered to get on a bus (to a hospital?) in Patras but had to ask the bus driver to stop and then collapsed. He had possibly had a cardiac arrest and in hospital they thought he was a foreign drug addict. He was unconscious and lucky that a Melbourne Greek visiting his father in the same room got the hospital staff on track. He couldn't remember anything for at least twenty-four hours and was disoriented, still very much so when we managed to talk to him on the phone. What a disaster!

John hired a car straight away and left at 4:00 pm for the three-hour drive to Patras. In the hospital John had to buy toilet paper and water for Dom as well as breakfast the next day. It was a six-bed room full of mayhem; next to Dom somebody died, very distressing for Dom. On the positive: they ruled out meningitis, did a brain scan, took brain fluid, organised a heart ultrasound and many more tests. But they could not find out what was wrong. John overnighted in Patras in a hotel and next day had Dom removed to a private hospital in Athens. Dom's health insurance by then had agreed to cover some of the costs.

In the private hospital he was checked out big time and there was nothing wrong with him, the doctors said, but he was still disoriented. John went to hospital every day all day and tried to support him, but Dom was freaked out and not able to be sensible in terms of trying to get more strength through eating, sleeping, and taking medication. We just bided our time on the boat. Eventually, after a week, his mother came out to support him. He had encephalitis, an inflammation of the brain, possibly caught in the youth hostel in Prague.

Monday, June 4
Everyday life is everywhere

Some days just don't start well. Finn dropping a full bowl of dry corn flakes was just the beginning (no vacuum cleaner). Despite the fact that we close the boat off with mozzie nets at dusk, Lizzie has been bitten six times, maybe at the fun fair last night, and due to her allergy some of the bites have already swollen big time and it hurts. Attempts at schooling had to be aborted, the antihistamines made her tired and she went to bed. Finn was not interested in his map project or to start the new literature project, so I ended up yelling and throwing books and sending him into his bunk, too, at 10 am. We are already one week behind with the schoolwork and will not get anything done today.

Obviously the main reason that everybody is stressed is Dom's collapse. John is at the hospital all day where Dom is still not much better and has an MRI done right now. Not much fun here at the moment.

Tuesday, June 5

John back to hospital, kids difficult with the schooling, but got something done. Very hot, went to supermarket. Kids stayed inside and played and read.

Wednesday, June 6

Very hot! Got everybody ready to take the hop-on-hop-off sightseeing bus, waited for almost an hour in front of the archaeological museum, asked two people, turns out although the stop is called museum, it doesn't leave anywhere near the museum. By that stage the kids had lost momentum and wanted to stay on the boat. Had diver for underwater, and had laundry collected again. Did ARC admin. John on afternoon shift with Dom, Jenny on the way.

Thursday, June 7 Antje's birthday

Today Dom's mother Jenny will arrive in the afternoon, so John won't go to the hospital today and we sightsee in Athens. We find the 9 am double decker hop-on bus and sit upside. We get off at the Acropolis and join the queues. It is hot and we start walking up the hill toward the temples. There is a great amphitheatre Herodes Atticus, that is used for opera nowadays. The Parthenon itself is being restored, but despite the scaffolding it is very impressive. The 360 degree view over Athens is breathtaking, and we climb over old marble and rubble and enjoy its size and importance. The new Acropolis museum is very well laid out on top of ancient ruins, that one can see and walk above on thick glass. There is a beautiful video installation in the foyer, of lions, deer and duck, and the kids get a sticker poster to complete with sculpture stickers on a trail through the museum. The museum is very light and spacious and well laid out. Then we rejoin the bus and drive around Athens for two hours. There are the usual four- to six-story apartment blocks everywhere, no freestanding houses to be seen. Traffic is thick and hectic, the streetscape not very charming. Athens in a day seems enough, although again I did not get any birthday clothes shopping done.

Dom McDonald

Friday, June 8

Cleaning, packing, shopping

In the evening went to O'Connells Irish bar for the first Euro2012 game Greece against Poland that ended 1:1. We adults are enjoying having a less crowded boat without the oldies, sleeping in their double berth at the front, and only having little meals with less washing up and shopping.

Looking back at the first part of our journey during the European spring we had some of the best experiences of this sabbatical then. Montenegro, Albania, and the Ionian Islands had been immensely interesting and not crowded at this time of the year. We did not just rub hulls with charter boats but had met some nice live-aboard cruisers, notably from Australia. The kids got on with each other surprisingly well and had not missed other children too much, and we were hopeful we might meet some kids during the summer holiday months. Losing Dom to a medical nightmare obviously was unexpected and changed life a lot on board, especially in regards to schooling. Thank god he subsequently recovered fully from his illness. We did mind that in many harbours our thirty-year-old Swan, our dream boat, only years ago considered huge and a Rolls Royce, was looked at as a beautiful classic, uncomfortable and impractical, in contrast to the apartment-style modern boats with bathing platform and cockpit table, not to speak of a shower.

Chapter 9.

Aegean Disaster

"If you did not get lost in Mykonos you've never been there." Lizzie

Sunday, June 10

We left before 7am, on a hot morning, and initially motored. But soon we could sail with No. 3 and reefed main, and later motored with full main up. Between two islands the wind whipped up over 25 knots and a choppy sea. Goes to show that one should always be ready for a bad sea state and wind here. We met frequent freighters that we had to dodge. The kids were in the saloon listening to Percy Jackson and quite content. When the waves got higher we sent them to their bunks, and in the end put the computer on in Lizzie's bunk with a few movies as it was Sunday. Finn threw up once. We were in Finika at 5 pm after 10 hours and easily found a spot on the concrete dock stern to with anchor. The anchoring worked perfectly and we were relieved. After a drink in the harbour bar we went to a taverna and had a typical Greek meal. Afterwards another drink in the harbour joint, to watch the second half of Spain against France.

Monday, June 11

Made a rough passage plan for the two weeks till Oehnes, our friends from Hamburg, arrive. Will try and see three more Cyclades Islands, Paros, Naxos and Mykonos. Difficult school morning until 12, rock climbing and a swim from the boat afterwards. The water was really warm, a pleasant contrast to the frosty sea temperatures we had before. Lazy afternoon with reading (John & me), computer games (Finn) and drawing (Lizzie). Evening game France against England in the harbour bar.

Thursday, June 14

We shortened our stay in lovely Finika by a day because the weather forecast was for a big blow from Friday onward, and we wanted to be safe with a good berth in Mykonos before the gale arrived. Mykonos marina is unfinished and has a bad reputation, but is very safe. So we decided to sit the wind out there. On our arrival there were two spots alongside the pier and a few back to a pontoon. We went alongside, very well knowing that the boat would be caked in dirt from the unpaved desert next to us, but it was the right decision. The wind started blowing a day earlier, and the boats backed to the pontoon had huge problems with their anchors entangled.

So we are happily sitting with the wind howling 35 knots outside, sun shining, and have done some schoolwork and tidying up. No showers here, no electricity for the fridge, crumbling jetties in a European money-funded marina that the Greeks didn't finish as so often, a disgrace. Mykonos town is a few kilometres away and we haven't decided yet when we will conquer that touristy hot spot. We will be here until the middle of next week. John is working.

Saturday, June 16

We are still in Mykonos and will likely only leave end of next week due to this massive gale. The wind is howling over the deck with between 35 and 45 knots, and the boat is caked in sand inside and outside. The wind has an enormous force, and though our berth is quite safe, both John and I did not really sleep last night due to the movement of the boat and the strong wind. The kids have not been out all day, as walking is difficult and the sand painful. We watch and help a charter boat trying to moor and fear it would be lost on the rocks but it just make it. John is completely over the Cyclades, and we won't be seeing any other islands when we finally will be able to leave for Samos. Quite an experience. The kids as always have been kept going by listening to CDs, Narnia this time.

Lizzie's Diary

"Yesterday we went to Mykonos Town with a bus. When we were there we looked for a new hat, but we didn't find one. My mum got a new dress, it is very pretty. Then we saw a shop and I got pretty shoes. They are white. My mum and I went into a shop and I got a hat. It is orange but then we went looking for a restaurant, a pizza place. I had Hawaii pizza. In the afternoon we went swimming. I love snorkelling and I saw a small crab."

Mykonos town

Wednesday, June something

This is day 7 of Mykonos and we are thoroughly fed up. The boat gets so dirty here we will never get it clean again, honestly. On several days the wind was so strong that we could not leave the boat. We have been into town three times for shopping, and the architecture is very quaint, but otherwise lots of jewellery shops, souvenirs and fashion. No nightlife opportunity for us with the kids. Mostly we have been inside the boat, sitting out the storm. Yesterday John got quite excited when some boats came in and the wind dropped to 25 knots. But when interviewed, one French boat had seen 53 knots on the way, not for us. On Saturday we seem to get our lucky break and will try to sail the 100 miles to Samos to pick up Bummi, Helgart and Nico. We have not seen the Cyclades at all, and don't care right now, as the boat is bouncing up and down in 30 knots as I write.

Mykonos marina

Lizzie's Diary, June 20

"Yesterday we went into town but this time Evie our neighbour came as well. We took the bus. When we were there we went to go to the post

office, we looked and looked, we found a supermarket, when we came back my dad had found the post office. My brother and I climbed on a tree. When my mum came out of the post office we went looking for a crepe place. When we found the crepe place we had been on the day before. Finn had a crepe with Nutella, I had a crepe with sugar. It was nice in town."

When John saw a water truck drive along the quay he did not hesitate. With a fire hose he washed "Senta" down from top to bottom, the kids in their swimmers squealing with joy at the huge shower. Soon after a few of the other suffering boat owners followed suit. We paid about 25 euros for thousands of litres.

The Greek gods were angry, a sign from above. Election Sunday mark II and we were holed up in Mykonos marina in a forty-five-knot gale. The unfinished Mykonos marina, to be precise, a multi-million-euro development financed by Brussels. The marina that was bucketing sand all over our boat, our hair, teeth, and interior surfaces from its desert-like marina quay. The marina that had electricity boxes but no power. That had no water and no mooring ropes but plenty of obstacles for the brave "anchorer" in one of the prime Greek tourist spots. The brand-new wreck of a marina in which we waited out the mid-June storm for ten very long days. Our two-month cruise through the Ionian and Aegean islands left us puzzled and bemused how this barren, cheerful, relaxed country has managed to have such a big influence on the world economy.

Greece was the birthplace of civilization. Nowadays it feels like it is its doom. With a coastline of more than seven thousand miles and uncountable islands, its sunny climate and friendly population has attracted many a tourist, sailor, and Shirley Valentine. But with no industry to speak of apart from tourism, food stuffs such as olive oil and feta, and some materials the corrupt political elite with big pockets had to be found out eventually. The euro entry had been a cheat and the public finances are a complete mess. Less than

50 percent of the population pay income tax, and there are many more budgetary horror stories.

The first Greek election we witnessed in early May in Vathi, Ithaca, home of Odysseus the Brave. One might have thought the election was held in some foreign country, as the Greek islanders continued to play cards, chat, and ignore the TV screens telling the nation that the main parties had been smashed and the extreme right and left fringes had gained immensely. Europe got nervous at these results, even more nervous. The island locals were just worried about the missing tourists, and rightly so. After rioters on Athens streets burnt German flags, no German boatie or other tourists were brave enough; officially numbers were down by only 20 percent.

My political octogenarian German mother, on her daily walks and beer stops with my father, was not afraid to ask the local shopkeepers and waiters their opinion on the election and Greece's financial situation. Souvenir shop owners and bakery women chanted no, no to the Dreaded Drachma Question. Everybody wanted to keep the euro.

Greece had profited from being part of the European Union profoundly. There were big billboards on every island saying how much money the European Union had put into this or that infrastructure project. But there were also building ruins everywhere. We heard from a local that after the European contribution of 75 percent to 90 percent to an infrastructure project, the Greeks didn't finish the projects, so after ten years it fell back to the council, and some cousin of the mayor could pick this multimillion euro infrastructure project up for one euro and finish it within three weeks—hearsay, of course.

We noticed empty houses on prime waterfront land, e.g., in Fiskardo, Kephalonia, one of the pearls of the Ionian. Local photographer Kevin from London told us about the inheritance laws that keep the thirty-odd heirs of a property from selling it. Some towns are well maintained but deserted; their huge houses owned by expat Greeks in Australia or the United States, empty places.

In Athens, watch for a run on banks, the European papers said. We managed to get some euros out of the second bank machine. Also reported: No more foreign medication exported to Greece, no export insurance any longer. What was true we didn't know; certainly life in Piraeus seemed to go on as always, the locals were power walking past our boat at night.

In Mykonos marina's tavern the young boss who went to Nottingham University and embodied the new Greece said, nodding toward some older Greeks eating their fish, "They don't get it." He and some fellow restaurant and hotel owners offered the council to pay half of the cost of putting bitumen down around the marina, but they were rejected.

Some warnings circulated amongst our fellow sufferers holed up in Mykonos in the gale: fuel up as long as you can, no more fuel soon, there will be power cuts. We raided the ATMs for euros like everybody else. Don't want to run out of money here.

Saturday, June 23 at 748 nm

It was still blowing, but not quite as hard, and we had timed our departure on day 10 of our unplanned stay in Mykonos carefully. The helpful Belgian cast off our lines at 7 am and we motored into big swells under No 5 jib. Lots of water washed over the deck. When we were able to bear away after the Mykonos lighthouse in the passage to Tinos we made fast progress in calmer seas. Nobody was sick, and after 60 miles anchored in the bay of Fournoi. The anchor had to be reset three times, but then we seemed safe and went for a swim. Saturday was TV day and we all watched "Surf's Up" before a happy hour drink in the cockpit.

Samos, "lush, seductive and shaped like a pregnant guppy, seems to swim away from Asia Minor"[13] only 2,500 metres from the Turkish coast, severed from the mainland in an ice age. In ancient times it was a rich and powerful city-state and the birthplace of the philosopher and mathematician Pythagoras. Repeated

---

13 *Rough Guide to the Greek Islands*, 2009

wildfires in the recent past had destroyed a quarter of the island's vegetation, but there was still enough natural beauty left to make the 478-square-kilometre island one of the most attractive in the Aegean.

Thursday, June 28

Since leaving Mykonos our Greece experience has improved dramatically. Our drive around Samos was really interesting, and the north coast waterfalls a great fun experience. We walked through a rainforest along a creek and then waded through a gorge to the waterfalls. Our little expeditions away from the coast are always a great success.

Samos waterfalls

Lizzie's Diary

"*Yesterday we hired a car. The car is yellow. We went to look for the waterfalls. We got the car stuck, we left it there and found a waterfall. We walked and walked and walked and found a tiny one. We kept on following the water. We got to a small river. We put on our swim stuff, Finn went in first, I went after that, then came my mum and my dad. After we swam to the waterfall then we went back. We ate at a tavern where there are a lot of bees. Today our friends will arrive."*

The new marina in Samos near Pythagorio had been talked down by other cruisers, but we really enjoyed the showers, supermarket, and cool breeze through the boat. Bummi, Helgart, and Nico Oehne arrived even a bit early on Tuesday, and the next day we leisurely sailed to Agathonissi where we anchored in a typical Greek bay. The swimming was superb and we decided to stay a day and watch Germany play Italy in the semifinal of the European soccer championships in George's tavern. The majority of us sampled goat, while careful John stuck to a Greek salad. The view from the boat to the village was picture postcard Greece, and Bummi and Helgart were over the moon as they had travelled through the Greek isles twenty years ago and had fond memories.

Chapter 10.

The Dodecanese with Friends

"Griechischer Wein ist so wie das Blut der Erde.
Komm schenk dir ein,
Und wenn ich dann traurig werde, liegt es daran,
Daß ich immer träume von daheim, du mußt
verzeihen." Udo Jürgens

The Dodecanese Islands lie against the Turkish coast, the farthest island group from the Greek mainland. Due to their strategic position the islands have a turbulent history. After centuries of rule by Persians, Athenians, Romans, Ottomans, crusaders, and others, the islands joined Greece in 1948. There are castles, forts, and other classical remains everywhere, and the islands have contained a mix of cultures and architectural styles. In recent history they were the scene of ferocious battles between German and British forces in 1943–44.

Tomorrow just 12 miles to Arki, so a swim in the morning, some schoolwork, and then off.

Sunday, July 1

We have spent two blissful days in Port Augusta on the island of Arki. We swam off the boat, had the rubber ducky in the water and sailed the Optimist. It was very hot.

Finn and Nico sail the Optimist

A great meal at Manolo's taverna with goat and squid that we had seen Manolo clean in the harbour in the afternoon. This is the life, finally some holiday feeling. Apart from the hours of school in the morning.

Sirtaki

After a cracking but too short sail we got a good spot on the dock in Patmos, and in the afternoon went off to see St. John the Divine's monastery. We took a taxi there while our friends walked up the mountain. Our little family had a stop at a café in the lovely village with its narrow alleys to wait for the monastery opening. The monastery was a very special place. 14 monks still lived there, in its best days it was over 100. We talked to one friendly monk with a very long beard that had been born in the UK and not been an orthodox monk that long. The monastery had a beautiful chapel with very old parts, a museum with parchments from as early as 900. And lots of yards and staircases. We walked down the donkey path back to Patmos, easier than expected.

Patmos

Bummi bought some dorade fish off a fisherman at Arki yesterday which he will cook tonight. The kids are allowed TV and will watch Percy Jackson. I end up preparing the fish in foil, unfortunately they have lots of bones. Tonight is the soccer final, Spain against Italy, which will happen without our attention. Germany didn't get through against Italy which was really disappointing.

Lipsi

Bummi and Helgart had been in Lipsi 25 years ago, they disappeared to explore, found a beach and were away all day. We did some schooling, looked at the church and hung out on the boat. In the evening Bummi fished with Finn and Lizzie, we had a cheerful evening in the cockpit with lots of rum and Coke. Unfortunately vital boat bits were left on the dock. We sail to Kos after an irate morning when John found out about the missing passerelle bracket and dinghy seat.

Kos
Wednesday, July 6

Stayed in a marina, mooring very tricky, mariner pushed us in, very touristy, took John forever to sign out in Kos town, atmosphere tense, separate meals. We are leaving Greece, hurrah. After a long battle with the authorities last night with John in a bar yelling I hate this country we got signed out and leave for Turkey today. A sigh of relief.

Chapter 11.

Lovely Turkey

"Everything we see in the world is the creative work of women." Mustafa Kemal Atatürk

All of our cruising friends who had visited Turkey had been raving about it as a sailing destination. A diverse cruising ground with friendly people and excellent food, lots of historical sites, and a green coastline a bit softer than barren Greece. Also my homeland Germany has a strong connection to Turkey with more than five million Turks working in Germany, now in their third or fourth generation. Having lived in parts of Hamburg with a huge Turkish population I have always had a soft spot and an interest in the country between the Orient and Occident.

Turgutreis
July 4–9

We left Kos in the morning after failing to secure a berth in Bodrum as planned. We were surprised, we had never been able not to get into a marina before but that seems quite normal for Turkey. So we decided to motor the seven miles into the wind to Turgutreis where a new big marina waited for us. We were not sad at all to leave Greece behind, and new adventures in exotic Turkey beckoned. The wind was up and there was spray over the deck as we approached Turgutreis. Dense modern housing covered the hills around the harbour, but they looked quite neat and not unattractive. The wind died as soon as we entered the marina and two marineros helped us into an easy berth.

John and I were amazed at the speed and efficiency of the marina office, customs, harbour police and harbourmaster that cleared us into the country. No endless waiting, stamps, filling out of forms like in Greece, these guys had computers, what a relief. The marina had great facilities, cost a steep 90 euros a day, and we decided to stay a while and do laundry, water, gas and other necessities. Oehnes left after a few lazy days to get back to Hamburg. The kids mainly enjoyed the pool, we lounged on the side and felt the holiday spirit for the first time. Waiters brought drinks and club sandwiches, this was the life. After four afternoons in the pool Finn looked like a strange monkey with his brown and white face where the diving mask had been, while Lizzie's hair had turned green from the chlorine. As temperatures reached more than 35 degrees we decided to give the ruins of Efesus a miss. A visit would have meant a four-hour drive there and back. We all got lazy; the envelope with schoolwork had been posted back to Oz and no new work had been received, bliss.

In Turgutreis we saw our first mosque and visited the bazaar. The choice of Turkish delight, spices, glass lamps and other knickknacks was astounding. The markets had a great atmosphere and became a highlight of any city visit we did in Turkey. At fruit and vegetable stalls I found to my surprise that whatever and how much I handed over to the stall owner to weigh, it always cost two or three Turkish lira. I wonder what the Turks would have paid. Saying "thank you" in Turkish was a challenge and John never got quite the hang of "tesekkür ederim."

Turkish bazaar

Lizzie's Diary, July 9

"On Saturday we watched Hoodwinked 2, it is very good. My favourite character was Twitch, he is a squirrel. Finn likes wolf most, wolf is a wolf. The next day we watched Mirror, Mirror. It is another version of Snow White. It is very funny. My favourite character was Snow White."

The Republic of Turkey is a large country on both sides of the Bosporus, the waterway that divides Europe and Asia. The 75 million Turks have an average yearly GDP of $15,000. The country is 99.8 percent Muslim, but the Turks practise a moderate Islam. It is a country of vast geographical and cultural differences between cosmopolitan cities, touristy coastlines, rural mountains, and remote Black Sea provinces. Its economic growth is fast, its people industrious, and Turkey has for years tried to connect itself to Europe with an application to join the European Union. Mainly due to its poor human rights record the EU membership has not come any closer, though.

When in Turkey...

"Straddling the continents of Europe and Asia, Turkey tries to be a bridge between West and East. The portion of Turkey's land in Europe may be small (about 5 percent), but the country's largest city, Istanbul, is located there. With nearly 13 million people, Istanbul is the third most populous European urban area, after Moscow and Paris."[14]

Turkey's northwest corner is famous for the World War I battlegrounds of Gallipoli while Ephesus is the best preserved Roman ruin site of the Eastern Med. In its heyday Ephesus was the capital of the Roman province of Asia with 250,000 inhabitants.

---

14 *National Geographic*

Turkey has boomed as a sailing destination for spring and autumn charter tours and base for retired European sailors. In the summer months it is less popular, as temperatures soar to above forty degrees, and the Meltemi blows strongly from the north. After our Aegean nightmare we were worried about wind conditions. For no reason, as it turned out. We did not get a single Meltemi day. It got hot, though.

A bus trip to Bodrum was necessary because the marina office should have held some schoolwork for us. As it turned out, there was no big, white envelopes for us, but we toured the well-known town anyway. It has a reputation as the Saint Tropez of Turkey. We did not experience that side of the touristy town, but looked at some Turkish gulets (classic Turkish yacht) in the harbour and explored the vast Castle of Saint Peter, built by the Crusaders in the 15ᵗʰ century. Confronted with the invasion of Seljuk Turks, the Knights Hospitaller, headquartered on the island of Rhodes, needed another stronghold on the mainland and started to build the castle in 1404 under the German knight-architect Heinrich Schlegelholt. The castle is well-preserved, interesting and great fun to walk around for the whole family.

Castle of Saint Peter

Tuesday, July 10

On Monday we sailed 50 miles into the Gulf of Gökova to Sogut, a great sail in blustery conditions, Senta loved the wind. But even on the water it was really hot, at least 35 degrees, and by the time we went in around 5 pm we were very tired. We got a berth on the yacht club pontoon and after a life-saving refreshing swim in the harbour dragged ourselves to the restaurant. John and I should not have had the three Sambuccas each after the meal, but we slept ok with the fans all going full speed. Retired sailors had warned us about the heat in Turkey, they go home to Northern Europe in July and August. We don't have those choices and stick it out.

Turkey has been an extremely positive surprise. It is a very modern society with no Muslim fundamentalism evident. In Turgutreis the muezzin called to prayers several times a day. But on the streets women walked in shorts, miniskirts and tiny tops. Everything is clean and well maintained and people are friendly. We loved the clothes market in Turgutreis while the food market was fantastic for stocking up with fresh produce. But life here is more expensive than in Greece, we have spent more money here on restaurants, food and marinas. At least everything works and it is worth the money.

Our jetty Gökova Yacht Club is part of a sailing school Global Sailing founded by a Turk who had sailed around the world with his family and afterwards started this sailing school. The grounds and equipment of the sailing school are very impressive, it is like a park, with birds in cages, bridges, a lovely restaurant and heaps of boats in neat rows waiting for learn-to-sail programs to begin.

Today we have started school again although it is school holidays in NSW. But we will otherwise fall behind, as we don't do school when we have sailing days or sightseeing days. Finn is very unwilling to work, and John is tearing his hair out. The biggest challenge on this trip is not the sailing, but the parenting with its endless challenges. On the positive side, the children spend 24 hours a day with their father as well as their mother, which rarely happens in other families. And they are really enjoying John's company. But having no escape from them is sometimes not easy for us.

We used to drag a bag with nappies, wet wipes and bottles around, now it is five kilos of Donald Duck books, the Kindle, crayons, paper etc., and that is just for going shopping, going to a restaurant, just in case there is down time.

Wednesday, July 11 at 986 nm

We motored to Cleopatra's Beach around the corner. In the anchoring bay of this little island there were already uncountable Turkish gulets with tourists. But we found an outside spot to throw the hook and took the dinghy ashore. Around 10 am it was already very hot. We had not brought swim stuff, so did not join the masses swimming in front of the cordoned-off beach that Cleopatra allegedly had brought from Africa for Mark Antony. We wandered to the well-preserved amphitheatre on a green hillside and rested for a while in the shade before returning to the boat. We motored on to English Harbour where the English fleet had been hiding at some stage. Tied to a tree we try to cool down in the water, but it has at least 25 degrees. I heard tales of boat freezers defrosting in Turkey as the cooling water from the sea is too warm.

Cleopatra's island

Friday, July 13

We must be starting to relax because I woke up and found it was 7.30, unheard of lateness. Even Finn was already awake. The kids started to fight straight away and John and I pasted a smile onto our faces with a firm determination to have a good day.

We are in a bay off the Seven Islands, with only one gulet "Jasmin" next to us. The cicadas are deafening, and the extremely salty water very clear. We are anchored at the bow and have a long blue rope at the back to a tree, Opa's blue Schwimmleine, a maritime family heirloom. In contrast to Greece these shores have low vegetation and some pine forests but little inhabitation. It almost looks like Pittwater, Kuringai national park near Sydney. The temperatures are mid-30s, but a breeze makes it bearable.

July 12–15 Sakli Koyv at 1010 nm

We are lazy, staying for a few days in this beautiful bay. We get the Opti out and go sailing, and when a French catamaran arrives the grandfather takes his two grandsons sailing with him supervising in a chase boat. An evening drink on the French boat K9 gets cut short when the French boys get too wild. The next day we do some party planning for our homecoming party, a favourite with the kids. We swim, sail and watch "My Fair Lady" on TV.

After an early start at 6 am to quickly get out of the Gulf known for its strong head winds and choppy seas, we have a much better trip than expected. The anticipated swell is not too bad. Soon we see the lighthouse on the high rock at Knidos, the once prosperous Dorian port city from 400 BC. In Knidos the architect Sostratos designed one of the seven antique wonders of the world, the lighthouse of Alexandria.

The harbour is in a spectacular location right under the extensive ruins of Knidos at the end of the Datça peninsula. The ruins are scattered over *three kilometres. But we miss the opening times. Instead we eat fish in the harbour tavern, tasty but expensive at 90 Euros.*

Knidos taverna

Monday, July 16

We climb the path through the ruins really early because of the heat. There is lots to see, and the view to all sides is stunning. From the amphitheatre we look straight down onto "Senta" and the other boats in the marina. Due to the changing winds at this strategic point ships in ancient times often had to wait for favourable winds at Knidos. The ship taking Saint Paul to trial in Rome around 50 AD had to take refuge at Knidos.[15]

15 *Lonely Planet Turkey*, London 2011

Knidos amphitheatre

We motor to Datça and get a spot on the tourist town's quay without problem. "Datça is an easy going mix of locals, salty expats and trendy Istanbulu holiday home owners."[16]

A big Dutch ketch "Alondra" has problems getting into the spot next to us backwards, we know the feeling. On board at least two families, atmosphere tense. The wife has hugely infected wounds on her legs, I wonder what from. Along the new promenade we walk to a little lake with a waterfall and have a swim. We also swim from the beach. It is super hot, around 40 degrees. After hamburgers for dinner on the boat we stroll through town, and in a gallery buy a picture of the Galatha Bridge for Finn's birthday. A Turkish super star violinist plays in the open air theatre at the harbour, and masses of people stream there.

Tuesday, July 17 at 1068 nm

Datça shower near the theatre, cold. Tried to get money, machine broken. Bought more bread. Really hot. From Datça to a bay opposite Marti Marina.

---

16 *Lonely Planet Turkey*, London 2011

Sailed away next to Dutch Rhodes-design "Alondra." Lovely beam reach for 20 miles in a Northeasterly breeze force 3-4, motored at the end. Anchor and rope tied to rock, very picturesque, high mountains, fjords. Swam with new green crocodile, huge success. Fish and salad for dinner. Finn difficult.

Wednesday, July 18

Schoolwork didn't go well, ratty, unhappy children. Still opposite Marti Marina, recommended by Filippo Masci. After some attempts at school with no result we motored over to the marina, had a look around, shopped in the very good supermarket (lots of German magazines) and had a pizza lunch in the restaurant near the pool. Lots of annoying bees. We went back, had another swim. Barbecued chicken on salad for dinner.

Cooling down

Friday, July 20

Motoring through a shallow passage between some islands near Bozburun we anchor along a spit with several other boats. The swimming in the turquoise water is heaven, the kids play with Croci, and John and I swim over to a German Southern Wind 72 to have a chat. Turkey's founder Atatürk's former yacht "Savarona" from the 1930s is anchored off the town and is just beautiful.

Savarona is one of the largest private yachts in the world. She was built in March 1931 in Hamburg for an American, Emily Roebling, granddaughter of the engineer who built the Brooklyn Bridge, spending about 4 million US dollars. The boat is named after an African swan living in the Indian Ocean area. In March 1938, the yacht was sold for 1.2 million US dollars to the Turkish government to be used as a presidential yacht. Atatürk loved this yacht but could enjoy her only for six weeks before his death on November 10 of the same year.

The yacht is 136 metres long, has a beam of sixteen metres, six metres of draft. She has two powerful diesel engines (2 x 3,600 hp) and can travel at fifteen knots of cruising speed (maximum speed eighteen knots). There are between forty and forty-five crew members on board. The yacht usually stays in Istanbul from October to May, then in the summer she sails the Med.

Savarona stayed moored at Kanlica Bay on the Bosporus until 1951, than became a training ship for young officers of the Turkish navy. She was badly damaged by a fire in October 1979 and not used until 1989, when she was leased from the government by a businessman, Kahraman Sadikoglu, who renovated and refurbished the yacht, taking three years and spending about 25 million US dollars. Steam turbines were removed and a modern diesel propulsion system was installed, interior was styled by a well-known designer, tons of fine marble was used, and so on. After her restoration, *Savarona* has been chartered out to the jet set. She was refitted in 1999 to meet the latest international and luxury standards.

The yacht has a great eighty-six-metres-long brass staircase copied from the original one, seventeen large suites to accommodate thirty-four guests, living areas, a large dining room, sun decks, recreational facilities such as a Turkish bath and a movie theatre, a small hospital room, water sports facilities, and a helipad.

Lizzie's Diary, July 22 Bozburun at 1109 nm

"We are in a nice bay. The water is so clear you can see the bottom. You can swim really good. The water is warm and clear. You can see some fish but they are small. Finn's birthday is in two and a half days. My mum bought bread that is round. Yesterday we were in a small city. It has three supermarkets. We met a nice man who is American, he spoke English, he told us to go to a nice restaurant."

Bozburun

We motor across to the town dock and do a bit of shopping in the three little supermarkets. John gets lured into a carpet shop where an American-Turk gives us good insights into life in Turkey and America. We have lunch at the recommended "Möwe" restaurant, run by a Turk who had worked in Germany as a teacher and had a German wife. A blues band plays in the lively town square, where everybody gathers around 9 pm.

Bozu Büku
Sunday, July 22

Our Hunters Hill friend Shayne Smythe had recommended the middle restaurant pontoon of the three restaurants in Bozu Büku. It looked more like a hut from the wobbly pontoon, but we walked around the structure along the stony path and first met a donkey, always a pleasure. We found the goat hut that Shayne had mentioned, but nobody was around, so we just watched the goats hop over the stone wall surrounding the poor little homestead. After a swim from the pontoon we enjoyed the delicious mezze buffet in the restaurant with a few glasses of cold white wine. Lizzie loved the stray cats and dogs that were hanging around our table.

Bozu Büku

Monday, July 23

We changed our plans flexibly after John had a long chat to the naval architect Devrim next to us, whom he had helped tying on his fenders the day before. A really nice young man with a French girl friend.

He recommended Albatros marina, as had the German from the Southwind 72. Then our Sydney friend Stephen had David Hightower text us his Turkish connection, and it turned out to be the same yard. We were off. We arrived at Albatros marina near Marmaris at 2 pm. Our welcoming committee was three guys on the dock, and the backward mooring manoeuver went perfect. The German foreman arrived a short time after and we talked through the work we wanted done. The German Southwind owner had told us about the high prices in Palma, so we wanted to get as much done here as possible. After a short while we had the laundry man appear, the life raft guy and some more. What a place. Marmaris was in sight, never seen so many gulets.

Tuesday, July 24 Finn's 10th birthday

It was an early start. Finn up at 5 am, in bed with John until 5.40. The kids had been very excited, we had made decorations for the cabin all day Monday, and especially the little figures as a chain that Finn drew were outstanding. A lot of thought went into them. The night before we had been sipping rum and Cokes in the cockpit as usual and the kids found it hard to sleep. When they finally did, I prepared the birthday table and was happy that it was a good selection of gifts after all, I thought we might not have enough. Books, DVDs, a new snorkel, a painting of Istanbul. Lizzie got a few things, the boat was quiet during the morning, everybody enjoyed the leisure time. I updated the website due to our excellent WiFi, what a relief. John dealt with tradesmen and we spoke to Oma, Opa and Hans Martin.

Birthday Boy talking to Oma

We took the dolmuş into town, super hot, around 40 degrees, on the way saw huge Netsel Marina and a West Marine shop. At the bus station we managed to tick off the internet café, supermarket and office supply store. Finn got McDonald's chips, and by this time we were tired from the heat. We started looking for a restaurant recommended by Lonely Planet and again experienced Turkish helpfulness. A shoe-shop saleslady phoned the restaurant for us, gave us directions, and a waiter met us at the tourist information. "Restaurant Ney" was hidden in small alleys and steps behind the castle. We could have never found it. Up some very uneven stairs we climbed onto a roof terrace. The only guests in this tiny restaurant we had a fabulous meal. The mixed mezze platter had quite a few different bean dishes that turned out delicious, as well as some unidentifiable other vegetables, all very good. There were some crisp rolls filled with cheese, and the speciality, Turkish ravioli in yogurt sauce, divine.

Happy we made it there, we walked down to the marina where I started the quest for Finn's school material and by luck bumped into John in the West Marine store next to the DHL office. We spent a couple of happy hours spending money in the chandlery, buying new hats and safety items for the Atlantic rally. Exhausted we got back around 4 pm, and the kids were allowed to watch two of Finn's new DVDs. We had drinks with some marina men and the owner Attila on the terrace, very pleasant.

Wednesday, July 25

School didn't work, Finn played Lego, Lizzie tired, has to learn seasons and months, didn't know her birthday month, I just gave up. The whole family took a taxi to the life raft workshop, we saw our life raft being blown up, very interesting and good fun for the kids. I visited the good bakery nearby, as the life raft place took quite long, John checked all sorts of things. The kids were unusually patient, tranquilized by the heat. In the back of a van back to the marina, exciting. Dinner in the marina restaurant was again very good. The owner Attila chatted about his Atlantic circuit.

Life raft test

BOAT MAINTENANCE

"Our boats are too complicated; we don't have time for anything romantic." A French sailor

Every time we headed for a big marina I was filled with some dread. John would revel in the facilities available, repair shops, chandleries, engine mechanics, and turn the boat, our home, into a bomb site. John had rightly decided that to have the ARC preparations and safety updates done in Turkey would save us a lot of money. So an intense week of boat work began.

The tradesmen at Albatros Marina near Marmaris were outstanding in the quality of work, were fast, and did not overcharge. The electrician and the computer man, however, could again not get our Wi-Fi booster antenna working. The polishing staff put a shade cover over the boat, in almost forty degrees sensible, but still work must have been really hard for them. We also had some bits of the teak deck resealed. The engine service as always disrupted the kids' routine, and schoolwork was difficult with the engine cover in our living space and people crawling around with oil and filters. Plenty of matrimonial conflict at engine service time throughout the trip; we had the engine serviced around eight times, I guess.

***Senta* at Albatros Marina, Marmaris**

Only now, having read Mike Litzow's enlightening cruising account of sailing from Alaska to Australia, do I understand what was likely going on in John's mind during the trip on the boat, when he was often overwhelmed by the amount of tasks needing attention. A boat is a puzzle of a thousand pieces, and each of them will need attention at some stage. Litzow writes: "To me, as I stood on the dock looking back at the boat, *Pelagic* appeared as a collection of problems: problems that were inconsequential and problems that could be serious; problems that were known, or suspected or (worst of all) that were neither, and therefore might take me unawares far out at sea some day."[17]

Senta was almost thirty years old, and although constructed well with equipment of the best quality, she had many complicated systems that John needed to maintain and be able to repair. There was the engine, most importantly, the batteries, the plumbing, the Mastervolt system that somehow regulated the electricity of 110

17 Mike Litzow, *South from Alaska*, Sydney 2011

volt, 240 volt, and 12 volt. There was the standing rigging that kept the mast in place and the running rigging that worked the sails, the autopilot, the centreboard, the fridge and freezer, the instruments, gas system for cooking, the bilge and toilet pumps. The list could go on and on. And as there are so many moving parts, some of them exposed to the forces of wind, water, and sun, something breaks all the time. The subject of boat maintenance is the bane of our trip. But as Litzow also correctly says, "It's not luck that got us, or any other sailor, to the point of casting off the lines and heading out for a year or three. There is luck involved, and the ability to organise your life around a vision, but also more work than many of our contemporaries can imagine."

Friday, July 27

Atlantis swim park in Marmaris, what an experience! We took a taxi there, mayhem, lots of big slides, doughnuts, spent 2 hours there, lots of English people and Dutch. Not for the faint hearted. Supermarket afterwards, taxi to chandlery West Marine, endless waiting in super heat in the car before John came out. We watched the Olympic opening ceremony in the marina restaurant til 1 am. Tomorrow Glenn arrives after lunchtime.

Sunday, July 29

Glenn safely here we all took a dolmuş around 10.30 into Marmaris and walked through the shopping precinct off the waterfront. Bought some cheap t-shirts and shoes. The small knight's castle was well preserved and only took a short while to look at. Our main reason to go into town, the restaurant Ney was closed, very disappointing, so we went to the Panorama restaurant which had a great view and mediocre food.

Monday, July 30

Stand by to stand by! Estimated time of departure was 11 am, we left just before 5 pm. The rubbish bin was the last thing to get fixed. The atmosphere was tense. No schoolwork done. Quite a long way out of the Bay of Marmaris and around the corner for the time of day, arrived in Ekincik at 7.30 and decided to go onto the restaurant dock. The whole estate at Ekincik was very nicely developed, with sandy colours and lots of maritime decorations.

With two young men on the dock we made a booking for the following morning to have a boat take us to the Dalyan river delta.

We raced up the steep hill to the restaurant terrace, and after some to-ing and fro-ing got a table at the waterside terrace edge. There was no menu, they had some starters on a trolley and we chose the octopus salad for 19 lira and the stuffed tomato. John had a fish, Glenn some lamb and Lizzie and I a chicken kebab. The burning coffee kept the bees away. Nice place, expensive as all of them, but we were too stressed and tired to really enjoy it.

Tuesday, July 31

At 9 am we boarded a little wooden boat that could have taken 20 people but the five of us had it to ourselves.

Touring the Dalyan River

The nice quiet captain first drove along the coast toward a huge cave. We soon entered the Dalyan river delta and noticed a long tourist beach with sun umbrellas on our right. The captain surprised us by stopping next to a boat anchored off the shore. It turned out a guy lured loggerhead turtles to the boat with a blue swimmer crab on a line as bait. They appeared after only five minutes, two big ones, one small. They had easy names like Elvis and Princess Diana and the guy made a real show of it. Great experience!

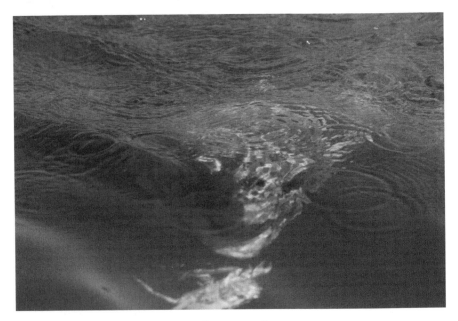

Dalyan turtle

Our captain then drove us through narrow sea weed channels, very tranquil, through the gate of a fish farm and out again. We stopped along a jetty and waded on a flooded path which the kids loved. It was a steep climb up a hill to look at the Kaunos amphitheatre, a strategic position overlooking the whole river delta. Kaunos was an important Carian city around 400 BC. Right on the border with Lycia, its culture reflected aspects of both empires, the Lonely Planet tells me. After an ice cream we walked back to the boat. Saw two donkeys, a tortoise crossing our path and a cow. Further up the river the outstanding cliff-side Lycian Kings' tombs cut from rock around 400 BC up on a mountain came into view. Here some background about the Lycians for the history boffs.

"The Lycians were an ancient and mysterious civilization. Lycia fought for the Persians in the Persian Wars, but on the defeat of the Achaemenid Empire by the Greeks, it became intermittently a free agent. After a brief membership in the Athenian Empire, it seceded and became independent (its treaty with Athens had omitted the usual non-secession clause), was under the Persians again, revolted again, was conquered by Mausolus of Caria, returned to the Persians, and went under Macedonian hegemony at the defeat of the Persians by Alexander the Great. Due to the influx of Greek speakers and the sparsity of the remaining Lycian speakers, Lycia was totally Hellenized under the Macedonians. The Lycian language disappeared from inscriptions and coinage. In 188 the Romans gave Lycia to Rhodes for 20 years, taking it back in 168 BC. In these latter stages of the Roman republic Lycia came to enjoy freedom as part of the Roman protectorate. After the fall of the Byzantine Empire in the 15th century, Lycia was under the Ottoman Empire and was inherited by the Turkish Republic on the fall of that empire. The Greeks were withdrawn when the border between Greece and Turkey was negotiated in 1923. The ruins of ancient Lycia are seemingly everywhere. For reasons unknown, perhaps isolation, recycling of the building stone was minimal compared to other regions."[18]

We stopped at the mud baths for two hours, recommended by our captain. Finn did not get in but took some photos. The rest of us hesitantly stepped into a muddy basin, caked ourselves with the mud, let it dry for five minutes and showered off. It was very smelly and a strange thing to do, smear mud all over yourself, but great fun. Then into the thermal bath which was quite hot, Finn went in that one too. More showers and back to the boat where our sweet captain was waiting. We all thought our skin looked

18 Wikipedia

much better. Near Dalyan we stopped at a waterfront restaurant and had a small lunch of mezze and a few kebabs, all delicious. A blue swimmer crab snack on the way back, and we were tired and full. Great day out, extremely memorable.

Mud bath

Wednesday, August 1

School hard work, left late, difficult bay, anchor manoeuver didn't work, line broke, too close to a charter Bavaria.

Thursday, August 2

Motored around the Gulf of Göcek, looked at bays and settled in Wall Bay, as Rod Heikell called it, goats, nice vegetation. We stayed a few days and later came back again, one of the nicest places in Turkey. Very relaxing.

Lizzie's Diary

"Yesterday we went swimming. My mum got us a swim noodle, it is yellow. We took the dinghy to Cleopatra's baths. We went twice. It is a beautiful place. I drove hard over the waves. Finn and mum swam back. It was great fun."

Allegedly Cleopatra swam in this bay, and there are some old ruins and tunnels under water, fun to snorkel through.

Cleopatra's bath

Sunday, Aug. 4 or so 1215 nm

Never been so hot in my life, constant sweating. We are in Ece Marina Fethiye, and our Sydney friend Glenn has been on the boat for over a week. He joined us at Albatros Marina at the end of our latest refit. Since then we have anchored in numerous bays around the Gulf of Göcek and *mainly spend the time swimming three times a day in 30 degree water, so not much cooling down. No internet whatsoever.*

Here in Fethiye it is over 40 degrees Celsius during the day and late 30s at night, it is soooo hot. We don't feel like doing anything. Us adults hose the kids and ourselves down on the dock all the time. This morning I saw a big turtle look straight at me off the jetty. Only one week left on the boat for now. Next Sunday we fly to Istanbul for six days, then on to Guernsey to cool down.

This is our only chance to see some of the London Olympics on TV, so we go to a marina bar a few times and watch women's weightlifting of all things. Turkey has an athlete competing in that, it seems. It is an incredible sport, a huge Chinese woman wins. Then there is shot put for women, a Bulgarian woman we call "Bob" wins, but later gets stripped of her medal due to illegal substances intake, hormones is my guess. Another day Lizzie and I watch women's gymnastics, she loves the costumes.

CHAPTER 12.

ISTANBUL

We left the boat in Fethiye for our Cornish friend Gary to pick up with some mates and sail to Mallorca, while we were sightseeing in Istanbul and recovering from the heat in Guernsey.

Our five days in Istanbul in mid-August were a huge success. Glenn came along, and we all caught up with our good friends the Vladimirov family. Together we discovered one of the most beautiful cities in the world. With around 14 million people right on the border between Asia and Europe, and a history of thousands of years, it is a breathtaking city, and there was so much to see. We walked from morning til late afternoon every day. The "Hotel Amira" in Sultanahmet was perfectly located to be able to walk everywhere or take the tram. The roof terrace a great spot to relax on afterwards with a drink, well deserved in the evening. The fasting month of Ramadan meant we could not get alcohol with some of the daytime meals, a good cleansing exercise for our liver. Istanbul is a soft, friendly city to see as a tourist, everything is easy and stress free. The kids tramped along all day and did not complain, they were mesmerized too.

Spice market

We saw the Haghia Sophia, the Blue Mosque, the Topkapi Palace, the Galata Bridge and much more. The underground water cistern featured in a James Bond movie had a beautiful atmosphere, and we got lured into having our photo taken there in traditional attire. In the Grand Bazaar we bought a new rug for our dining room from a Bulgarian merchant, not the typical Turkish type but a cow hide, and John treated me to an "authentic" Prada bag.

The beautifully ornamented, carpeted and lit mosques were soothing resting places also for us. We never went during prayer time, though. In contrast to the touristy Turkish south coast there were more women wearing headscarves and long coats in Istanbul. And after sunset the place was sheer chaos as everybody came out to eat and socialise due to the Ramadan fasting during the day. The Haman Turkish bath was a bizarre experience, the massage therapist naked to the waist was a hoot. While I was washing myself down in the women's bath to my surprise a guy walked in. Not prudish, those Turks.

"Mum, we need a new carpet!"

One of many grand mosques

Sitting on the hotel's roof terrace looking over Istanbul's roofs toward the Bosporus while the muezzin were calling for evening prayers from the nearby grand mosques was very intense and pure magic.

View from Hotel Amira roof terrace

Lizzie's Diary, August 16

"We went to Istanbul. We went to the Blue Mosque, it was amazing. We weren't allowed to wear shoes inside. We went to the Spice Market. It had all sorts of spices, red and green and brown. It was amazing. My dad got Turkish Delight and it tastes delicious. Mum and a friend went to the Turkish baths. Finn and I were allowed to watch television. I like Istanbul."

CHAPTER 13.

A BREAK FROM THE HEAT – GUERNSEY

Lizzie's Diary, August 12

"We got up early in the morning to get to Istanbul Airport. We had trouble with our bags, but we thought they were safe. In Düsseldorf in Germany Finn got Pringles and I got lollies. We found our luggage, and we went to a plane and it went to Guernsey. We took a cab to our hotel. What a glorious meal. I ate noodles. I like Guernsey. We have a nice hotel. We went to St. Peter Port, mum had a surprise but it didn't work. So we went to bed."

Our departure from Istanbul was tricky; I had a gastro bug, so threw up in the taxi, airport rubbish bins, and wherever necessary. A difficult, long trip to say the least. We stayed in the Hotel Jerbourg on Guernsey for five nights, and it was just wonderful to be in moderate climates and green, lush countryside. I had sailed here twice in the early '90s and had always wanted to come back, and it was also on John's list of places to see. The Channel Islands off the coast of France belong to the British Crown but have some French influences; they have a warm climate and beautiful landscape. Their "Britishness" felt like coming home. The whole family enjoyed the moderate climate; we even had some fog. Only the pool temperature was too chilly for all except Lizzie. There was enough to do, though: the kids ran around in the hotel gardens, climbed trees, shot bows and arrows, and were very independent. We did not bring enough long trousers as the change was too drastic for my packing skills.

Saint Peter Port, Guernsey

I still had severe gastro for the first day so John took the kids mini golfing while I stayed in bed catching up on UK television, bliss. When I was back on my feet we explored the capital, Saint Peter Port, and its impressive castle, took a day trip to the island of Herm, and walked around the cliffs near our hotel. In old age I might become a hiker and bird watcher.

Boats on Herm

Those of you who have read the book *The Guernsey Potato Peel Society* know that the islands had a very bad time under German occupation during the war, and there are bunkers everywhere. We took the kids into a huge underground structure, the German hospital, which was really eerie and made a deep impression on them. Life has not always been as good as it is for them now.

Thursday, August 23

Just after lunch we took the fast ferry from St. Peter Port, Guernsey, to Saint Malo in France. After two hours we approached the coast. The entry into Saint Malo was thrilling at low water, as all the rocks were exposed;

they have a huge tidal range here. We stayed in the Hotel Elizabeth, booked for the name, which had a modern maritime décor and was inside the walled city. The city walls are really high and the walk around was thrilling.

PARIS

In our little hire car it took us four hours to get to Paris. I drove a fair bit of the way as John had the gastro now and was not feeling well. We returned the car to the same hire station we used on our last visit to Paris eight years ago when Finn was a toddler. We had booked three nights in Paris, which had been Lizzie's wish as she wanted to see the Eiffel Tower. Despite peak season we got rooms in the Hotel Lutece's sister hotel, Deu Iles, which was equally nice, also located on the Isle de Saint Louis. We walked to Notre Dame and took the metro to the Eiffel Tower.

Paris

It took forever to get up this Paris icon, but John whiled away the time chatting to people, this time a Lebanese family considering residency in Australia. After almost two hours in the queue with them we were almost ready to sign their immigration forms. The tower was way too high for my vertigo; we obviously went all the way up with me clinging to the handrail, and was I really happy to be down again half an hour later.

We walked to the Louvre, sailed boats in the pond, and had a magnificent meal at our café Marly in the Louvre forecourt. Heaven! We met up with my friend Götz for happy hour and had an early night. On the second day we explored the natural history museum with its zoo, skeleton collection, and amazing evolution display. They really spend money on education, the French. Savoury crepes for dinner and everybody fell into bed. Paris treated us well, as always.

National Museum of Natural History

Chapter 14.

Around Mallorca in Four Weeks

Mallorca is often misjudged as a common package holiday destination. Still, a lot of European sailors have long known the island as a prime cruising spot. The stunning coastline of this biggest Balearic island with its uncountable anchorages and picturesque villages makes for interesting cruising. We sailed around Mallorca in a leisurely two weeks and stayed another two in Palma.

Wednesday, August 29

Since our arrival here in Palma on Mallorca Monday morning we have been super busy. Unpacking, heaps of washing, that John heroically processed in the steamy harbour laundry for hours on Monday. Yesterday a mega shop at Carrefour with a taxi there and back, an engine service and new single sideband radio, so the boat in a mess and mechanics crawling around. We are in a top berth in front of the bar of the Real Club Nautico, super, the kids have been in the marina pool every day for hours. We are berthed between two bigger Swans and feel really privileged to be here, over 1000 boats in this marina. My parents will arrive tomorrow, and on Saturday German friends will fly in, busy social calendar. School has restarted again as well, sigh.

Here in Mallorca we finally have a stable internet connection so I can upload a few photos. The photo side of our website has been very frustrating, and you won't see my best photos but a random selection depending on how often I had to try to upload.

Real Club Nautico, Palma

The weekend Sep 1–2 our friends Claudia and Lutz from Düsseldorf visited, and we did some sightseeing together. As always some alcohol was involved, and on day one while the girls enjoyed some Sambuca the boys did a rum tasting. We were all really cheerful. Next day we took the old train from Palma to Sóller, through mountains and tunnels, very picturesque. Lunch in Sóller was superb, we must have found the only Italian restaurant in town, run by a German.

Lizzie's Diary, September 9

"On Saturday our friends arrived. We went up in the top restaurant at the Yacht Club. The food was great. On Sunday we took the tram. There are lots of tunnels. We went under the biggest mountain. When we got off the tram we were in a little town in the mountains. We ate at a small restaurant, the food was great."

Train to Sóller

On their last day, Tuesday, we sailed to Puerto Andratx on the southwest coast of Mallorca. Lutz and Claudia went on the bus back to Palma and the kids hopped into the marina pool. A very nice set-up here with cafe, restaurant and pool. We will stay a few days and visit our friends David & Rikki Dawes who live in the Mallorcan hills.

Tuesday, Sep. 11

Mallorca has after Turkey been the most positive surprise of the trip. The island is known for cheap package holidays, hooligans and the Ballermann, so we had not expected such stunning cliffs, beautiful island interior with wine, almond and olive groves. We found nice harbours, charming promenades and even a sandy beach. Sailors are fortunate to be able to explore Mallorca's diversity from the water.

Below are some not-so-well-known facts about Mallorca from the web. Mallorca is the largest island in the Balearics with 3,640 square kilometres and around 870,000 inhabitants. In its capital, Palma, live almost half of all Mallorca residents, more than 400,000.

- The name Mallorca derives from the Latin *insula maior*, meaning "larger island," because Mallorca is the largest island of Spain. This later became *Maiorica* and eventually ending up as *Majorca* for the people of the UK and *Mallorca* for just about everyone else.

- The national anthem of Mallorca is *La Balanguera*, which is an adaptation of a poem based on an ancient and popular Mallorcan children's song about a spider.

- People have lived on the island of Mallorca since about 5000 BC, and it was occupied by the Romans in 123 BC. Tourists have only been coming to the island since 1952.

- The island has been invaded a number of times over the years, the most famous being King James I of Aragon who launched an invasion which landed on Santa Ponsa, Mallorca, on September 8–9, 1229, with 15,000 men and 1,500 horses.

- In 2008, 22,832,865 passengers passed through the airport in Palma, with an additional 1.5 million arriving by sea.

- Palma is famous for La Seu, its vast cathedral originally built on the site of a previous mosque. Although construction began in 1229, it didn't finish until 1601.

- Cap de Formentor forms the eastern end of Mallorca's Formentor peninsula. The Mallorcans also call the cape the "meeting point of the winds."

- In 2005, there were over 2,400 restaurants on the island of Mallorca according to the Majorcan Tourist Board.

- The latest tourist initiative on the island of Mallorca is "oleotourism." Literally translated this means "olive oil tourism." Many of the island's centenarian olive groves and olive mills have turned into museums, and the gnarled, ancient trees in their natural habitat are bringing a new "green" trade to the area.

- The current legislation in Spain states that it is completely legal to practice nudism in public. The fact that certain beaches have been classified as nude beaches in Mallorca does not mean that only nudists are allowed entry...in the same way that it is possible for there to be nudists on non-nudist beaches.

- Each year over 35,000 cyclists ranging from professional cyclists to cycle tourists visit the island of Mallorca.

- Should you order wine from any Mallorcan restaurant on the island, it will most probably come from Binissalem. The best-known wine from the region is known as Bodega. The local red variety, Manto Negro, represents about 50 percent of the red grapes planted, the others being Cabernet Sauvignon, Callet, Tempranillo, Monastrell, Syrah, and Merlot. The local white variety, Moll (also known as Prensal Blanc), represents about 70 percent of the white grapes planted, the others being Macabeo, Parellada, Chardonnay, and Moscatel.

- At the beach of Es Trenc, which is visited by more than 500,000 tourists each year, twenty-five tonnes of sand are carried away from the beach each year on the bottom of people's sandals, between their toes, and on their towels! This sand has to be replaced regularly.

- The local pastry, the ensaimada, is only available in Mallorca.

- Tap water in Mallorca is safe, but everyone drinks mineral water because the tap water doesn't taste too good.

-The private family slaughter of a pig, *fer matances* as it is called on Mallorca, is perhaps the island tradition that has evolved the least of all those that are still preserved. And so the slaughter that is still carried out nowadays is more or less similar to what was done two hundred years ago. Many families, especially in the villages, still kill a pig or two per year and produce the star product, the sobrasada sausage.

Lizzie's Diary, September 19

"Last week we were in a little bay. We were going to go to a cave. We got tickets but we couldn't go so we went into town. It was nice. We went to a little tapas bar. The food was great. Then we went back to the cave and

went in. It was amazing. It was ginormous and great! We sat on a bench and heard music for a long time. When we left we went home."

Finn's Diary, September 15 Puerto Christo, Mallorca

"Yesterday we went to the Cuevas del Drach which means caves of the dragon. We bought tickets at ten to 12 but the tour at 12 was full so we had to go into town. Then we had lunch in an old-fashioned Tapas bar run by two English people. We came back to the caves at twenty to two and the queue was very long but after that I thought the caves were amazing."

We have been sailing around Mallorca now for a week and have reached the northeast corner, so have left the magnificent rocky cliffs behind. Yesterday we took the bus to Pollensa, an ancient village.

Finn's Diary, September 10

"Yesterday we took a bus from Puerto Pollensa to Pollensa. We put Grandma and Grandpa in a café and climbed up 365 steps (I counted) to see a chapel. We also had an ice cream. Later on we had lunch with Grandma and Grandpa. We then took the bus home and are doing schoolwork. Later on we went swimming. Dad and I took a walk."

Pollensa

Porto Colon
Saturday, September 15

School went well this morning according to my diary, which was rare. John and I had looked at real estate in the bay the night before, lots on offer and cheap, Spain is not in a good way. We get a recommendation for a local restaurant, quite a walk, but the food is great and the place really quirky. On our dock we discover an Australian flag and meet Mark and Karline on their Bavaria 42 "Maloo" who are also ARC participants. We hear that Mark is from Aubury, New South Wales, and Karline from Austria, they have lived in Germany for the last years and are sailing to Australia. They will become very close friends in the months to come.

Tuesday, Sep. 18

We have circumnavigated Mallorca and returned to our prime spot at the Real Club Nautico in Palma today. Felt like home, to sit on the terrace and munch a club sandwich. The last two nights were spent in the anchorage of the national park Cabrera Islands, a beautiful spot with many fish around the boat. You have to get a permit to stay there for up to three nights. Due to his cold John could not swim and wound me up by making the fish crazy with bread while we were swimming close by, lots of shrieking. The rib tender of a huge powerboat came across to us and the Australian owner had a chat. Within minutes he volunteered which private schools his children went to, that was so Sydney!

Cabrera Islands

Today, just before we reached Palma harbour, a big dolphin crossed our bow, swam under the boat and appeared at the back, everybody saw it, just great. The overfished Med has not a lot of marine life left in the water but out here in Mallorca it feels that some nature remains untouched.

Mum and Dad fully reinvigorated will leave the boat Thursday, and we will likely head off Saturday to make our way to Gibraltar. Some technical issues left as always, first technician coming this afternoon.

Sunday, Sep. 23

Still in Palma, will leave on Tuesday. While the kids have been enjoying five star comfort with Oma and Opa in their hotel Gran Melia Victoria for the last two days, we have been polishing and scrubbing the boat and dealt with more electronics problems. Don't know where we went wrong, we should be in the hotel. At least the kids were happy in the pool and watching German TV while we had them out of our hair, all good. It has been great to have the grandparents on the boat for such a long time this year, three months, good for them, the kids and us.

Oma and Opa go home

John and I managed to fit in a sumptuous Tapas lunch yesterday, we also shopped for some clothes, bumped into UK navigator Hugh Agnew in town, as one does, and caught up with our fellow ARC participants, Mark and Karline. This morning there will be kids wailing when we drag them out of the hotel back to normality and take them to the cathedral for mass. We really like Palma, a place to retire to. Monday our good friends Rodney and Mary Ann will arrive from Cowes to take part in Oyster week, so we will meet for drinks, I haven't seen them for eight years or so, will be great.

The miracle happened, the electronics guy Mark got the WiFi booster working. The brand new router was broken, he simply installed a new one for 40 Euros and we were connected, unbelievable.

We had drinks with some other ARC sailors, Kerstin and Robert from "Trinity" who were working hard at getting their boat ready for the crossing, mainly generator problems. We don't have one, nor a water maker, it is enough work to keep the simple systems going.

Monday, Sep. 24

Last day in Palma with full on program. School in the morning, last lunch with my parents, cooking for the next few days and drinks with our Cowes friends Rodney and Mary Ann.

This morning Palma felt like Sydney, thick smoke in the air from a bush fire, a big problem here too. Kids super ratty at breakfast, very rewarding. I am so little concerned about my looks nowadays that I cut my hair with nail scissors in the public showers this morning, the ends tangle all the time. No one will notice. Long sail to Ibiza tomorrow in not so good conditions, hope we won't get too sick.

Wednesday, Sep. 26

Yesterday we aborted the attempt to sail to Ibiza. We left at 8 am well prepared, but the seas were huge and confused, and the wind 25 to 30 on the nose. So after a few hours bashing into it, with most of the team sick, we veered off to Port Andratx where we have been before. It was such a relief when we found a berth and were safe, it was pretty wild out there. So now we have to go to the mainland in one go tomorrow, around 15 hours for the 105 miles with luck, we hope it will be calmer. The next front is arriving Friday and we want to be ahead of that. Andy our brilliant electronics man from Palma is back on the boat, always something new.

Finn's Diary, Sep. 26 at 2821 nm

"Yesterday we woke up early as we were leaving for Ibiza which is west of Mallorca. We encountered strong head winds and heavy swell, so we decided to change course and headed for the port of Andratx. Once we had a safe berth we went swimming in the pool and had dinner. It was a normal day."

Chapter 15.

Mainland Spain

Saturday, Sep. 29

A lot of action in the last few days. After the unplanned stop in Port Andratx we left Thursday 5 am after getting up at 4 am. In pitch darkness we motored out of the harbour and almost ran down a floating dinghy and debris in the harbour entrance, fallout from the wind the days before. John and I both had the same thought, was it worth to get that dinghy, but in the end we did not pick it up. We pulled up the sails and got on the road for our 113 mile trip to Denia on the Spanish mainland, where my German uncle has a holiday house. The light came up at 7.30 but no sun. We motor-sailed through huge dark clouds, reefed the main in between, and tried to keep our average speed up with the engine. Finn was sick, Lizzie was bored, I could not go down below as I would have been sick. There was rain, lots of dolphins hopping around the bow, and scary dark fronts moving toward us. The waves from the aft were enormous. It was really hard on everyone and casts into doubt our future ventures. After 17 hours at 10 pm we entered Denia and got a good spot on the dock. My legs were shaking. Kids asleep by that time. Only food all day a few biscuits. The next day we had another engine man, sigh.

Spanish Main, here we come!

At least we got there before the next huge blow and on Friday, our 10th wedding anniversary, we connected with my father's brother Onkel Olaf and his wife Elke who own a holiday house in Denia. For those of you who went to our wedding in Stade you would remember what a happy affair it was, and we were very pleased to have a celebratory lunch with my close family at the Restaurant Arena with Spanish bubbles.

Lizzie's Diary, October 4

"Last Saturday we were in a big city, it rained and rained and when it stopped Uncle Olaf and Tante Elke came on the boat. We took the car to a restaurant named Arena. The food was great. Then they took us to their holiday house, it was amazing and small."

Family is so important

We then drove to Valencia to look at a boat, and on Saturday got onto the engine man, did the washing etc. As we are waiting for new batteries we will be late for our onward journey and I am fretting a bit. On Friday, while we had the day off, the wind was so strong that in the next town the ferris wheel of the local fun fair collapsed onto the roller coaster and injured 50 people. We were so glad to be here and safe. Autumn in Spain!

Sunday, Sep. 30

Finally a quiet day with just family time. We are waiting to get new batteries tomorrow. The kids scootered, we ended up in a Harley Davidson gathering, and watched Lord of the Rings. Too rare, those normal days. I cooked a chicken curry and a tomato soup for the next few days. Better prepared this time is my motto, we might be going 24 hours nonstop, we are behind schedule. Housewifely annoyances of the moment: fried no 3 of toothbrush battery chargers in as many weeks, each Euro50 a pop. Those chargers don't like our boat electricity. So we have been manual brushing for weeks and have fur on our teeth. Other annoyance is the poor quality of laundry services where after the delivery back I have sniffed at the clothes to see whether they had been washed at all, they were still so dirty. The white t-shirts and shorts are mainly yellow now, and stains are here to stay. My other annoyance is iTunes which I have never managed and just have wasted money on buying the same two films which take days to upload. Enough grumpy old women whinging.

Denia

Monday, Oct. 1 at 2960 nm

The batteries came, were installed, and euro 2400 later at almost three o'clock we left Denia for Altea. It blew with 25 knots on the nose from the southwest, so under engine we arrived before darkness at 6.30. Chicken curry, reading and bed. The new Ken Follet, second in his trilogy, was out on the Kindle, I was hooked. Finn also got the new Percy Jackson on his Kindle and read 800 pages in a day, he was slightly disappointed about the end.

Tuesday, Oct. 2

Leave at 7.30am for an 80 mile trip, dark, tired. Amazing sunrise on high orange cliffs. Wind on the nose, main up, later No 5. Made pancakes on the way, saw pilot whales. A Dutch super yacht leads us into Cartagena, a huge port, new marina with finger pontoons, bliss. At 7.30 tied on by marinero in golf cart, drives kids to marina office. Shame we don't have time to look at the city, seems interesting. But we have to move to get to the Canaries on time.

Skipper John

Along this whole coast we drive through islands and islands of debris, rubbish, but also trees, vegetation, they must have had big rains ashore. We really have to watch the floats and not drive through them.

Saturday, Oct. 6 at 3245 nm

We are in Benalmadena next to Torremolinos on the Costa del Sol, and it just looks like it, high rises everywhere. Kids and John had a swim on the beach this afternoon, and we are now waiting for my oldest friend Antje to join us for the trip to the Canaries. Gibraltar tomorrow and for the next few days, really looking forward to it, John and I went there 12 years ago when we were courting.

Sunday, Oct. 7

We approached Gibraltar under engine between lots of dolphins on a misty, sunny day and the rock was clouded in fog. We had had thick fog at times motoring up from Benalmadena. Lots of freighters were anchored in the entrance, waiting for freight? It was a buzzing scene with bunker boats, tug boats, fishing vessels and yachts filling up the bay on the way to Marina bay. Next to the lighthouse to our surprise stood a mosque. The Moroccan coast was visible right opposite, how exciting. We headed straight to the fuel dock and filled up. Our allocated berth was a long way in, we motored slowly along the runway. Our friend Basil Diethelm on Swan 48 "Sumatra" was already there, also heading for the ARC start in the Canaries. The holiday was over, now for the crossing!

Rock in fog

JOHN'S PRACTICAL TIPS
FOR MAINTAINING A BOAT

1. The boat should be ready to go when you step on. It is better to keep working and pay competent professionals to get it right. Do not head off with the family on the boat and start fixing things to be able to continue. They will be frustrated with the wait, and the whole journey will start off on the wrong foot. You will lose enough time just packing and getting ready for sea. If you have to do some extensive work go to a nice place and get the family ashore for swimming and exploring.

2. Look for yards with competent, nonexpensive staff, e.g., in Turkey. Large charter fleets often have a yard with good troubleshooters. Their staff doesn't have a lot of work midweek when the charter boats are out. Work in yachting hubs like Dubrovnik, Mallorca, or Gibraltar will be expensive.

3. Try to do everything at once, take a week or two in that yard and work through the lot rather than spending your leisure time constantly working on her.

4. In regards to spares, go for the bits that can stop your main motor. The bolt on kits, fuel lift pump, water pump (bolt off, bolt on to fix it quick, spare impellers to rebuild it later), belts, fuel filters (lots), starter motor, steering cables.

5. Preparation is better than cure. And know your boat; it is your problem out there.

6. Check belt tension and oil regularly and always before setting off on big trips.

7. Know where all the skin fittings are and what they are for, check them for leaks regularly, have double clips on them and service them periodically.

8. Have a split boom preventer to the front of your boat; check the gooseneck fittings regularly.

9. When wintering in the tropics don't buff the polish off until next season close to launch.
10. Have a list book and write the jobs down as you see them. Start years before you leave. Have "needs first" and "desire" lists separately. The book will never be completed.

PART THREE

CROSSING
THE ATLANTIC

"**F**irst, the ocean, the steep Atlantic stream. The map will tell you what that looks like: three-cornered, three thousand miles across and a thousand fathoms deep, bounded by the European coastline and half of Africa, and the vast American continent on the other side: open at the top, like a champagne glass, and at the bottom, like a

municipal rubbish-dumper. What the map will not tell you is the strength and fury of that ocean, its moods, its violence, its gentle balm, its treachery: what men can do with it, and what it can do with men."[19]

The last part of our sabbatical was going to be the most challenging one, and I was apprehensive. The sail from Gibraltar to the Canary Islands would take around four days and be the first real test for the long ocean passage we were attempting in November. My main worry was seasickness, as both kids and I suffered from it. Three weeks on the Atlantic feeling really sick would be a nightmare, not only for the kids. I would be cooking, looking after them and the guys, keeping the boat in order, and standing a night watch. Not much fun while feeling crooked. If the delivery trip to Gran Canaria went well we would all feel more positive about the ARC rally across to the Caribbean.

Of course it would help immensely that my oldest friend Antje would be with us to get the boat to the Canaries. She had taken two weeks off from her family duties, her husband, and her two teenage children to sail with us from the Spanish mainland to Lanzarote. Antje's parents had been members of our local sailing club in Stade, as had my parents. We had known each other since age ten. But we became firm friends sailing my dinghy as teenagers and both went to university in Hamburg. I remembered that Antje could sleep anywhere and did not get seasick. She was a more competent sailor than me and very hardy, as she spent her sailing summers in the cold northern climates. The only thing was: she was a racer at heart, and our twenty-ton *Senta* did not naturally lend herself to peak performance.

19 Nicholas Monsarrat, *The Cruel Sea*

CHAPTER 1.

THE ROCK

"Of course those apes *could* travel around in Spain if they wanted to, and no doubt they *do* want to; and so, how sweet it is of them, and how self-denying, to stick to that dull rock, through thick and thin, just to back up a scientific theory."[20]

Motoring down the Spanish mainland coast had been uneventful and not very rewarding; Costa del Sol, Costa Brava, Costa Blanca, there was not much to see and we had long days on the water. Also lots of fog, which is always creepy, and we often had to dodge dangerous floats of debris in the water. We were blessed, however, with a fantastic approach to Gibraltar. The fog lifted slightly, and we could see the famous rock and uncountable freighters moored around it. The ships reminded me of Hamburg and my home river Elbe with its busy commercial traffic.

"Let's watch the World War II submarine film *Das Boot* on DVD at some stage as it has thrilling scenes in the Gibraltar Straits," I suggested. As we nosed around the point we were surprised to see a mosque, right there, near the lighthouse, what a location!

20 Mark Twain, *The Innocents Abroad*, www.twainquotes.com

Gibraltar, on the southern tip of Spain at the entrance to the Mediterranean, is an oddity. Still a British territory, its inhabitants are fiercely British and have voted against reunification with Spain time after time.

"It has an area of 6.8 square kilometres and a northern border with Andalusia, Spain. The Rock of Gibraltar is the only landmark of the region. At its foot lies the densely populated city area, home to almost 30,000 Gibraltarians and other nationalities.

"An Anglo-Dutch force captured Gibraltar from the Kingdom of Castile in 1704 during the War of the Spanish Succession on behalf of the Habsburg pretender to the Spanish throne. The territory was subsequently ceded to Britain 'in perpetuity' under the Treaty of Utrecht in 1713. It was an important base for the Royal Navy, today its economy is based largely on tourism, online gaming, financial services, and shipping.

"The sovereignty of Gibraltar is a major point of contention in Anglo-Spanish relationships as Spain asserts a claim to the territory. Gibraltarians rejected proposals for Spanish sovereignty in a 1967 referendum and again in 2002. Under the Gibraltar constitution of 2006, Gibraltar governs its own affairs, though some powers, such as defense and foreign relations, remain the responsibility of the UK Government."[21]

Sunday, Oct. 7 at 3245 nm

The marina right next to the runway was easy to find, we spotted two ARC flags, fellow rally participants, and decided to take fuel first to have full tanks for the trip to the Canaries. John did not like the berth that we got allocated by the marina office as it was very hard to get into backwards. He drove in ok, but had a go at the marinero, who was not amused at all. At least the berth was close to the promenade. Since John and I had been in Gibraltar 12 years ago on my boat "Bella Gioia" the marina precinct had changed a lot. Big apartment blocks now towered over the yachts, and famous chandlery

21 Wikipedia

Sheppards had moved into a back yard of a high rise. On the plus side, there were numerous bars and restaurants and less of a derelict feel to the place.

Our friend Basil from Sydney, who was delivering his son's Swan 48 "Sumatra" to Gran Canary for the ARC, came for happy hour drinks. I had first met Basil at the Swan Cup 2000 where he was moored next to my boat with his Swan 44 "Sarabande." He had circumnavigated on "Sarabande" several times and we had bumped into him in marinas all over the world. It was harder to see him and his wife Angela in Sydney, they were always on the move.

Basil Diethelm

We had dinner with Basil at the steak restaurant on the promenade. Mark and Karline from "Maloo," the Australian Bavaria 42 we had first met in Mallorca, cycled past on their practical, foldable boat bikes and stayed for a drink. Their boat was moored in La Linea, the brand new Spanish marina just across the airport runway.

In the morning Basil showed us the way to the Morrisons supermarket, which was very big and had lots of English brands. Nice to buy some well-known foods after shopping in Greece and Turkey for months. We stocked up for the four to five day crossing ahead and took a taxi back to the boat. Grocery unpacking on the boat is always stressful, as the fridge is very small and cupboard space at a premium. The half price Margaritas with Basil at a bar on the water went down really well after that effort. Later Mark and Karline came to our boat and we had more drinks with them on Senta. We enjoyed the Australian banter.

The children met two English girls on the dock with exotic names one couldn't possibly remember, and soon they had a gang of kids running and playing on the dock. I was busy cooking some food for the crossing. As it happened we had to throw it out. The chicken curry had gone off straight away despite the cool temperatures. Strange, maybe the movement of the boat.

To our dismay we saw on www.weatherguru that the weather forecast had changed dramatically and we quickly decided to leave two days earlier than planned. That left just one day of sightseeing in Gibraltar. The boat will never be completely ready, so we just had to go.

Kids on the dock in Gibraltar

Tuesday, Oct 9

Our darling dog Pauli had to be put down in Stade, Germany today. She has stayed with my parents since we left Australia and had enriched their lives. All of a sudden she had an enlarged heart, stopped eating and after three weeks of misery my mother had her put down, only ten years old. We did not tell the kids straight away but were sad for weeks ourselves. I could not stop thinking about her.

Pauli 21.8.2002–9.10.2012

That Tuesday we walked up the busy Gibraltar High Street to find the post office. We planned to send another parcel back to Australia. It was quite a walk, the kids were on their scooters. Due to a cruise liner in town the place was hopping. While I dealt with the parcel in the post office Antje, John and the kids looked at shop windows. It took maybe ten minutes. When I came out they had lost Finn. He was nowhere to be seen, so John went one way down the pedestrian street, Lizzie and me the other and Antje waited at the post office. After Lizzie and I had been walking for a long while to no avail we approached two Bobby policemen who sent out a walkie talkie message to their colleagues. The family gathered at the post office and soon Finn walked toward us accompanied by a policeman. He was visibly upset, he said he had just looked at a window and when he turned around everybody had gone. So he walked in the direction we had planned to go. We were so relieved to have him back.

On the way to the post office

We did not take the cable car up the rock as the queues were too long, but spotted some monkeys on a park bench, which was just as good. The famous monkeys exist nowhere else in Spain. Mark Twain explains: "So the theory is that the channel between Gibraltar and Africa was once dry land, and that the low, neutral neck between Gibraltar and the Spanish hills behind it was once ocean, and of course that these African animals, being over at Gibraltar (after rock, perhaps, there is plenty there), got closed out when the great change occurred. The hills in Africa, across the channel, are full of apes, and there are now, and always have been apes on the rock of Gibraltar— but not elsewhere in Spain! The subject is an interesting one."[22]

---

22 Mark Twain, *The Innocents Abroad*, www.twainquotes.com

Famous Barbary macaque

At 6pm we had drinks on "Sumatra" with Basil and Mark and Karline. The fog set in and it got damp and miserable. It was autumn after all. Back on the boat we drank hot tea and did some reading, a cosy evening.

Chapter 2.

Into the Fire – Crossing to Lanzarote

"I must down to the seas again, to the vagrant gypsy life,
To the gull's way and the whale's way where the wind's like a whetted knife;
And all I ask is a merry yarn from a laughing fellow-rover
And quiet sleep and a sweet dream when the long trick's over."[23]

Wednesday, Oct. 10 at 3294 nm

In the morning the fog was so dense we abandoned the idea to take a taxi up to the rock. Instead we walked across the runway to Spain, a fun experience, and went into the airport to get money, Gibraltar pounds that apparently we could not use in the UK, weird.

---

23 John Masefield, *Sea Fever*

On the Gibraltar runway

Later Antje and John got the boat ready while I cooked another few stews for the next days. On the dock more ARC people appeared to say hello, two English families with kids from Gran Soleil 52 "Fabiola" and "Open Blue." On "Fabiola" there were two boys Finn and Lizzie's age, while the "Open Blue" girls were smaller. Little did we know then what good friends they all would become. We heard that they were going to stay for a few more days, sightsee and provision. Mark and Karline were off for a trip to Morocco, with ferries and trains. Very few sailors were game to stop in any Moroccan harbour on the way to the Canaries. The marinas did not offer good protection and people were concerned about safety. We had not considered it at all, we just wanted to get quickly to Las Palmas. Basil gave us another good tip: Lizzie and I walked to a pizza place and got a few takeaway pizzas we could eat on the first evening and not have to worry about cooking.

Our hasty departure also meant that there was less time to get worried about this first major ocean leg. John was very experienced in the ocean, but I preferred day trips (I like my sleep) and am prone to seasickness. So we had avoided overnighters in the month before. I was not worried about too much wind, steep seas, etc. My only worry was that I would be too sick to look after the kids. The four-day crossing to the Canaries would give us a real idea of our abilities and whether it was feasible to take the kids across the Atlantic. I could still fly out from Las Palmas and greet John and the crew in the Caribbean. But I preferred to sail there, with the kids, in the ARC rally.

John and I had planned to do the ARC in 2002 on *Bella Gioia*, our Swan 40. Lists were written, seminars attended. But then Finn was born mid-July that year and I was not so naïve to want to sail across an ocean with a newborn, my first child. So here we were, ten years later.

We left at 2 pm, John super stressed from doing last minute things. We motored into the bay and turning a corner had a gusty 30 knots on the nose. Basil had warned us to put a reef in straight away which was the right advice. The wind soon eased and we motor sailed, short tacking up the Spanish coast to avoid the current. We counted eight other boats and it felt good to be in company. The wind generators at Tarifa appeared, where 12 years ago we had tacked endlessly on "Bella Gioia." This time it was a beautiful evening. We thought we could just make it out of the strait and across the immensely busy shipping lane before darkness, and fortunately it worked out exactly that way.

Sunset in the straits

I had the watch from 11 to 1 and 5 to 8. My first watch went really quickly due to the freighter traffic that I had to monitor, but the last watch was very long, and at sun rise I found it extremely hard to stay awake. We adjusted that watch a bit in the following days. "Senta" motored against a light southwesterly with the main up, sometimes the No 3 jib or the No 5 during the following days. Antje was a bit disappointed that we only could sail for two half days all in all. At night we wore full wet weather gear as it was really damp from dew and quite cold too, socks on. Antje and I chatted a lot during the day and she was a great sailing support to John.

Antje on her watch

After day one with some boredom, eased by a TV treat, the kids settled into a good routine and listened to tapes and entertained themselves with reading and drawing. Maybe because of the Stugeron nobody got sick, what a relief! We had soup at lunchtime and stew in the evening, the kids got pancakes twice on this trip. Finn shared John's watch from 8-11. We could see the lights of Casablanca and Rabat at night. To have the African coast just there, so close, felt threatening to me, which was completely irrational. Strange to think that Moroccan families were having their evening meal while we were sailing along their coast.

On the second day we were approached by an open wooden fishing boat, we were surprised, how far do they go out to fish, we were more than 30 miles off the Moroccan coast. The two men made signs we should watch their nets, they also wanted to sell us fish but we did not let them get too close. That night we encountered a long row of flashing lights that we could not place. We decided it must be nets and altered course toward the Moroccan coast to drive around the nets. We encountered them again, nerve wrecking and annoying. John was very happy about his AIS, however, being able to determine the frequent freighters' course is a great safety feature.

The MPS – not for long

During the morning a whale blew quite close to the boat and showed his back, and by the time everybody had clambered into the cockpit he did it again, very exciting. We saw a second one a bit later. This would be our only big whale sightings for the whole of our tour.

Sunny, wobbly, not enough wind on day three. Get up at 9, and around 10 play battleships with Finn. Two dolphins surf around the bow, and we also spot a turtle swimming by. The kids listen to "Treasure Island" while the adults play with the baby-blue blister (MPS) to gain some speed. The warmed-up pizza for lunch is still good. At 4 pm we take the blister down and try sailing angles with the main and No 3 jib. But the angles mean we are off course by 30 degrees so we put the engine on again. Chili con carne for dinner. Overnight fishing boat scare (fishing boats are a worry to sailors all around the world as they often carry strange lights and their course and type of net is unpredictable) and little sleep for all.

Dolphins on the bow

Day 4, the 5am watch goes very fast, as does the boat, she is surfing, quite scary. The new course is very wobbly, we carry No5 jib, main and also have the engine on. 132 miles to go. We gybe before it gets dark, boom onto the other side, always a major manoeuver with just the three of us. Overnight John is on the tail of an Oyster 54 "Persian Pearl" according to the AIS.

"Guten Morgen, Mama!"

We are nearly there. Up early to gybe again as soon as daylight dawns. John has overtaken the Oyster on his watch. Approaching Lanzarote in the morning the sunlight is beautiful, we motor into Puerto Calera marina in the afternoon and have a necessary shower first and a fantastic Spanish tapas meal afterwards. The salted Canary potatoes with green and red sauces are delicious. Great berth in front of the Irish pub, opposite an ARC boat, "Tallulah Ruby."

Fire Island, Lanzarote

What a relief! The first crossing had gone well. Four days from Gibraltar to Lanzarote and nobody had been seasick. Finn, 10 and Lizzie, 7 had after a first difficult day settled well into life on the ocean and been as thrilled as us by the sightings of whales, dolphins and turtles.

On that Monday in mid-October, the day after our arrival in Lanzarote, my diary has little to tell. A Swedish boy, Kim, comes to play, and we have happy hour drinks with the *Oyster* people. The shops are nice and there is a sale on, so I buy myself new black jeans. Lizzie gets a blue cardigan and blue-white flowery blouse. John buys himself a green corduroy cap in which he looks like Ratty from *The Wind in the Willows*. We sit in the cockpit long into the evening and just enjoy.

After some admin on Tuesday morning with e-mails and other computer work we talk to *Maloo* on the phone. Mark and Karline had a great time in Marrakesh but are still in La Linea near Gibraltar and say that a big weather front is expected, so they will be stuck there for a while longer. Our decision to quickly leave Gibraltar seems to have been the right one.

We hire a car to explore the island, Antje squeezed in the back between the kids. The landscape is black, rocky, and completely barren but visually very attractive. It has not rained here in years. The black fields framed by low stone walls get their moisture solely from dew overnight. On the approach to the Montana del Fuego, the fire mountain, we see a herd of camels with tourists on their backs but give that ride a miss. We do, however, pay for the bus trip on a ring road around the mountain that is very worthwhile. An amazing reddish lunar landscape that suffered volcano eruptions as recent as 1824. Lanzarote had volcanic eruptions for six years from 1730 to 1736 and a smaller one in 1824; its current status is classed as dormant. Out of the bus at the viewing point a tourist guide throws a tree branch in a hole in the ground and it catches fire. He also pours a bucket of water down a pipe, and a tall steam pillar erupts from the pipe.

Camels in Lanzarote

Lunch in a simple restaurant on the roadside is tasty and Finn even gets chips. The island is not big; within half an hour we are on the other side to visit Cesar Manrique's home and studio.

The local artist and architect had a major influence on the planning regulations in Lanzarote. He recognized its tourist potential and lobbied successfully to encourage sympathetic development of tourism. One aspect of this is the lack of high-rise hotels on the island. Manrique's home itself is built on a 3,000-square-metre lot, on the site of the Lanzarote eruptions in the eighteenth century, and was built upon Manrique's return from New York in 1966. The rooms on the first floor, including the artist studios, were created with the intention of keeping with Lanzarote traditions, yet making them more modern with open spaces and large windows. The basement contains five areas situated within volcanic bubbles, the rooms bored into volcanic basalt. There is a central cave with a recreational area and a swimming pool, a barbecue, and a small dance floor. Manrique died in a car accident at Tahiche, Teguise, very near his Lanzarote home, in 1992. He was aged seventy-three.[24]

Manrique's house was one of the most interesting architectural designs we had ever seen. The whitewashed living spaces in the volcanic bubbles with bright red and yellow leather seating looked fantastic. The kids loved the bridge over the courtyard pool as well as Manrique's windvane sculptures. A very versatile, gifted man.

---

24 Wikipedia

One of Cesar Manrique's wind sculptures

To finish off the grand tour of Lanzarote with a shopping spree John dives into a hardware shop. Lizzie still remembers to this day that she got lost between the shelves. Meanwhile I check our e-mail in an Internet café. Dinner at the marina tapas restaurant crowns another interesting sightseeing day.

We have sailed more than four thousand miles by now, mid-October, and it already feels like an achievement, although the big trip is yet to come, 2,800 miles across the Atlantic. But first a mere fifty miles to sail for us to Gran Taja on Fuerteventura, which translates into "Strong Fortune" and is the second-largest Canary Island after Tenerife. But in contrast to that lush bigger sister, Fuerteventura is barren, and its economy is mainly based on tourism. Apparently the island is home to one of the two surviving populations of the threatened Canarian Egyptian vulture, but we did not spot a single one. Little chance too, as we did not tour the island. We now really wanted to get to Las Palmas and settle down before the ARC.

The marina in Gran Taja had a typically cruising fraternity atmosphere. We met Cindy and Robert from American boat *Tenacity*; he is a sail maker, she an artist. Robert later did some canvas work for us and Cindy painted a beautiful painting of *Senta*. We would see a lot of them in Las Palmas, and Cindy's art lessons were hugely popular with the children.

In Gran Taja the kids and I spend hours gluing tickets, photos, postcards into the kids' diaries, their least favourite pastime and hence lots of work. I hope they will look at them as adults and say: "Look, all those places we have been to."

A Russian boat came in and moored next to us, quite expertly. Antje and I were intrigued by the muscular, trim guys that were doing push-ups on the deck. Were they soldiers on a yachting exercise, secret agents on a team building mission? Or what else? In the evening I approached the only woman on the boat. Turned out she was a psychologist and the guys were from a company, their trip focussed on team building, very modern. The woman, who had never been on a boat before, was supporting them psychologically. Now we knew.

Celebrating Russians

We take the kids into town with their scooters, the promenade is slippery and both fall over. Ice creams help the healing, we find a bakery and a supermarket, and in the evening have pasta with anchovies and olive sauce.

After an early departure the next morning and 15 miles motoring in flat water, quite unexpectedly we meet confused seas at Fuerteventura point. The wind gets up to 15-25 knots with four metre swells, we carry the No 5 jib and the main. Antje and I are on watch all day, John minds the kids. Lots of shipping traffic approaching Las Palmas.

The hard way to Las Palmas

We dock at the marina of Las Palmas, Gran Canary at 6.30 pm after an exhausting 12 hour sail in huge seas and big winds from Fuerteventura. Kids and I quite sick. After checking in at the reception pontoon, the grumpy marinero was supposed to show us the berth. "Senta" is very hard alngSabb

to manoeuvre and, as always, John motored into the aisle backwards while we were looking out for the berth. But the RIB with the unfriendly marina helper was nowhere to be seen. "Where is he, can you see him?" John got agitated. With 20 tons of boat under him gaining momentum he almost missed the spot and could not get the boat around fast enough when we finally saw the guy. Fortunately we just did not hit our neighbour Swan 44 "Selene," and on second attempt John got "Senta" easily into her spot for the next weeks. We will be here until Nov 25, the start of the ARC rally and are happy to see plenty of ARC flags in the marina already. Opposite is our friend Basil Diethelm on "Sumatra" and also a German Swan 51 "Cherie." The partying will only start mid-November but I guess there will be plenty of boat drinks before.

After two weeks on "Senta" my friend Antje is flying home and I will be sad to see her go, we have had great sailing and lots of deep conversations you can only have with old friends.

Chapter 3.

Five Weeks in Gran Canary

"A real sailor does not own a boat, the boat owns him." A perceptive sailor.

Las Palmas has over 400,000 inhabitants and is a busy place with heaps of traffic, a huge port and big marina. Dirty and noisy! I am sure we will know it well by the time we leave.

Gran Canary, originally meaning "Great Island of Dogs," is the second most populous island of the Canaries with around 840,000 inhabitants constituting approximately 40 percent of the population of the archipelago. Located in the Atlantic Ocean about 150 kilometres off the northwestern coast of Africa, it is about 1,350 km from Europe.

Gran Canary was populated by the Canarii who may have arrived as early as 500 BC. After over a century of European (French, Portuguese) incursions and attempts at conquest, the island was conquered on April 29, 1483, after a campaign that lasted five years, by the Kingdom of Castile, with the support of Queen Isabella I. The capital city of Las Palmas was founded on June 24, 1478, under the name "Real de Las Palmas," by Juan Rejon, head of the invading Castilian army. In 1492, Christopher Columbus anchored in the port of Las Palmas and spent some time on the island on his first trip to the Americas.[25]

Due to its pleasant winter climate Gran Canary is a major tourist destination for sun hungry Northern Europeans. I had been there three times before, on sun baking holidays with my mum in the European winter.

Frolicking in Las Palmas

The walk into town on the promenade above the marina would become very familiar soon. The kids always took their scooters, it was a 15 minute walk for us past the local sailing club Real Club Las Palmas across the pedestrian bridge over the highway. Through some side streets with pharmacy and electrics shop we found the central market where we would buy fruit, vegetables, meat and eggs for the crossing a few days before the start. On the main shopping street the department store El Corte Ingles had everything we wished for. We bought school shoes for Finn for next year and ballerinas for Lizzie, I got a pair of red jeans and John a new Swatch. The basement food store at El Corte Ingles had a fantastic selection but not so much bulk, we would have to take a taxi to the outskirts to another El Corte Ingles Megamart.

We have Basil and some of his crew from Sydney over for drinks, and later Antje and I enjoy a final Sambuca, our tipple since we were 16. She would fly out early the next day.

Last sambuca

"Laundry, all morning," my diary says on Monday, October 22. Spain had not been good laundry-wise in contrast to Croatia, Greece, and Turkey, where industrious people had collected sailors' laundry. In Mallorca John spent a whole day in a steaming hot marina laundry. The second load we gave to an English laundry service in Palma de Mallorca, and 150 euros later the clothes returned still really dirty. In Las Palmas, we learned the hard way that one should not attempt washing clothes on a Monday when the laundry is humming with people. And one needs to be friendly with the women from chandlery Rolnautic, who supply the kilos of coins one needs for washing machines and dryers. We spent a lot of time in this laundry over the five weeks we were there. One laundry for a marina of five hundred boats, crazy. Also the laundry detergent is supplied by the machines; you can't put your own in. Consequently Lizzie suffered from big pussy spots on her behind for weeks to come.

Thursday, Oct. 25

John washes the deck, kids do school, hard. Robert comes over for canvas work. Kids swim at the Club Veradero. In the evening rain.

This would be almost our final attempts at schoolwork. We sent the last few envelopes with assignments back in mid-November so the kids could enjoy the pre-ARC atmosphere. Also the school year in Australia was coming to an end, and although we did not quite finish everything we had made a big effort over the whole year and were ready to quit. More about the issue of homeschooling in the back of the book.

Can't believe we have been in Las Palmas on Gran Canary for almost a week. We have been into town only once in that time, otherwise chasing parcels, finding post offices, starting school again and cleaning up the boat. It is a great atmosphere on dock L, four Australian boats and plenty of talk, e.g. with our friend Basil and Mike Thurston at the Sailor's Bar. The marina is vast but run down, I have the showers to myself at 7 am which is good because I am using the one shower that works. There are over 400,000 people living in Las Palmas, and the marina is under a six-lane expressway. But we have become members of a yacht club Club Maritimo Veradero next to the marina that has a good feel (and bar) and a pool for the kids. Sightseeing is next on the agenda, maybe a bus trip tomorrow if the gang is up to it. We have all been to the hairdresser. Here in unemployed Spain with up to fifty percent of people out of work the hairdresser was Chinese, naturally, and could cut hair well. There seems to be no internet café in Las Palmas and the marina WiFi can't cope, great!

Lizzie's Diary, Oct. 31

"Last week we took a hop-on-hop-off bus to Christopher Columbus' house. There are old maps and an old compass, it is very, very big but you can only see the downstairs. On the roof of the rooms there is a painting, on the rest there are carvings. In a cathedral we took the lift to the roof and had a great view over the city. Then we went to the top of the cathedral."

The house in which Christopher Columbus allegedly stayed for a few nights, the Casa de Colón, is one of Las Palmas' most attractive buildings with ornate doorways, beautiful latticed balconies, large courtyards, and carved wooden ceilings. This palace was the residence of the first governors of the island, and it is claimed that Christopher Columbus stayed there in 1492 while one of his ships was repaired. The old maps of Columbus' three voyages were really interesting to us so shortly before our own crossing.

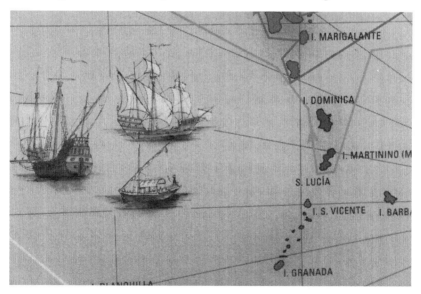

Columbus' voyages

In early November we have been here two weeks and time has flown by. We have had drinks and dinners with Basil and Mike Thurston,

303

have pottered around the boat, one project a day. Some of our friends have been stuck in Gibraltar with huge winds and we are just so glad we cut Gibraltar short. The provisioning is in full swing while detailed planning for the ARC will start soon, it is still relatively peaceful now.

We spent over 800 euros on the first lot of shopping which was mainly tins and bulk stuff like kitchen towels and flour for bread. El Corte Ingles delivered the crates the next day and the unpacking was less painful than feared. We got everything in but are dreading the next shipment. Now here is a lucky duckie:" Provisioning in Las Palmas was problem-free for me – my husband did it! He was the logistics officer in the Swiss army and has vast experience in that area," said Tatjana of "Mis Amoress."

Derek made it here safely yesterday after an epic journey from Australia, announced that he does not drink alcohol any longer which made us feel guilty and went to bed. So John and I celebrated his arrival with way too much Sambuca.

On Sunday we did some schoolwork and otherwise took it easy. Lizzie had a girl from another boat visit which did not go well, the chemistry did not work. Artist Cindy and Danish girl Isabell came over in the afternoon for some art school. Dinner on "Drina" with Mike cooking a fantastic leg of lamb with all the trimmings.

On this first Tuesday in November back in Australia everybody is asleep after a busy or boozy Melbourne Cup Day. We have been in holiday mode but still managed to do a monumental food shop for the crossing and visit the amazing department shop El Corte Ingles in town again for video camera tapes etc., very successful. It is hard to plan a menu for four adults and two kids for three weeks without access to shops. Also the movement of the boat will likely be such that people can't use knives and forks but just forks and spoons to eat, hence lots of curries. And where to store the food in this overcrowded boat with all the Lego and toys. Challenge of a life time.

Derek, one of John's oldest sailing friends from our suburb, has fitted into the life on Senta perfectly. The last crew member, John, will arrive middle of next week. There have been more boats joining jetty L, the best in the marina we think.

Next week the ARC social program will start and we will be out every night, also seminars every day. The kids have made a lovely Danish friend Isabell and had another arts day with Cindy from "Tenacity"; they learned how to draw animals with great results.

Chapter 4.

Arc in Full Swing

"I gotta feeling, uuuuuh, that tonight's gonna be a good night, that tonight's gonna be a good night, that tonight's gonna be a good, good night."[26]

The ARC (Atlantic Rally for Cruisers) in the year of our participation, 2012, was in its twenty-seventh year and with around 260 entries bigger than ever. First organised by cruising legend Jimmy Cornell, it is now in the capable hands of World Cruising's Andrew Bishop and his yellow-shirted team. Over two hundred boats start every year at the end of November in Las Palmas, Gran Canary, and sail around 2,800 miles in fifteen to twenty-three days to the Caribbean marina Rodney Bay in Saint Lucia. The ARC is the largest transoceanic sailing event in the world. And as any sailor would know: with two boats meeting on the water, a leisurely cruise turns into a race.

The ARC—although a rally—has a racing division and a rating system for the cruising participants, and let me tell you, some

---

26 "I gotta feeling" by Black Eyed Peas

skippers can get quite competitive. More importantly: the safety requirements for taking part, such as up-to-date life rafts and vests, EPIRBs, Internet capability, and much more, are substantial, and safety checks before the start are thorough. Some participants believe sailing in numbers is safer than alone, but we think the ocean is big and in the end you have to be confident to solve your problems alone. Most sailors take part in the rally for the camaraderie, parties, and lifelong friendships formed. We had signed up knowing there would be like-minded families with children so our kids would have a fun time before and after the rally, and a better time on the go, knowing their friends were out there too. We had an expensive SSB radio installed by German expert Jörg from yachtfunk.com, so the children could take part in a kids' radio net on the ocean.

The ARC seminars were all well run and interesting, and we attended most of them. The provisioning one expertly presented by ARC photographer Claire led to a general panic. She mentioned the possibility of rig failure leading to a lengthy crossing of more than four weeks. More food, we need more food!

A typical pre-ARC day, Wednesday November 7: Grey! After school more shopping, Hiper Market and El Corte Ingles, euro 484. Cook a curry and carbonara sauce to freeze. Danish girl Isabell on the boat to draw with Lizzie. I walk to marina office to chase some mail, no luck. Early dinner then drinks on Swiss boat "Mis Amoress." Owner Marco is my age, so also turned 50 this year, and is a hoot, we get on like fire. His little girls aged four and six speak an impressive four languages, his doctor wife Tatjana will help many ARC participants with minor ailments.

Dock L

An epic journey is undertaken to find a church for Sunday mass. Around forty euros in cab fares later we are in; the mass is in Spanish, naturally. That night my diary says we socialize with Heidi and Peter from *Stormvogel*, who are from a little town opposite my hometown on the river Elbe. Their boat, although very beautiful and not old, is still a bit of a project. We have so much to talk about.

Tuesday, November 13

Pancakes for breakfast, should pacify the crew (wishful thinking). At 10 am John and I walk into town, we find a Chinese shop for plastic egg containers and more kitchen stuff, and waste an hour at El Corte Ingles looking for a spare pair of glasses for me. In the end the euro764 price tag for Silhouette glasses the same as mine are too much, I buy a 20 euro pair in the pharmacy, for emergencies. Have food delivered, late lunch, frustrated and exhausted. At 4 pm the kids enjoy a playground meeting with Carolyn, Cameron and Sophia from "Sirius." At 6.30 sundowner with Mark and Karline, and at 8 pm the first ARC event kicks off, the Rolnautic Welcome Fiesta with a live band at the catamaran basin with kids, good fun. The next morning we have our meat delivered from a butcher at the market, Euro150 vacuumed and frozen, very exciting. The freezer is ready for it. We buy relatively little in contrast to other boats, some steak and lots of chicken breasts for ocean-friendly risottos and curries.

Ten days to go til our start across the Atlantic and the ARC social program is in full swing, comparable to the silly season in Sydney before Christmas. The kids are really enjoying the company of around twenty other kids. Last night at the family barbecue the table soccer games girls against boys were loud and exciting.[27]

Around 130 boats have arrived and we wonder whether the other 130 boats, that have also entered, will arrive in time. Dock L is super sociable, which is what we like. Today there is a full day of seminars for the adults while the kids promised some diary writing on the boat supervised by "Drina" s crew girl with the poetic name Capers. They really enjoy the sun downer happy hour between six and eight and have gone to bed way too late. Lizzie tried to open her eyes this morning and looked at her swollen dark circles in horror. Tonight our other crew member will arrive, John from Sweden and we are looking forward to meeting him.

---

27 **ARC boats of significance to us:**
Chili Cat: Charles, Heather, Luca, and Isabella Manfredi, *Drina*: Mike Thurston and Capers, *Fabiola*: Gill, Lisa, Cameron, Samuel Duncan, *Intrepid Bear*: James, Sarah, Milly, Thea, Harry Simpson, *Kalimba*: Peter, Leandra, and Dylan, *Kazayo*: Gonzalo and Carina with kids, *Mad Fish*: Russel, Emma, Oli, and Ethan, *Maloo*: Mark and Karline Shipard, *Open Blue*: Tim, Freddie, and kids *Rafiki*: Rob, Cully, Emily, and James, *Savarna*: Keith and Pam Goodall, Pat and Roly, *Sirius*: Andrew, Carolyn, Sophia, and Cameron, *Stormvogel*: Peter and Heidi Wiedekamm, *Storm Svale*: Mike, Tanja, Isabell, and Joshua St. John, *Sumatra*: Basil Diethelm, *Trinity*: Robert and Kerstin.

ARC kids' first play

It is Saturday, and we have only a week to go and are still working all day every day to finish the preparations. The romantic vision of white sails before glorious sunsets, the relaxing nature of sailing is a myth. Hundreds and hundreds of mundane tasks are involved in keeping this almost 30-year-old boat on track. John has become great friends with the chandlery man Morten, while I have used the chauffeur services of German Renee on the dock. Storing mountains of groceries into small spaces is only one of the tasks. Most of the food is crammed into cupboards, I can't find anything and still have things to get as I am panicking about running out. ARC food expert Claire has warned that we should be prepared for 30 days or more in case the rig comes down, great thought.

Which sail plan to use on this downhill ride is the topic of endless discussions between the guys. A few affluent owners have bought a parasailor (a kind of spinnaker with a hole in the middle) which allegedly is the ideal downwind sail with no mainsail up. We have prepared for twin headsails on two poles but will have problems securing the optimist on the deck, as it is tethered to one pole. A good preventer system to stop the boom crashing over in an involuntary gybe is vital to avoid boom damage. John has devised a good, elaborate system of lines led all the way to the front of the boat.

Groceries everywhere!

I am trying to bake bread in a pressure cooker as well as in my new superdooper thermal cooker ordered from David at www.mrdscookware.com. Get one! The bread, however, if you can call it that, does taste a bit rubbery, but not that bad. However, it truly looks disgusting! I could eat it but nobody else will, knowing my fussy family. So back to kneading and traditional baking. Precooked rice is easier to handle. I have bought freezer bags with a vacuum pump so the rice is sealed and flat, great to stack in the freezer. Freezer and fridge capacity vary hugely depending on the type and age of boat. We have a boat-sized small front-loading fridge with two shelves and a very spacious freezer with two baskets and space underneath. Keeping the food frozen means motoring for four to five hours a day as we have no generator and no other means of making power than the engine.

The weather is changeable, sometimes we wear shorts, sometimes long trousers and take cover from a few showers in between. The sun downer gathering is very popular, and we also have had some great parties, like the official opening last night. There was a magician and Finn—as always—volunteered to get onto the stage with the magic man and did a great job. The kids watched the Rio style dancers until after 11 and everybody was super tired today.

Tonight the owners' dinner, tomorrow an Olympic procession where Finn is going to carry the Australian flag. Lizzie is busy socialising with her new girl friends and has become a real little teenager, only slightly less stroppy.

ARC girls

The owners' dinner exceeds expectations. We share a table with a lovely New Zealand crew of outstanding sailing pedigree from Hanse 52

"Savarna" and are joined by Jimmy Cornell and his wife Gwenda as well as ARC boss Andrew Bishop, lots of interesting conversations.

But more stress on the horizon. Our new crew member John from Sweden is not working out at all. Lizzie rightly notices:" He does not look like the photo." Rather pale and pallid. On the first night after his arrival he stays out til 5.30 in the morning, wakes the whole boat getting into bed and then sleeps until 1.30 that day in the living room of our boat, while everybody is busy preparing for the crossing. He then goes for a long walk, we are so not impressed. Derek finds out about his sailing capabilities and after that negative report we decide to send him back. A hard decision, he has quit his job and made arrangements and we might get nobody else so close to the start. But better just to manage with the three of us than to carry somebody across an ocean who is not pulling his weight. Skipper John is, rightly so, very stressed about the whole thing, but we are relieved to have made the decision now. We might find somebody in the remaining time, there are a lot of people walking the docks offering their services.

Australian contingent

The ARC procession along the marina promenade with hundreds of sailors grouped in their nationalities bearing flags is oddly touching.

Our Australian group of around 25 people walks right behind the German contingent, so we mix and mingle. Finn carries the Australian flag proudly.

Finn carrying the Australian flag

In the afternoon of the same day the Swedish sailor leaves we have Nathan on board for an interview, an English ex-Royal Marine who would like to join our boat. One of Basil's crew members had met Nathan on the bus from the airport. We all like him straight away and sign him on. He would become an invaluable crew member and good friend. This was meant to be.

Completely exhausted by the mental stress of the crew issue we then decide to host a sun downer party in our cockpit for various family boats. The crowd of kids peacefully eats pasta Bolognese and watch TV while the parents compare notes about preparations. What a day!

Pasta on *Senta*

The ARC atmosphere can't be beaten. The dock is full of nice people most of whom we know now, the sun downer is the hub of cruising information, and the kids have started kids club and enjoy the play dates on each other's boats. This is why we joined. Tonight I met some old Hamburg friends that are participating in the rally, sailing is always a small world. The kids did some Opti sailing in their half day kids club and also some beach games, while John and I had computer and satphone instructions by mailasail nerd Ed til our heads swam. Dinner at the Sailor's Bar was wolfed down, another big day. Our new crew member Nathan from England has helped Derek all *day with getting things right on deck and will move onto the boat Thursday.*

ARC kids

A major worry for me has been dealt with Wednesday, four days before the start. We go to the fruit and veg stall No. 48 in the big market hall, and the lovely old Spanish lady that speaks no English led us to the back into the cool room where her brother takes ARC orders. He is competent, knows his produce and with his long list ready makes ordering easy. I do not go overboard but admittedly have no exact idea, unlike some other boat chefs who have worked out recipes in kilos and grams and made detailed volume lists. We buy peppers, onions, tomatoes, apples, oranges, lemons, few bananas, carrots, cabbage (remains uneaten), aubergines and zucchini.

More shopping!

It is the night of the costume ball, the theme is "masks." I had bought six red and black devils masks in Gibraltar and we combine those with red or black clothes, it looks great. The disco at the end of the marina is hopping. The music fantastic, everybody dancing and the kids stay until 11 pm. The crew from "Mis Amoress" is dressed as doctors with face masks and John is being convinced to pose as an accident victim. He is wrapped in toilet paper and put on a stretcher, hilarious.

Senta crew masked

Not long now, everybody is partied out, tired. The boat is almost ready and most of our friends went for a last shop today at Corte Ingles, we kept bumping into each other in the aisles, the shop had a party atmosphere. The kids have so enjoyed hanging out on each other's boats. Our new English crew member Nathan is fully integrated and has been a great help to Derek in finishing off the boat preparations. As an ex-Royal Marine and lifeboat captain his safety and medical experience will be invaluable.

Chapter 5.

The Start

"The path to success has no shortcut." Schoolyard poster

The day before the start. We process our last loads of washing, do I hate! that laundry. We are ready, happy to go. Only the weather forecast doesn't sound too good. In preparation we all decide in accordance with packet instructions to take Stugeron seasickness tablets the day before the start; the kids get Stugeron drops. The 9:30 ARC checkout goes without hitch; with mixed feelings we march in the crowd to the skippers' briefing held in some big Las Palmas hotel.

On the way I get a phone call from our weather router Meeno Schrader in Kiel, Germany, and he says, "It is going to be ugly for the first few days, wind on the nose around forty knots." John and I look at each other and quickly decide to start anyway, but turn around and head back into the marina for a few days. That is allowed. We do not want to ruin the crossing through a bad few days at the beginning.

The ARC magazine says: "The rally departure, planned for the end of the third week in November, allows boats to arrive in the Caribbean just before Christmas, whilst benefiting from the first settled Atlantic seasonal winds, which blow steadily from Africa to the Caribbean from December through to April." This is the theory! Now for reality.

The atmosphere at the briefing is tense; we are not the only ones worrying about the weather. Some of our friends almost didn't make it to Las Palmas due to the bad weather. Hurricane Sandy in the United States wreaked havoc unexpectedly late in the hurricane season and the trade winds do not seem established. After some introductory remarks by Andrew Bishop, ARC weatherman Chris Tibbs gives an overview of the weather in the next few days—no good news there. People look worried.

Andrew Bishop takes the microphone again and—we don't believe what we hear—says that only for the second time in the ARC history it has been decided to postpone the start, the cruising division will not leave until Tuesday. Stunned silence. Then the crowd roars with relief, the applause is deafening. What a great decision!

Las Palmas forest

The afternoon is a total blur for the adult members of *Senta's* crew. One after the other we pass out, and the whole boat is asleep for hours. Only the kids are live and active. Turns out the Spanish Stugeron tablets against seasickness have five times the dose of the English ones, and I let everybody take two. We are completely out of it. What luck we did not have to head into the ocean.

Impromptu ARC sundowner drinks are organised this Saturday; the ARC staff know their customers, and most participants are elated. Risking your gear and family peace on the first few days is nobody's idea of fun. The racing division organised by the RORC (Royal Ocean Racing Club) will start as planned on Sunday, and cruising boats wishing to start with the racers are welcome. In the end only seven cruisers take that option, the remaining 190-odd boats wait till Tuesday.

On Sunday noon we walk in blazing sunshine along the promenade to the start line. I end up teaming up with Kiwis Pat and Roly who as Admiral's Cup participants know exactly where the committee will lay the line. We get a great viewing spot, and when John arrives he organises beers and soft drinks for our friends and us. John and I cheer on our dock neighbour Adrian on his Swan 44 *Selene*, who is starting in the racing division. A delicious lunch in the old town with Roly and Pat makes this a perfect day. On Monday we walk the docks and say goodbye to all our new friends. The marina is swarming with people. Marching bands are playing on the pontoons and last-minute preparations are underway.

Watching Start 1

TUESDAY, NOVEMBER 27 AT 4,082 MILES, 1,521 ENGINE HOURS

An early start, naturally; we are all too excited to sleep long. At 7:00 am John, Nate, and I walk up to the shower block for the last time and are surprised to see a little crowd gathered in front of the showers. Turns out that due to our later departure the shower access cards have been blocked, so the guys can't get into their washrooms. The ladies', however, are open, so the boys get invited in and we all share the facilities. You do want a shower before sailing for up to three weeks.

Trying to get out

The start! At 10:00 a.m. we leave the dock like (almost) everybody else. The start is scheduled for 11:00 a.m. There is a ten-boat-wide and fifty-boat-long queue trying to squeeze out of the marina. Mike and *Mis Amoress* wave us off; *Fabiola* is right behind us. It is tight! John somehow gets us through the marina entrance without a collision. We hoist our main in the traffic exclusion zone, but something is flapping. We lower the sail again, pull it up for a second time, and now get into trouble with a police boat. We bear away and head for the line. A rain squall goes through, visibility is poor. We are all in full wet weather gear with life vests on.

We are off!

"Stick to the Kiwis, they know what they are doing," John instructs me. I follow Hanse 52 *Savarna* through the crowd of boats. We are near the front. Swan 51 *Northern Child* pushes past us from behind, very powerful. We unfurl the number 3 jib and head for the line. "Bang," the start, we are off. That worked really well.

Next to us sails Australian Amel *La Boheme*, the Norwegian Swan 44 *Embla* is behind us, and we are looking good. Who calls this a rally? With only 2,800 miles to go the start is important! Swan 48 *Amoress* is over the line and gets penalized with a few hours added to their time. We head for the southern tip of Gran Canary toward the dunes of Maspalomas that we had visited weeks ago, following *Savarna* until we can't see her any longer.

After the start

CHAPTER 6.

CROSSING THE ATLANTIC

"A marvellous stillness pervaded the world, and the stars, together with the serenity of their rays, seemed to shed upon the earth the assurance of everlasting security. The young moon recurved, and shining low in the west, was like a slender shaving thrown up from a bar of gold, and the Arabian Sea, smooth and cool to the eye like a sheet of ice, extended its perfect level to the perfect circle of a dark horizon."[28]

DAY 1: TUESDAY, NOV. 27

After our splendid start we sailed close to the coast and at the higher-wind acceleration zone on the southern end of the island put a reef into the main sail. A pod of grey-pink small dolphins played around our bow, cute. Everybody ate some red soup and tried to settle into the motion. During the first night nobody got any real sleep because the boat was pitching and surfing so much in up to forty knots of wind. The waves were huge, quite scary. We still saw lots of ARC boats sailing into that first night.

28 Joseph Conrad, *Lord Jim*

A quiet moment

Our evening routine for the whole crossing evolved as follows: We all had dinner around 6:00 p.m., I then put the kids to bed and put my head down myself, while the boys washed up and somebody stood watch. During the night we had the autopilot on all the time. John had the watch before me from 10:00 pm to 12:00 am but hardly ever had to wake me; I could somehow feel when it was time to get up. I was on from 12:00 am to 2:00 am, then Nathan. The person heading off watch wrote some wind, miles, etc. data into the ship's log before lying down. John and I slept in the saloon berths, Nate eventually on the floor below my bunk, and Derek in the lively bunk in the front.

Sleep tight

Day 2: Wednesday, Nov. 28 at 4188 nm

I try the SSB for weather information, feel sick all day, lie down. Kids in bed, Finn sick. We have soup for lunch. The sun is out in the afternoon, I take part of John's afternoon watch as he has not rested and has a headache. Nate catches a little tuna that makes five filets. Another tuna bites, but gets thrown back as he is too small. We are not as fast now, and are on a westerly course due to Wetterdienst instructions. No dinner for Karen, guys eat ginger beef, kids are weak. Lizzie spoke to Sophia (Sirius) and Emily (Rafiki) at 7:00 pm on the SSB kids net, works really well. Moon and stars are out for the night watch, two, three boats, everybody got some sleep.

Kids' SSB net

As John is not mad keen on fishing we got instructions from Gill about getting the fish and then killing them. We had invested in a gaff to drag the body in and a small plastic bottle filled with aquavit that should kill the fish painlessly. Gill had written extensive notes and we were going to have a try. So what amazing success, to catch a tuna on the first evening.

Derek wrestles the catch

DAY 3: THURSDAY, NOV. 29 AT 4388 NM

In the morning shook reef No 3 out to 1½ and ran full No 3 jib. We got much better speed. 8:00 am breakfast, Lizzie in the cockpit, all feeling better. Beginners mistake: during the night two bowls of stew on the carpet, one thermos flask broken, three bowls of muesli in the sink, one mug handle broken off, lots of bruises. The rolling is not so bad from night two onwards, but the odd wave throws the boat around just when you are moving hot beverages or try to dress or undress. Down below is despite the movement a haven of calm, all you hear is the sound of water slushing or racing along the hull. I have not had the stomach yet to start turning the vegetables in the nets above our bunks like instructed. The first few days the kids sleep and drink a lot, but eat very little, especially Finn. The soup and stew last for days which is great for me. The boys are really good with kitchen duty.

On day three some of the capsicum is getting wrinkly, so I am thinking about chicken fajitas. Manage to send emails to race control and home after hours of trying with the SSB. Amazing technology, old but good. Mailasail email via satphone doesn't work, what a surprise. The 1:00 pm SSB radio sched, where you have to report your position, weather and events, was a shambles as two net controllers tried to get the positions at the same time. We heard Kerstin from "Trinity" and Mike from "Drina", and Nate put their positions into a grid. In the afternoon during John's watch the rod started to reel, and soon John handed the rod to our "youngster" Nathan to reel in a medium sized Mahi Mahi with a yellow belly. A lot of aquavit was needed to sedate the struggling fish that made fantastic dinner. The kids were super excited about the catch, and afterwards watched part three of "Lord of the Rings." We are going well!

Afternoon TV

My new night routine after my watch entails sending out e-mails and receiving positions and weather; the airways are not as clogged at 2:30 at night and the mails transmit faster. The daily sched and position reports become very important as they tell us where our friends are, how fast everybody is going, and what weather they have. We also hear about breakages and fish caught. John, Mike, and some other Aussie guys establish an additional Aussie net at 2:00 pm every day. The SSB was one of the best investments we have made for the boat.

DAY 4: FRIDAY, NOV. 30 AT 4508 NM

A rolly night with not much sleep for all, a sunny morning, though, and all are up around 8:00 am. John and I look at positions and Lizzie gets impatient, so I make pancakes for the kids. Finn is still sick. Lizzie and I read a German book, and then she chats to the boys in the cockpit. She wears a life vest and is clipped into a strongpoint with a harness while in the cockpit, as we all are. Sticking to a strict safety regime is vital on such a venture. The boys hand steer for a while.

DAY 5: SATURDAY, DEC. 1 AT 4756 NM

The night was unsettled, Lizzie was up twice with growth pain. In the morning we decide to gybe onto port tack. The gybe takes over an hour but goes well, hopefully we will stay on this tack til St. Lucia. It is grey and rainy, I look at emails from "Fabiola" and "Trinity," read to Lizzie. Lunch of bread, cheese, eggs, ham. Leave message for Bummi in Hamburg, it's his birthday. TV Harry Potter 7 part 2, Nate, Derek and I watch too. Chicken fajitas for dinner. Wild ride at night, we furl the headsail in a bit. Scary and rolly!

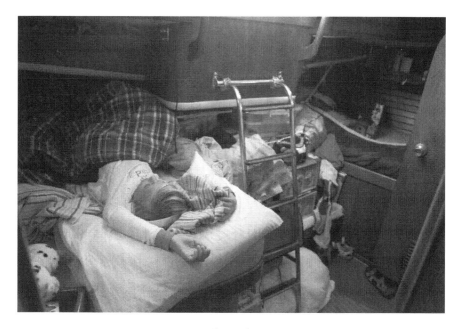

Kids' cabin

Day 6: Sunday, Dec. 2

I get up really early, John had whistled. We put the motor on, but it unexpectedly dies even before breakfast. At least we had a SSB message with weather from Meeno Schrader himself. He says: keep going, conditions will remain tough. Lizzie, Nate and I chat in the cockpit, while John changes the fuel lift pump successfully. Breakfast finally at 11.30. I play cards with the kids, read to Lizzie, listen to the SSB. John is tired, did not get enough sleep. German movie "Vorstadtkrokodile." We eat pasta with vegetable sauce, have to get rid of the peppers, aubergines and zucchini. The night is bad, lots of squalls, we furl in the headsail again, head north. Rain! John does double watch. A flying fish gets found on deck. Huge swells! "Great Escape" and "Lady Anne" are close by. Lizzie has a bladder infection, we find the tablets and make a warm water bottle. There is an email from the grandparents in Germany.

Helping to steer

DAY 7: MONDAY, DEC. 3

Gybe the No 3 headsail and put the pole away, we are beam reaching. It is rolly and we are roughly back on course. I try to bake bread, make soup for lunch. Kids watch "Vorstadtkrokodile 2." My freshly baked brownies are very popular. I update the log, it is such a relief not to be sick, I can function well but am intimidated by the conditions. Huge waves from different directions toss the boat around. It blows 25-30 knots ESE, no sign of steady trade winds. At least it is sunny. The seas and wind calm down in the evening, we eat the rest of the soup with freshly baked bread. The night watches are uneventful, lots of flying fish, "Andante" close by.

I had been worried that time on the crossing would pass very slowly, that after a week we would be completely over the whole thing and just want to get ashore. But that is not the case at all.

The days fly by, are not boring and rarely stressful, and we all are enjoying this special time on the boat. I do believe a bit less speed during the night would be better, but the guys know we are doing well and don't want to slow the boat down. I try listening to some music on John's iPod during my watch but find that I concentrate on the music and not on the boat and weather.

DAY 8: TUESDAY, DEC. 4

Slept long, sunny morning, new boat positions and weather came in on the SSB. Something breaks at the front of the boat, some track, and John is pissed off. Kids play cards. Breakages and spills report: 1 litre of milk on the floor. Finn empties bag with Tortilla chip crumbs over chart table and two computers in a rogue wave. Super mess, the vacuum is needed. Veggie omelette for lunch. Kids watch "Vorstadtkrokodile 3." I change the clock one hour back. The weather forecast is not clear, John is cranky. Dinner is tortellini and ravioli with pesto and salad. The salad has kept well, the peppers went off first, mandarins are eaten up, not enough apples, bananas on day 9 go into banana bread, the kiwis are also soft now. Tomatoes holding out very well, we have too much cheese and still lots of yogurt left.

DAY 9: WEDNESDAY, DEC. 5

Quiet night at good speeds, beam reaching on a steady course. One reef and No 3 headsail. All are in good spirits though Lizzie has a cold. We shake the reef out and unfurl the big genoa. I phone German weather router Sven Taxwedel on the satphone to hear about the approaching low. He says it can't be avoided and will produce lulls, a difficult few days ahead. Kids get history audio CDs, very interesting. Lizzie and I bake banana bread and beer bread, pancakes for lunch. We play cards, she wins.

Where did I spend my time?

Kids watch "Treasure Buddies." Finn is lying in the corridor in front of the bunks with a pillow, in everybody's way. I cut the first pancake (he always gets the first one as the oil is not too hot yet) into bites. He flips, the bits are too big, he wants the pancake whole, a typical Asperger moment. So I take away the plate, give him a whole pancake and eat the first one myself. In the afternoon the kids start to fight, Finn wants to steer, Lizzie gets competitive. We try to have a buffet dinner with our new beer bread but a rain squall arrives and all goes pear shaped. John earlier talked to

Nick Black from "Charm Offensive" and Ian from "Sundancer II." Into the night with full main and No 3. For the midnight watch the boat is going like a train, more than 8 knots, it feels too fast, rounds up, the auto-pilot can't cope. John and I furl headsail in and put engine on for charge, nobody sleeps a lot that night. In John's early watch at dawn we reef and unfurl the jib, better balance.

Well balanced

DAY 10: THURSDAY, DEC. 6

Rain. Nate spots a huge school of dolphins. Kids stay in their pyjamas, why not. Lizzie feels much better, has warm raspberries and hot cocoa for breakfast. Fresh supplies dwindle, the last kiwis, a few bananas and apples left. A possible shortage of milk and tea looming, those English habits. Derek and Nate love hot beverages. It is grey with squalls and thunderstorms as predicted by weatherman Taxwedel yesterday. 1200 miles to go, around seven days which would get us in around Dec 17, with luck! Huge thunderstorm late morning, torrential rain and strong winds. Nate and Derek are outside when a huge wave goes over the boat and into the cockpit. We lose one cushion and Derek's life vest inflates. It is a total lockdown below with temperatures like a sauna, it lasts 1½ hours. The boys are drenched. John hears on the SSB that "Skyelark" is through it. We turn the engine on at 12.15, crank the fans on and write emails to Hamburg and "Chili Cat." Chicken stir-fry for dinner. Most amazing fiery sunset. Nate hears a whale blowing next to the boat. A quiet night.

Sunset

DAY 11: FRIDAY, DEC. 7

The engine is on. We are lucky, no thunderstorm hits us during the night, but we see plenty of lightning. No rain. Everybody catches up on their much needed sleep. At 7am John drops a cable from the sweets cupboard above me on my face, a wake-up call? I get up and join John and

Finn in the cockpit. Nate is there, too. We have a cup of tea, a late break-fast and motor sail. I tidy the fridge and the freezer. Finn and John have a shower in the cockpit. Lizzie listens to her new Barbie CD, the flat water is fantastic. Finn reads in the cockpit, it is a lovely, sunny day. Later we watch "Pirates of the Caribbean 3."

The fun starts in the evening. A black front looms on the horizon. We put the engine on and furl in the headsail. A freighter appears, "Tasman Sea," on collision course. John talks to an officer on the VHF, but ignoring the rules of the sea where we have right of way he does not alter course. So we have to motor around him, the engine surges and threatens to stop, now, of all times. Likely a fuel filter issue. When around the freighter's stern we start sailing in a new north easterly and switch the engine off for John to deal with the filters in the morning. Thank god he was such a car boffin in his youth. I am tired during the night watch, endless and dark.

Keeping busy!

Day 12: Saturday, Dec. 8

I slept til 8 am next morning, the boat swerved and banged a lot before breakfast. The engine box is open, high stress, filters, diesel, in the end it is ok. A good day, egg and bacon sandwiches for lunch and pasta with tomato/anchovy sauce for dinner.

Day 13: Sunday, Dec. 9

Speak to my mother, she is sick, shingles, a worry. We chat to Mike from "Drina" at the lunch sched and compare notes. We are getting great speeds of constantly over 8 knots up to 10 knots during the day with full main and poled out No 3 jib. Chicken soup for lunch. Kids play computer games. John and I have the first rum and Coke in the afternoon shift, we have not missed drinking alcohol at all, until today it has been a dry trip. The children watch "Valiant." At six we reef down for the night, and I cook pancakes for the kids. Finn rejects the first and eats only half of the second pancake, such a worry. I fry steaks and add self-made red potato chips and tomato for us adults. Grey skies. I have time to read "Atlantic Children" by Juliet Dearlove, the story of a family sailing around the Atlantic with lots of parallels. We slow down to 7 knots into the night.

Day 14: Monday, Dec. 10

540 miles to go, unsettled night despite a reefed-down boat, we are trucking at 8 to 9 knots with squalls. I get lucky in my watch, there is no rain and the wind is ok. Derek again sits his watch in torrential rain. No sleep for me after the watch, the boat is swerving. John talks to cruise liner "Costa Luminosa" who is not on collision course. At 8 am it is still dark, we should change the clock again, but it will be difficult to remember the UTC schedule for the SSB radio. The gas is empty, we have a late breakfast after the bottle is changed. Finn listens to German audio "History of the World," Lizzie does drawings. Sausages with onion marmalade for lunch. It is great to have an almost empty fridge, the nets are empty, we have tins and frozen meat left. In terms of the fleet's positions there are huge differences depending on the strategy. Boats on the rhumb line did much better than boats heading south til the butter melted. We were somewhere in the middle. Nate hand steers a record speed of 13.4 knots and ties with me. Then he gets Senta to more than 16 knots, we are flying in NE 25-30 knots of breeze.

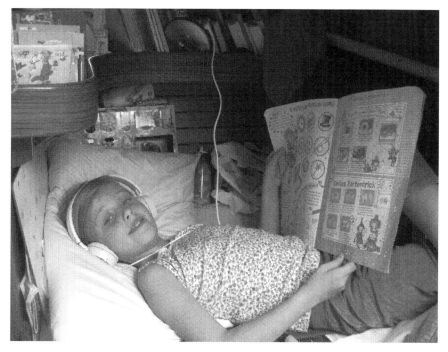

Still happy

DAY 15: TUESDAY, DEC. 11

A clunky night with little wind and lots of noise, we pointed northwest for a while, not where we want to go, got little sleep, everybody tired. A sunny morning with Nate and me in the cockpit reading, John and Derek are sleeping in. Lizzie has a cold shower. At noon we shake the reef out, the wind drops. Lunch is ravioli pesto for the men, leftover lasagne for me,

---

sausage and corn for Lizzie and toast for Finn, I am running a restaurant here. In an uneventful afternoon I read a Caribbean pilot book while the kids play. We watch "Tintin" and have lemon yogurt chicken for dinner, it is a new recipe and a bit dry. We have a fast ride toward the morning.

DAY 16: WEDNESDAY, DEC. 12

Second last day on the water. It is sunny with big swells from the back, NE 25 knots. The toilet at the back is broken, thank god so late in the crossing.

DAY 17: THURSDAY, DEC. 13

The sun rose and we saw the hills of Saint Lucia to our left, in a morning haze, just like that. Our little crew was up at 5:00 am, only a few miles to go now. Finn sat on the deck and looked across at the land, Lizzie chatted happily in the cockpit. We took some photos and John spoke to Ian from *Sundancer II* to find out whether he needed assistance to get into port as his engine had stopped working, but Ian, the old racer, crossed the finish line under sail just ahead of us. A yacht with a big ARC flag was anchored in the bay and took down the finish times. It was sunny and hot, and tropical smells wafted across from the land. We were there, it was unbelievable how completely normal this felt. In sixteen hair-raising days *Senta* had trucked across the Atlantic. She had done us proud, and the time at sea had passed so fast. It had been great!

But now normality set in. We had to get out ropes and fenders, talk to the marina office, and get a berth. We passed through the narrow entrance of Rodney Bay Marina where typical Caribbean boats were laid up in front of colourful shacks. It was easy to take the wrong turn in this marina, and John had to motor back, but got spotted by Roly from *Savarna*, who waved.

Saint Lucia finish

Our dock was right at the end of the marina and was going to be the kids' dock, but so far only *Fabiola* and *Intrepid Bear* were there. Our Kiwi friends had raced around to our berth and helped with the lines. Gill from *Fabiola* appeared, big hugs. A man came with a cart of rum punch, very welcome even at 6:00 am, and we cracked a few bottles of champagne. Lisa from *Fabiola* came over in her nightie, the boys Cameron and Samuel in pyjamas, we sat down below and compared stories. For nonsailors the excited conversation would have sounded like Chinese, but we all had done the same thing. Crossed the Atlantic Ocean. We were elated.

WHAT LIZZIE LIKED ABOUT THE CROSSING:

- It was good to have a hot cocoa every morning.
- The sticker and colouring books I got for the trip.
- The Advent calendar from the first day of the crossing.
- Happy to be inside the comfy cabin when it was raining.

- See lots of rainbows.
- Lots of time with Mum, e.g., reading books and playing cards.

WHAT FINN LIKED ABOUT THE CROSSING:

- Fishing, we caught five fish.
- Look at stars.
- Talking to friends on the SSB.
- Watching movies and listening to History of the World on CD.
- Steering the ship.
- Reading on my Kindle.
- Not so good: the rainy squalls and unpredictable waves.
- Sometimes sick.
- It was not too long.

MY ARC SUMMARY:

- It went much quicker than expected.
- It was busier than I thought; the little down time was used for resting.
- Through the daily SSB it was not lonely; the chats were an important part of the day.
- The constant rolling did not matter much for sleeping but surprise moves made cooking and working in the galley much more difficult than expected.
- Even in the cruising division it was more a race than a rally.
- Fresh food lasted longer than we thought and we had too much of it.
- The kids did not ask once "Are we there yet?" They were fantastic. Finn lost some weight but he survived.
- The cabin was cosy and calm at all times.

The winning team

We had lots of congratulations e-mails once we were again connected to the modern world. Our family and friends had followed
our course across the Atlantic on the excellent ARC tracker. We
also updated our website www.finnandlizzie.de with some photos
and diary entries. Wi-Fi in Rodney Bay as everywhere was tricky,
but our booster antenna made a difference and we were among the
few with a decent connection.

Lizzie's Diary

"When we arrived in St. Lucia Gill helped us dock on. "Fabiola" came
over and had a glass of wine and rum punch. Finn played with Cameron
and Samuel. The next day "Intrepid Bear" came over to us and we played
Playmobil and it was really fun. The next day "Sirius" and "Chili Cat's"
Sophia and Isabella came to play and it was really fun. The next night we
went to the Toga party."

Chapter 7.

Saint Lucia Party Time

"...under all the parade of human effort and noise, today is like yesterday, and tomorrow will be like today; that existence is a wheel of recurring patterns from which no one escapes; that all anybody does in this life is live for a while and then die for good, without finding out much; and that therefore the idea is to take things easy and enjoy the passing time under the sun." Herman Wouk, *Don't Stop the Carnival*

Life in Rodney Bay was easy; we were relieved to have completed the crossing and relished the laid-back ambience, the hot, steamy Caribbean atmosphere, steel drums and all. The marina development in the 1970s had been the first large harbour built specifically for yachts in the area and had all amenities. A few hours after arrival, and well after the first shower, John and I took our little blue bag with boat papers and passports and looked for the harbour office. The customs and registration formalities were surprisingly pain free.

The Saint Lucian people were friendly and confident; one did not have to feel guilty to be in their space. We had lengthy breakfasts in cafés along the walkway, chicken rotis for lunch, and sipped rum punches in the bars in the evening. A short dinghy ride took us to Spinnakers Bar on the beach, where the ARC Olympics took place with tug of wars, surfboard battles, and other games.

Lizzie and Nate joined the Australian *Sumatra* team, and Lizzie did especially well at the limbo dance. Nate, however, secured the win for the Australian team with his striptease, an easy task for an ex-Royal Marine. Then on to the evening fun. The Gros Islet jump up is legendary, but we were warned not to stay out too late there with the kids as it gets very busy. So we strolled over to the local village of Gros Islet. At the petrol station on the way a women was singing karaoke very well; the kids loved it. We tasted a few plates of street food barbecued on the road and sipped rum punches. Loud music was blasting from open doorways, often not reggae but duff-duff music.

Fun on the beach

Saint Lucia for years had a bad reputation regarding safety, but with the arrival of the ARC and the financial prospects for the island the authorities have made a huge effort to clean it up. We never felt threatened anywhere and believe that the friendliness and pride of its people are the real attraction of the Caribbean nations. We had read about burglaries on boats but did not lock our boat at night as our bodyguard Nathan was sleeping on the deck and we generally felt safe.

The first inhabitants in Saint Lucia were Arawak Indians and the Carib people that named the island *Hewanorra*, which means "island where the iguana lives." It changed hands many times in its history and is now a sovereign island country. Saint Lucia is part of the Windward Islands and is located north–northeast of the island of Saint Vincent, northwest of Barbados, and south of Martinique. It covers a land area of 617 km² and has a population of 174,000 (2010). Its capital is Castries.

It's hard to find up-to-date statistics, but in 2001 per capita GDP in Saint Lucia was $4,400, the country's main earners being bananas, tourism, and small manufacturing. Although banana revenues have helped fund the country's development since the 1960s, the industry is now in a terminal decline, due to competition from lower-cost Latin American banana producers and reduced European Union trade preferences. The country is encouraging farmers to plant crops such as cocoa, mangos, and avocados to diversify its agricultural production and provide jobs for displaced banana workers.

The volcanic Saint Lucia is more mountainous than many other Caribbean islands with the highest point being Mount Gimie, at 950 metres above sea level. Two other mountains, the Pitons, form the island's most famous landmark. They are located between Soufrière and Choiseul on the western side of the island. Saint Lucia is also one of the few islands in the world that boasts a drive-in volcano.

The capital city of Saint Lucia is Castries (population 60,263), where 32.4 percent of the population lives. Major towns include Gros Islet, Soufrière, and Vieux Fort. The local climate is tropical, moderated by northeast trade winds, with a dry season from December to the end of May, and a wet season from June to the end of November.[29]

Sadly we had missed the new James Bond movie in the cinemas, but *The Hobbit* was out, and one afternoon the whole family took a taxi to the Saint Lucia cinema. Fast and furious dwarves, a different world from ours here in the laid-back Caribbean. A few days later Finn decided he would like to take Emily from *Rafiki* to see the film again, so I enjoyed the film again with both youngsters. All the kids were having play dates on each other's boats all day long—they had pancakes for breakfast on *Sirius*, waffles on *Mad Fish*, spaghetti Bolognese with a movie on our boat, and a birthday party for a whole group on the marina lawn. They just had a ball.

More boats started to come in, and at the ARC drinks in the evening we heard the stories. Robert and Kerstin of *Trinity* had one of the worst crossings. Double-handed, the journey across the Atlantic is tough in any event, but they experienced significant technical problems and completely lost their electrical power. As in their boat almost everything is power driven they ended up hand-steering all the way without navigation and without most other safety and creature comforts. Horrendous!

---

29 Wikipedia

Heidi and Peter

Our other German friends on *Stormvogel* were still out there, also with serious mechanical problems. There was no wind and they were drifting at three knots, no engine. What a rough trip they had had after a heavy squall damaged vital boat bits. I felt for Heidi and her men. Finally they were towed in by their friends on *Mauni*, at 3:00 am. The ARC welcome committee plus Kerstin and I stood on the dock, and the rum punch flowed even at this time.

The last boat to come in was an all-girls crew on a smaller boat that had experienced major problems. They came in early in the morning, and when we were having breakfast in a café and they were enjoying a celebratory beer, one of them let her head drop on the table and just fell asleep.

Lizzie's mozzie bites are bad. At 9 am on Monday the ARC kids club visits a pirate ship (replica) but the kids say it was boring. After I bake a cake with Lizzie she has to lie down for hours as consequence of the bites and medication. Finn plays with Cameron and Samuel. Nate fixes the toilet, John fixes the bilge pump, Nate fishes and finds the dropped dinghy anchor on the sea bed, relief! At 5 pm ARC cocktail party at the Ocean Club. Despite the weak rum punch it is good fun, lots of friends. Finn goes back to the boat alone and "Mad Fish" bring Lizzie home later.

The ARC toga party is on for Wednesday evening. Senta has fitted sheets, so we can only kit out Nathan with a white toga sheet. The venue, a night-club, is a taxi ride away. Open air. Great band and dancing. The day after it's the girls' day out, more than 12 weary women pile in a bus and drive to a resort somewhere on the island. Lazing at the pool, massage, pedicure, a nice lunch on the beach. We return refreshed and beautified late in the afternoon. Husbands tired. All children still alive.

The heroic parents James and Sarah from "Intrepid Bear" together with Russell and Emma from "Mad Fish" organise an impromptu birthday party for some of their kids the Friday before Christmas. The gang enjoys games on the marina lawn and cake afterwards. It is the day of the big prize giving, the last day of the ARC. Buses and taxis drive us all to a big hall where we stand in little groups in the garden and chat about future plans. Some are going north, some south. Most of the family boats are heading south toward the Tobago Cays and Grenada, which is where we are going. So no good-byes for the kids yet, fortunately. The prize-giving is a longish affair as lots of prizes are awarded, not only for speed but also for looks and success in adversity. Rally control tells us that 102 boats took under 16 days and that 52 boats did not put the engine on, that is a quarter of the fleet. 33 nationalities crewed on boats from 27 countries. There was 42 kids on 21 boats, 21 boys and 21 girls, and 55 people over 60 years old.

We are surprised to come 21st overall and 4th in our group, an amazing success. But even better, the kids get to collect a nice trophy for the fastest family boat to arrive, and nobody expected that. I get a mountain of flowers for being the best female skipper (John and I always appear on the entry list together), and in his absence we collect Basil's prize for doing *well in the face of adversity. He stepped in for his sick son and sailed the son's otherwise disappointed Sydney crew across in excellent time and style.*

Best family boat

We have sailed to Marigot Bay, St. Lucia, in contrast to earlier plans, as there is a whole fleet of our friends with kids there, and we all wanted to celebrate Christmas together. Just a few weeks to go til our return, and we are trying to slow down. A nice sail of only 12 miles, and despite this being the high season we get a marina berth next to the super yacht "Sheherezade." "Chili Cat" takes the spot next to us and "Fabiola," "Sirius," "Mis Amoress," "Kazayo," and "Maloo" are on moorings in the bay.

CHAPTER 8.

CHRISTMAS IN MARIGOT BAY

AUSTRALIAN JINGLE BELLS
Dashing through the bush,
in a rusty Holden Ute,
Kicking up the dust,
esky in the boot,
Kelpie by my side,
singing Christmas songs,
It's Summer time and I am in
my singlet, shorts and thongs

Oh! Jingle bells, jingle bells, jingle all the way,
Christmas in Australia on a scorching summer's
day, Hey!
Jingle bells, jingle bells, Christmas time is beaut!,
Oh what fun it is to ride in a rusty Holden Ute...

*Yesterday we hired a bus and went with the "Chili Cat" Manfredis out for
a fun day driving around St. Lucia. We were glad not to drive ourselves,
as the roads serpentine up and down.*

On the roadside the locals were cutting up meat and selling it for Christmas. Our guide explained to us the intricacies of growing bananas that were covered in blue plastic bags here. The banana trees only carry fruit once in their life. We sang endless Christmas carols with Heather leading the choir. Our driver stopped for us to have a simple lunch of chicken, beans and beers in a hilltop restaurant. And then we went zip-lining. Kitted out with helmet, hairnets, tough gloves and harnesses the eight of us lined up to zoom through the jungle on twelve different wires high above the ground. The boys thought it was fantastic, the girls were not heavy enough so needed help from the staff to get to the other side. My body shape seemed not suitable as I turned backwards every single time when taking off, eventually crashed into the ramp and at some stage lost a shoe, so disheartened I stopped halfway and John joined me. Next stop were the mud baths, great photo opportunity and very relaxing.

The 40 million years old Pitons are the landmark of the island, we drove past them and look at the bay below us, should we anchor there on our way south? Maybe not. Early in the afternoon we saw hundreds of schoolkids walking back from school, in their very tidy uniforms, the girls with elaborate pleated hairstyles and white bows, beautiful. One of the highlights of our day, however, was our bus racing down the runway of the abandoned airport, thrilling!

Just the four of us, much later, had an outstanding meal on the water-side terrace of the "Rainforest Hideaway," a charming waterside restau-rant with tables arranged on a wooden deck overhanging the lagoon, a very romantic setting. Today I have been singing German Christmas carols all morning. It has been raining on and off but that didn't matter today. On Christmas Day we will have a family BBQ on the beach and hopefully the Caribbean sun will shine on us then.

Manfredis in mud

Monday, Dec. 24, Heiligabend

Fresh croissants for breakfast, yum! Cameron and the Manfredi kids came onto the boat to watch "Penguins of Madagascar Christmas." Our main German Christmas on Christmas Eve was great, despite the recurring rain. I talked to my mother three times to make sure they were ok without us, otherwise we hung around, drank fizz, tidied the boat and prepared for 3.30, the big present event. The kids were patient and appreciative, the presents a success and although the Spanish roast beef turned out to be a meat loaf nobody complained and we completed the evening with a James Bond movie.

Lizzie Christmas

On Christmas Day we have an early start with church at 8:00 am and a taxi collecting us—at least that was the plan. The taxi is late and the church service at 9:00, but eventually we sit in a huge church on a hill with only a few punters attending the service. They have a nice choir but sing too few carols for my liking, and the priest is not very good. The disappointment stems from John having attended a captivating, loud, and full of singing mass a few Sundays before, where he was greeted personally as a guest, and we had hoped for a similar service at Christmas.

At noon we gather on the sandy spit in the harbour entrance to celebrate Christmas in the Aussie spirit with a BBQ on the beach, six families, super fun for all. The children climb around the rock breakwater looking for crabs and shells while the adults lie around chatting and drinking. They swim, swing off a rope, there is plenty of food, and we only mosey back to the boat at 5:00 pm. Evening drinks on *Chili Cat* with Heather and Charles.

Christmas in full swing

This is what it was all about, this Christmas on a Caribbean beach, with a big group of people that we had not known four weeks before, but that through our common achievement of crossing a big ocean with our children had become very close friends, probably for life. This was the lifestyle we had dreamt about, lazing around on a tropical beach in good company. But this gathering was more about having a goal, sharing it with friends, and celebrating the achievement, as we all did in Marigot Bay. To see the children of different ages confident, independent, and happy bonding with each other, splashing, beachcombing, and fishing, that alone made the hard yards of preparation worthwhile.

Chapter 9.

Bequia New Year

"There are obviously magic moments, and I think the hardest thing is that you feel you should be 100% happy all of the time, and this cannot be possible. We then feel guilty when we are not going: 'Wow isn't this brilliant' all the time." Emma Hawkins, *Mad Fish*

We arrive in Bequia, a popular island in the Grenadines, at 5.30 pm, just before dark, and take one of Rory's moorings in front of the ferry terminal. A good spot in a big bay with the picturesque village Port Elizabeth as centre. Lizzie for obvious reasons loves the name. Drinks on "Savarna" followed by dinner at the landmark Frangipani Restaurant with "Savarna's" Keith and Pam from Auckland.

In the days to come we swim off the boat several times a day, and Nathan invents a jumping-off-the-boat game for Lizzie that they play endlessly. I spot a turtle swim by, we eat three big lobsters, visit a neighbouring Swan 48, buy some nice t-shirts and are in holiday mode. Being interested in nature and animals is a huge plus in a place like this. The kids, John and me take an open taxi to the turtle sanctuary in Bequia, *officially closed that day, which is lucky as we can visit it by ourselves. An elderly local, Orton G. King, takes care of hundreds of turtles of all ages here, feeding and healing baby hawksbill and green turtles until they are strong enough to survive the wild, real dedication and very interesting.*

The Port Elizabeth fruit and veggie market at the harbour is quite well stocked, although they don't seem to grow tomatoes and peppers here, fair enough. Lots of passionfruit instead. The stall owners are all over me, put produce into my face and are a bit too pushy for my liking. I buy less than I want as I feel hassled.

There had been long discussions in the ARC family gang about what to do for New Year's Eve, also Lisa's birthday, and as there was no firm conclusion the Senta crew decided to partly do their own thing. The French landlord of French-Caribbean restaurant L'Auberge des Grenadines on the waterfront, only a short dinghy ride away, had reluctantly fit us in at 6 pm to be out by 8.30 pm, and we were really happy about that plan. After a superb lobster meal in the completely empty restaurant we connected with the others, walked the streets a bit, hung out with them while they ate in a Mexican restaurant, and at midnight all toasted the New Year on "Chili Cat" in a prime spot for the fireworks.

The boss relaxed

Chapter 10.

More Windward Islands

"The Tobago Cays is a special place. It's what you
come to the tropics for."[30]

It's 12 miles to Mustique and we leave at 10 am. I am not feeling that good,
no surprise on the first day of the year. We motor past a wrecked freighter
high on the rocks and wonder how a local captain could have gotten his
course so wrong. Several moorings in Mustique harbour are vacant and
after trying most of them, John finally settles for one and we can go for a
swim. Late afternoon we visit the famous Basil's Bar where Mick Jagger
has done impromptu performances for years, but we find it overrated, the
drinks are not tasty and the hot chips almost inedible. Apart from the few
shops at the harbour, the island is blocked off for visitors because Mick
Jagger, Paul McCartney and other VIPs are on the island. Never mind!
    Lizzie the next day convinces her father to buy her the most expen-
sive bikini ever, very nice blue-red design. I get some running shorts with
Mustique written on the backside. Through our ARC friends the Hazemas
from "La Boheme" we hear that one can still see the island by booking a

---

30 *Yachting World*, 11/2007

lunch in the beach bar of the fancy Cotton House hotel. Our wedding anniversary is looming so we leave the kids in Nathan's capable care and join the Hazemas' taxi that drives us across the island. The houses that we can spot are not particularly impressive. The beach restaurant is also less fancy than expected and to my surprise I meet a sailing acquaintance from the UK that I had not seen for 15 years, her parents have a house here.

John starts chatting to the people on the table next to us and lots of drinks later the couple and their six-year-old let us climb into the back tray of their gold buggy and show us around the island. We stop at a famous beach and when we get into the cart again our guide says: "And did you see Mick Jagger and family in the left corner of the beach?" No, thanks for pointing it out now!

When we motor into the famous Tobago Cays through the shallow passage between Petit Rameau and Petit Bateau we see most of our friends in the process of leaving, "Fabiola," Chili Cat," "Salsa," "Mad Fish," and many more. Clearly we got our timing completely wrong, the kids are beside themselves. In silence we pick up one of three mooring buoys behind Baradol's sand spit in the picture postcard lagoon, nice location. Anchoring behind the outer reef seems not advisable in the increasing breeze; we see only "Intrepid Bear" out there, but they also leave soon. After the initial shock of having missed the party we have a good day in the end. In contrast to the Grand Central Station atmosphere at our arrival amongst 300 boats, the next day there is just eight left, three of which are Australian. We are guessing the charter boats had to get back to their base and New Year holidays are over.

This is paradise pure, the turquoise water, white sand, fish and turtles, the jewel of the crown of the Grenadines. We go snorkelling within the fence of the turtle sanctuary in little family groups, and soon everybody has spotted a green turtle. The boys and kids later build sand castles while I take photos. In the distance against the almost blinding sun we can just see Petit Tabac where Jack Sparrow had been marooned with his rum stash.

What would Jack Sparrow have done?

In the afternoon we hang out, read books and watch a DVD. The laid-back Caribbean way of life has finally made it onto Senta. Mark and Karline, on the mooring next to us, come over for sundowners. Overnight the wind picks up from 20 to 30 knots so we take the rattling cover down and Nathan sleeps inside, a rare occasion. The boat is quite wobbly, when does it ever not blow here?

Still safely moored in the Tobago Cays it is raining the next morning. We get fresh croissants and bread delivered by boat (expensive!) and hear "Fabiola" talk to "Open Blue" on the VHF. "Fabiola" got quite badly damaged by a Russian boat that had run into them. John speaks to Lisa and Gill about the legal side of the crash, Finn chats to Cameron about Lego. John and I make a rough plan for the next few days and I tidy up the medical cupboard. It is amazing what you find after not having looked for a while. As prudent our medical supplies were comprehensive, lots of antibiotics, tooth repair kits, gastro relief etc. We have been so lucky in the last 10 months, we have not used any medication apart from a few Panadol against hangovers.

We take the dinghy to the beach and build a huge sandcastle overlooking Jack Sparrow's island. The wind is howling but we are safe on our mooring. At lunchtime we go back to the boat to eat pancakes, this is the life. In the evening we team up with Mark and Karline and dinghy over to Petit Bateau. Charles from "Chili Cat" had recommended the grilled lobster from the shack there, so we have booked for the seven of us. The restaurant has one table and a little shelter where the couple is cooking for us. It is windy but the air is still warm. Our hosts drive every day the two hours from Union Island in their tiny motorboat, and the chef admits she is scared witless when they drive back at night. She expertly cuts the lobster in half (still alive) while Lizzie watches with interest. She then grills the crustaceans and serves them with a traditional banana dish, salad and potatoes. It is a feast.

Lobster feast

I wake up with a migraine the next morning, nothing to do with our lobster party last night. I take a migraine tablet and get on with my chores.

Suddenly, the French lady on the boat next to us starts yelling at Nathan hysterically: "Your boat is moving, do something!" to which Nate replies, "Not ours, lady, we are on a mooring." They quickly leave.

We head out through the shallow Penguin Channel leaving Jamesby to port. After a short, brisk sail we enter Chatham Bay on Union Island where "Chili Cat" and "Kazayo" are already at anchor. We head for the beach with the "Chili Cats." There is good snorkelling off the rock edge right on the beach. The kids have a great time. The beach bar serves rum punch, and we head back at 4 pm for dinner on the boat. In the evening the wind picks up, we have to run anchor watches, first time on this trip. A smashed up catamaran on the shore right behind us is a sobering reminder of what can go wrong. John, Nate and I take turns in watches of two hours on, four hours off, not very enjoyable. The boat swings violently on the anchor, an extremely restless night.

Not that easy – family shot underwater

After the kids have played on "Chili Cat" for two hours "Senta" leaves around 11am for a short motor to Clifton, Union Island in lots of wind.

After some discussions with a boat boy about the safety of a mooring we pick it up behind the Polish ARC boat "Malaika." We can just see the beautiful horseshoe reef inside the harbour where kite surfers plane back and forth. We go ashore late afternoon, Clifton feels really authentic, no tourists evident apart from yachties. We stroll up the lively high street, buy mangos, apples and passionfruit and have a drink at the Anchorage Hotel right on the water. They have sharks in a basin but don't serve food so we venture on and have a very good burger in a rooftop restaurant.

The chemist is not easy to find and in the end has no lotion against head lice for Lizzie, a lot of the ARC kids are infested, somebody blames it on us but who knows how it started. Same problems here as at home. We get back at 8 pm and go straight to bed, despite the howling wind all get a good night's sleep. Nathan a few days later realizes that somebody must have taken a mould off his credit card at the ATM in Clifton, his card gets cancelled, we got lucky.

CHAPTER 11.

FINALLY GRENADA

"Adventure exists, when the outcome of a journey is unknown."[31]

Over 7000 miles sailed. This might be our final sail before we put *Senta* away, and it is a cracking one with a reefed main and a number 5 headsail, *Senta* at her best powering down big swells, quite hard to steer. I don't tell John about the areas of volcanic activity we might have crossed on the way to Saint George; no bubbling water as far as I can see.

For whatever reason, possibly cost, we decide against mooring in the new Port Louis marina but squeeze into a berth next to the petrol station in the yacht club opposite. The lovely clubhouse with its wraparound veranda and chunky chairs has a true colonial feeling and serves cheap food, but all in all turns out a mistake. The showers are unusable as they are incredibly mozzie infested; so is the whole place. And our children have that unfortunate sensitivity/allergy against mosquitoes. We stop showering (again) and

---

31 Mike Litzow, *South from Alaska*, Sydney 2011

manage to stay for a few days before we move across to Peter de Savary's new marina.

Grenada covers 344 square kilometres and has an estimated population of 110,000 people. It is called the "Spice Island" as it is a leading producer of several different spices. Cinnamon, cloves, ginger, mace, allspice, orange/citrus peels, wild coffee used by the locals, and especially nutmeg, providing 20 percent of the world supply, are all important exports. The nutmeg on the nation's flag represents the economic crop of Grenada; the nation is the world's second-largest producer of nutmeg (after Indonesia). The island has also pioneered the cultivation of organic cocoa, which is also processed into finished bars by the Grenada Chocolate Company.

Tourism is Grenada's main economic force. Conventional beach and water sports tourism is largely focused in the southwest region around Saint George, the airport and the coastal strip; however, ecotourism is growing in significance. Most of these small eco-friendly guesthouses are located in the Saint David and Saint John parishes. The tourism industry has benefitted hugely from the construction of a cruise ship terminal in Saint George.

Grenada's early history was as chequered as any of the Caribbean states. First a French colony, then a British one, the island worked toward independence from the 1950s. Many of you might have a Grenada political crisis involving the United States in the back of your mind. This was the story. Independence from Britain in 1974 was followed by a coup in 1979, when the New Jewel Movement under Maurice Bishop launched a paramilitary attack on the government, resulting in its overthrow. The constitution was suspended, and Bishop's "People's Revolutionary Government" ruled subsequently by decree. Cuban doctors, teachers, and technicians were invited in to help develop health, literacy, and agriculture over the next few years. Though Bishop cooperated with Cuba and the USSR on various trade and foreign policy issues, he sought to maintain a "nonaligned" status. In 1983 the communist deputy prime minister overthrew Bishop's government and placed the prime minister under house arrest. Bishop was executed by soldiers when he tried to resume power.

The overthrow of a moderate government by one which was strongly procommunist worried US President Ronald Reagan. Reagan was particularly worried that Cuba—under the direction of the Soviet Union—would use Grenada as a refueling stop for Cuban and Soviet airplanes loaded with weapons destined for Central American communist insurgents. So Reagan invaded Grenada in October 1983. The prerevolution constitution became valid again and the leadership responsible for Bishop's murder was sentenced to death. The United States withdrew from Grenada in December 1983, and an interim prime minister was appointed until the elections in 1984.[32]

We tour the island, just Nathan and us, and decide Grenada is our favourite island. Lush, green, with colourful villages, a bit run down. What had made it especially popular with boat owners in the past was the fact that it was deemed hurricane safe. Hurricane Ivan in September 2004 put an end to that assumption. The devastation was of epic proportion. Boats stored ashore lay in tangles of broken hulls and rigs, boats on the water ranged from sunken to unscathed. Barely a building stood whole, barely a house had a roof. We heard from our local guide that Grenada's population is very young, as after the hurricane suicide rates among the elderly who had lost everything soared, very sad.

Following Ivan was Hurricane Emily on July 14, 2005, causing serious damage in Carriacou and in the north of Grenada, which had been relatively lightly affected by Hurricane Ivan. However, left with not much else after the hurricanes, Grenadians built on their traditionally strong sense of family and helped each other; there was a renewed sense of community, we heard. They rebuilt their homes, businesses, and the marine industry's facilities. Boatyards are back at capacity and have improved their boat storage with tie downs and better cradles. Cruise liners pull into the

---

32 Wikipedia

new cruise terminal. And yachties restock and relax in Peter de Savary's glistening marina.

The British entrepreneur and yachtsman (he mounted the British challenge for the America's Cup in 1983) was among the property developers who took a look at Grenada after Ivan hit. He first visited the island fifty years ago and clearly never forgot the place. De Savary hopes to convert the former swampy lagoon into the Saint Tropez of the Caribbean with hotels, clubs, private villas, and the marina. He has come a long way already. When we were there the marina was nicely filled, and after we finally moved into Port Louis from the other side of the lagoon we enjoyed the little T-shirt shops, easy restaurants, and large pool for the kids. Unfortunately we are a bit too early for the annual Grenada Sailing Festival.

Our island tour first takes us to a waterfall where a few brave locals hop off the top for EC$5. It is raining now, and we are glad we decided to give the big waterfall a miss, the one that some of our friends are now hiking to deep in mud, carrying their smaller children. We hurry on to the rum distillery, still in use. The sun is out again, tropical weather. The mountains of sugarcane residue are astounding while the molasses basins look like a sewage plant. This place is amazing; I love decaying industrial architecture.

The process of rum making seems quite complicated, and the machinery would have been comfortable in the *Titanic's* engine room. But at the end of it there is rum, in very nice bottles, and we get to taste it. Holy cow, it is firewater, and without hesitation we decide not to sample from the distillery's bottle shop.

The chocolate factory is slightly disappointing in regards to the actual manufacturing of chocolate. Does not seem to happen here, although they sell the stuff in a little shop. But the pretty guide shows us the fermenting cocoa beans and the interesting cocoa drying sheds as well as the little zoo belonging to the beautiful property, which delights Lizzie. We stroll around and enjoy the estate garden. In the end we watch a video about how chocolate is made, well.

Does not smell like cacao!

We have dinner in the club most evenings as it is cheap and good, chicken, fish, simple fare, and we are joined by ARC families like *Chili Cat*, *Intrepid Bear*, *Mad Fish*, and others. Most of them are moored in the marina and dinghy across. On our pontoon we meet a nice English couple that want to sell their Jeanneau 42 that they have owned for years and want to let go due to old age. It is a lovely, well-equipped boat, and for a few days we are very interested, but then the practicalities of owning two boats dawn and we give it a miss.

Hog Island's bay hosts the final hurrah for all present ARC family boats that manage to anchor in one spot so the kids can swim between the boats. I am surprised at the distances even Lizzie can cover, back and forth all day. The dads tow some kids around on a mattress, we go snorkelling, visit each other on the boats. In the evening the beach shack offers a fry-up, and we all go to celebrate Gill's fortieth birthday. The place is a bit chaotic, a few hashed-up locals present, the bar slightly understocked, the kids play behind the shack in the dark. But all in all a fun last evening.

Most of our friends had intended to complete an Atlantic circuit, some planned to cross the Pacific to Australia, and a few will hopefully sail around the world. In contrast to past decades, when retirees set off to go cruising without any time restraints, most people we met had a precise schedule for their cruise, either one, three, or five years. People ran stressful fixed itineraries, with relatives and friends flying into predetermined destinations. Some plans had to be changed along the way, though. A few families after the Atlantic crossing abandoned the idea of sailing back across the North Atlantic to Europe and shipped their boat home or had it delivered back.

See you again!

Into a choppy swell and howling wind followed by *Chili Cat*, we motor the few miles to Saint David's Bay, home to our haul-out yard Grenada Marine. They are no-nonsense people; John drives *Senta* straight into the travel lift, guys standing ready to help us get the luggage off the boat, she goes up, all done within an hour. Almost too fast. After ten months we are off the boat. The hotel is waiting. *Chili Cat* gets hauled on the same day. The Manfredis want to paint her bottom and stay on the boat. Over the next few days we hang out together in the marina bar that has good snacks and Wi-Fi.

The La Sagesse Hotel for three nights is a positive experience—our spacious room, the good restaurant, but most of all its fabulous location on the beach. After all those good-byes a few days ago, who would laze in sun loungers just there? The Duncans from *Fabiola*. She was being fixed up in Prickly Bay after her crash, with Gill supervising, and Lisa had taken Samuel and Cameron to the beach. The *Chili Cats* join the fun, the boys get canoes out, the girls build sand castles and splash forever.

The Caribbean clearly did not want to let go of us yet. When we arrive at the airport in a minibus, mountains of luggage in the back, ready for a two-day return journey, the airport is deserted. Turns out our flight was the day before, easy mistake to make (mine) after ten months on the boat, calendar packed away. We get back to Australia eventually.

FIVE BEST THINGS BOUGHT FOR THE BOAT:

John:
- Propeller
- Bimini/Dodger
- Electric Winch
- Inner Forestay
- Coffee Cup Holder

Karen:
- Bean Bags
- SSB
- Dodger/Bimini
- iPad
- Place Mats

Epilogue

"There is nothing more enticing, disenchanting, and enslaving than the life at sea." Joseph Conrad, Lord Jim

So how was the trip really? Honestly?

We got through living in a foreign city with no support system and coped really well.

Our child suffered the consequence of a badly run school and survived.

We adjusted to the realities of living with a unique child, and he prospered and relaxed. We agree with the experts, an Aspergers child is much happier without the constant pressures of normal life.

We didn't enjoy taking over the responsibilities of teachers but eventually got better at it.

We followed our dream and paid the price to do so.

Spending 24/7 with your partner and children is really hard, and life at home is easier in many ways.

But trying to slow down and getting back your brain and sanity was necessary, and it worked.

We knew that three generations are better than two, and tried hard to give something back.

It was all we had hoped for and much more.

What did John learn: He learned that the corruption of power is everywhere. Well-practised systems and procedures are critical for all boat manoeuvres. Don't transfer your own reality and wishes onto the kids, they have unpredictably different desires and enjoyments.

What did Karen learn: Even a rock solid marriage can wobble in the confinements of a small boat. But my husband is a technical genius and I still love him. Primary teachers are saints. I don't want to live on a boat forever. Even after 40 years of using them, I hate marina showers.

What did Finn learn: That it is possible to control one's emotions and not react on frustrations. He says: "I learned about other cultures, food and how people live. Also other languages."

What did Lizzie learn: That although her brother can be hard work it can be great fun to spend time with him. She says: "That many cultures are different from ours and you first have to get used to them. That the boat costs Daddy a lot of time. There is a lot of beautiful places but home is best."

ARC mother Emma Hawkins from "Mad Fish" with Oli and Ethan (and husband Russell) was speaking for many sailing mothers: "I wanted to spend quality time as a family and give my kids an amazing adventure that they would remember. I am not sure I would say that I am living the dream, as it is much harder than I ever anticipated, and I don't get much thanks from the kids for showing them amazing places."

THE FIVE BEST EXPERIENCES OF THE TRIP WERE FOR

John:
- Our on-land activities including Guernsey, Paris and all car trips
- my wife and children's great achievement in the Atlantic crossing

- Rum & Coke in the cockpit in the evening with Karen
- Dalyan River Tour
- Down time in Wall Bay, Turkey with Turkish flat bread

Karen:
- No seasickness on the crossing
- Rum & Coke with husband
- Dolphins, whales and turtles
- Catching up with international news
- Sighseeing trips ashore

And the worst was not wind, weather, danger and excitement but without doubt schooling our children, but we all survived. I want to add an interesting quote by Alain de Botton who believes that our school western systems do not teach enough life lessons: "I think our education system leaves us woefully unprepared for some of the real challenges of adult life, which include: How to choose a life partner; how to manage a relationship; how to bring up children; how to know ourselves well enough to find a job we can do well and enjoy; how to deal with pressures for status; how to deal with illness and ageing." The big challenges are still ahead of Finn and Lizzie, but maybe with this journey we have contributed to their confidence in themselves and their curiosity for the world and life.

I couldn't say it any better than Wendy Mitman Clarke in "What doesn't need saying"[33]

"We knew how wonderful it was to value the small things that would be taken for granted in our old lives, but which now seemed so precious. (What the ARC girls missed. Lisa: a freezer; Emma: a bath; Tatjana: a dishwasher; Karen: a shower)

We knew to feel the small triumph of making a passage to a new country, clearing in, and anticipating all that was fresh and unknown.

33 Wendy Mitman Clarke, Cruising World 5/2013 "What doesn't need saying"

We knew how it felt to struggle through a long night watch only to earn the grace of sunrise each morning and feel awed and honoured and lucky, knowing how tiny was our privileged minority.

We knew how frustrating it was to live with people in 45 feet of space.

We knew how hard it was to keep our floating homes operating well, and how expensive and complicated it could get to secure needed parts in far-flung places.

We knew how vulnerable we could be out there, at the whim of weather and forces so beyond our control, and how fulfilling it is to live a life deeply connected to the natural world, the wind, the clouds, the rain, the storm."

And I will finish off with what Tatjana from "Mis Amoress" wrote to me after the ARC about her experiences: "The most fascinating thing for me has been all the amazing people we have met and their life stories. The big majority were kind and friendly people, intelligent and successful but simple, dedicated and persistent, yet patient."

We did it!

Appendix

1. Technical Info *Senta*

Our Swan 46 *Senta*, built in 1983, was purchased to fulfill a specific purpose: to carry us as a family safely across oceans. If we had just wanted to cruise around the Mediterranean, any modern boat would have done. But we wanted top quality, seaworthiness, and a practical layout for our dream trip.

Senta has six bunks, some of them doubles, so she can sleep up to nine, and all berths can be converted into safe sea berths with lee cloth. There are two heads (bathrooms) and a galley in the corridor between the aft cabin and the salon. The big table in the living space seats up to ten people and is great for the kids' activities when underway. The children both have their bunks in the aft cabin, each with a shelf and a cupboard for their clothes. They have a toilet next to the cabin and a companionway into the aft cockpit that is covered by a large spray hood. That aft entrance is also used by anybody else wanting to safely get into the back cockpit. We use the front double berth when in port, but when sailing overnight John and I sleep in the more stable middle of the boat.

This particular Swan 46 has a rare centreboard, so only draws 1.75 metres when it is up, a great advantage heading into any harbor. She was fitted with two furlers for headsails so nobody has to get on deck to change sails. An electric winch in the aft cockpit controls several lines, e.g., the furling ropes, reefing line, and main sheet.

Senta was designed by German Frers, one of the most renowned boat builders in the world. The Frers relationship with Nautor's Swan started in1980. He designed the Swan 51 and the 651, then in 1983 he designed the 46 considered one of the most successful designs ever carried out by the Frers/Nautor team. With 109 hulls built and sold, it still remains the largest volume design of the entire range.

The Swan 46 MKI was produced from 1982 to 1990—eight-one hulls; the Swan 46 MKII built from 1990 to 1997—twenty-eight hulls. Ours is a Mark 1 with the hull number 11.

Masthead sloop with fin keel, centreboard, and spade rudder.

LOA: 14.36 m
LWL: 11.53 m
Beam: 4.40 m
Draft: 1.75 m
Displ: 14,200 kg
Designer: German Frers
Builder: Nautor
Year: 1983
Hull No: 11
Engine: Westerbeke
Water: 880l
Diesel: 4,76l
Instruments: Raymarine and B&G

Safety:
  Life raft
  Life vests and harnesses
  Grab bags
  AIS

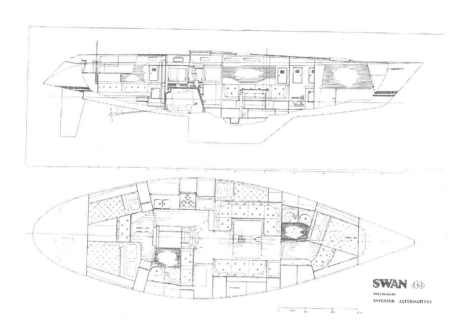

Drawing and cabin plan *Senta*

2. Practical Tips for Entertaining Kids on a Boat – You can't have too many Toys!

Safety: As our children have been on boats since they were newborns, safety is not really an issue on our boat. There are certain rules that the kids follow without arguing. They started to learn how to swim aged three and are by now competent swimmers. But if they want to move around the deck of the boat they have to wear life vests, and on the ocean be clipped on with a harness at all times outside the cabin.

"One hand for the boat, one hand for what you are doing" is the basic rule, so they hold on to something with one hand always. They know how to get down the companionway safely and to jam themselves in their bunks when big swells shake the boat around. And after a lot of discussions they have learned that they have to stop their constant bickering when we concentrate on mooring the boat. Our kids treat the dangers of the sea the same way inner-city children treat traffic or busy shopping centres.

Gear: Whatever your child likes doing best, have plenty of it on the boat. Finn was into Lego and books, and we had enough of both. Lizzie likes drawing, so we had different boxes of crayons, sticker books, stencils, water colours, picture books, and paper. At home or at sea the most important entertainment for our kids was audio books. They spent thousands of hours listening to Harry Potter, Percy Jackson, *The Chronicles of Narnia*, *Eragon*, Bibi Blocksberg, and Famous Five while playing. I had a large stash of surprises, books, etc. to hand out before long passages to make them a special thing and distract from the discomfort. We had big stackable plastic boxes for the Lego and Lizzie's toys under the companionway stairs that they could reach themselves. As we needed the table for eating on at night, they had to tidy away their toys and books every afternoon. I had birthday presents and Christmas gifts and decorations hidden away.

Choose from the following:
- Books, also geography and nature
- e-reader, Kindle
- Arts and craft material, fashion magazines, scissors
- Lego
- Board games, Monopoly, chess, Memory, etc.
- Musical instruments
- Little animals or dolls with one house
- Stuffed toys
- Computer games
- Sufficient movies
- Audio books on CD or MP3, headphones for bunks, head-phone splitter for listening with two earphones
- Inflatable water toys, dinghy, flippers, snorkel, goggles, canoe, sailing dinghy, air mattress
- Fishing gear
- Fold-up scooters

Boat work: Some kids are more interested in helping run the boat, some less. Ours fall in the latter category, but they will come up when we get into port, help put out the fenders, and Finn will throw a mooring rope at the back or jump onto the pontoon and take a line. *Senta* is a big, very heavy boat, so Lizzie could not do that quite yet. Both children steer for short periods, but the wheel is really too big. Other children will spend hours in the cockpit taking in the action; ours are just not like that and prefer to play down below.

Tatjana Walser from Swiss boat *Mis Amoress*: "We try to include the kids in everything we do so that they can see and learn from our everyday activities. So the girls cooked with me and I even survived the flour mess in the kitchen and having pancake mixture pouring around the galley. The kids enjoyed fishing, stars, and flying fishes on deck. Alexandra read *Baking with Globi*, a children's book with 120 recipes from Switzerland, many of which we tried out. This was THE book of the Atlantic crossing."

Finn figured out how to put a route into the navigation computer and was of help there. As at home, if any kids ask "Can I help?" you say yes and make something up for them to do. More ideas in the excellent article by Amy Schaefer "Crossing Seas with Kids" in the bibliography at the back.

Company: Whenever there is the chance of other children coming onto the boat, take it! While we met very few children during our cruise around the Med, the ARC compensated in full. We had kids on the boat every day. The girls played with Playmobil figures and animals, the boys with Lego and computer games. We had art classes on the boat and the kids swung around the rig in bosun chairs.

Activities: Arriving in a new port our children would get their scooters out straight away and we would look for an ice cream place, often on the way to the harbour authorities. I would read the travel guide before and devise a rough plan for sights or relaxing activities like swimming. Our kids don't mind looking at churches and fortresses as long as they hear the story connected to the place and there is enough fun combined with it, such as going to a souvenir shop or having a meal.

Try to have the kids keep a travel diary with glued in postcards and tickets.

The kids never tired of swinging in the rig in a bosun chair on a halyard; we actually put two chairs out so they could swing together or with their friends, hugely popular.

Ours were also allowed to play on the sun awning, not too wildly, and obviously it depends on the sun awning's robustness.

Get a star chart of the area you are sailing in and let the kids find star constellations at night. Talk about tides and the moon. Let them collect and identify shells or try to identify fish they have seen snorkelling.

Fishing is a great activity while sailing, but it requires an adult who has some knowledge and patience so the whole thing does not end in tears.

A nature experience is often not important to kids spoiled with fantastic TV nature shows. We have tried to teach them awareness of their surroundings and kindle an interest, but could not rely on nature providing lengthy distraction and entertainment.

This book has no chapter on first aid or medical issues for the simple reason that we did not get really sick in eighteen months apart from travel gastro. Lizzie had an infected mosquito bite and a light bladder infection, Finn got two new fillings in Denmark and a tooth pulled, but that was it. We had a good medical cabinet and excellent health insurance and did not need it; that's how it should be. Other families could write a book about the emergency departments of the world due to the wild nature of their children, but they experienced good treatment everywhere.

Emma Hawkins from *Mad Fish* with two boys about activities: "We have a kayak and a windsurfer on board. The kayak is more successful than the windsurfer, and we are looking for a second canoe paddle so that the board gets more use. We play lots of card games and board games and the Lego found its way out during a torrential downpour. During the crossing the boys tended to play DS, watch DVDs, and listen to audio books."

3. SCHOOL ON THE GO

"Thing about boats is, you can always sell them if you don't like them, can't sell kids!" Lin Pardey, *Bull Canyon, a Boatbuilder, a Writer and Other Wildlife*

I wrote the following about our home schooling experiences when we were still on the go, in the midst of it. It should not deter families from going. The fantastic teachers at Sydney Distance Education Primary School (SDEPS) tried to accommodate our circumstances at all times and make life as easy as possible for us. Margaret and Frank, you could not have done a better job. But it wasn't easy, at all. Other parents have better luck with schooling their children, like Leon Schulz (*The Missing Centimetre*) or take a tutor along, as our friends Marco and Tatjana from Switzerland did.

Cruising encourages creativity, independence, self-reliance, and a far broader view of the world than most kids possess. Cruising parents mention their children's sensitivity to nature, their increased sense of self-worth, greater attention spans, and curiosity. Homeschooling on board can offer engaging, real-world practical lessons that might seem remote if just learned from a textbook. However, that more or less did not work for us.

In contrast to most other developed countries, long-distance education is a highly developed part of Australia's school system as we live in a vast country and schooling has had to reach the remotest of communities. Nowadays Australians love to travel and correspondence schools help kids on longer journeys to keep up with their schoolwork. So when my husband took a one-year sabbatical and the family went on a sailing cruise around the Mediterranean and across the Atlantic we enrolled our seven- and nine-year-old children in SDEPS. There are similar long-distance schools in other countries, like the UK and United States.

We had been so naïve. When people were asking us about our adventure of a lifetime and the question of schooling popped up generally in the second sentence, I just said confidently, "No problem, we do long-distance education with the NSW curriculum, they won't miss a thing." With no teaching experience between us we were smart enough to take a nineteen-year-old student along to help with tutoring and the boat. He held his head on the table while teaching quite a bit, out of despair, I knew. I was close to crying on the other side of the table. But when he had to go home for health reasons after a few months, it was down to only us parents again.

Probably a different set of parents with a different set of children would have been more successful, and admittedly the kids' results were very acceptable, but we would have wished we had had a better time with it. For us, it overshadowed the trip.

But you will have different children, so a few words about the SDEPS program. The school material arrived in thick white envelopes roughly every four weeks in marina offices on our route whose addresses we had supplied to the school beforehand. Although the program runs in two-week sequences we had the school send us the work for at least six weeks at a time, as we could not time our mail stops that precisely beforehand.

The envelopes contained five or more great children's books for the appropriate reading stage and the school magazine, which was fun and informative. There were several maths packs with geometry, algebra, probability exercises, and much more. Each pack had exercises to fill out or we had to record the answers to a memory stick. There was also a test at the end and supervisor and student feedback about how the unit worked for us. The literature and grammar projects were mostly based around a book and the instructions very easy to follow. There were special projects of science, sports, and arts. It was extremely well prepared, foolproof, and could have been fun.

We should have been more aware of the inbuilt problems. But packing up our house for rental and the preparations for this long a trip all took priority. Our two children, bless their little hearts, can be a lethal combination. A nine-year-old with Asperger syndrome (a high functioning Autism) who does not like to (physically) write, has very rigid ideas about his projects and gets bored with most maths exercises on the same table as a highly creative seven-year-old that we sent to school too early and who struggles with writing and spelling are not good in the small saloon of a fourteen-metre yacht. Every day, Monday to Sunday, apart from when we were moving long distances and they might get seasick during school.

Even Leon Schulz, whose children seemed more self-motivated than ours, admits: "We had been mistaken to believe that school could simply happen between 0900 and noon—with eager kids who wanted nothing else but to work efficiently so they could go swimming or playing afterwards...I had hoped that they would work more on their own."[34]

"No school, nooooo, not yet. Not now. We want to go swimming first. Why do we have to do school again. I can do it all anyway. I am tired. I don't feel well. Noooo school." The wailing could be heard across the harbour. We steeled ourselves for a normal day in paradise, which would go like this: Get up at 7:00 am, make four different breakfasts for five people, or nine different for eight people depending how many friends we had on the boat. During breakfast I would read out facts and history of the places we were seeing in Greece and Turkey, Montenegro and Albania in the hope that something stuck. Clear the breakfast table and get the school folders out, school start is between 8:30 and 9:00 am. As soon as school time neared our son would escape to the toilet for a lengthy session while his sister complained that she had to start while he did not. "It is so unfair!" That's life, darling, get used to it.

---

34 Leon Schulz, *The Missing Centimetre*

I usually let her do some reading aloud and then did some spelling words with her before moving to maths or the current literature project. "I'm tired, Mama," this is only half an hour into the work. How do the teachers at home keep them going at that age? I resort to bribery, "A biscuit, sweetie?" It is going to be a long morning.

"This is stupid, I'm not doing it!" Our son looks at his maths work. "We don't have MABs, Mama!" What might MABs be? The dazed mother starts looking for the things in the maths pack supplied by the school. Turns out we were to assemble cardboard MAB blocks for calculating thousands from the oversized yellow printed carton I left on my mother's wardrobe in Germany because it didn't fit in the luggage. "Have to do without them, darling."

"We need scales for this maths exercise, Mum." There are no scales on the boat whatsoever. So off we go on Mykonos to look between a thousand souvenir shops and clothes boutiques for a kitchenware store. And oh, wonder, there is one. But it has no scales. At least that's what I gather; I don't speak Greek. "Have to weigh with our hands, darling."

"Mama, how do you spell 'are,' I have forgotten!" I am ready to cry, one of the most important words of the English language.

The substantial Olympics projects packs go straight in the bin. Without TV, Internet, and access to English-language newspapers the kids have no chance of following the games and completing projects on them, what a shame.

"What is the perimetre of our back yard, Dad?" Hard to remember from eight months ago, buddy, let's do the perimetre of that picture there instead.

"I don't want to write about this book, I don't like this book, I am not interested in this book, I'm not doing it." By this stage I say: "OK, if you want to stay stupid..." Not sure how a psychologist would rate that answer, but I am over this. Feeling helpless, inadequate, impatient, ratty while trying to be supportive and helpful, in the end being desperate.

Our relationship to our children is clearly suffering through this. A teacher has to have the patience of a saint. They need to get paid more.

On sailing days we finished around 11:00 am and left the port or anchorage we were in to go to the next spot. We often did not manage the daily four hours we were obliged to do and consequently worked at weekends and through the school holidays to get through the work load. It seemed endless and we were never on top of things. The teachers were very flexible, understood our problems, and made helpful suggestions. But we still dreaded sitting down for school every day.

I can only recommend that parents who are planning a long trip with their children and are considering distance education look closely at their program, their children, and themselves and decide whether it is worth the hassle. Or just let them enjoy the different experience and learn through life and travel.

The Walser family from Switzerland had a tutor on the boat for their two daughters. This is Tatjana Walser's account: "Schooling before and after the ocean crossing, yes. During the passage, no. We have our board teacher so he did the schooling every day two to three hours in the morning and the same in the afternoon. Depending on where we were we rented some space in the marina so that our teacher could settle a 'real' school. He would walk every day with our two girls (seven and five years) to the premises. I would provide them with the snack, a typical routine in Switzerland. We had lunch together on board or in a restaurant. In the afternoon again the same program.

"Before we left our home country of Switzerland we discussed the schooling of our two daughters with the local school officials. We bought school material and official books for the first five years of elementary school so that our girls are schooled according to the Swiss curriculum. Currently we are spending five months in Naples, Florida, and our daughters attend the local private school. So far it worked well. Our girls joined the school without any problem.

"Our daughters could speak English before we took off on our trip around the world, so the communication with other children on the way as well as here in Florida at the school proceeds normally. They manage to adjust to new conditions incredibly well, and I am as a mother amazed how (my) children adapt to the new situation and the new environment quickly and smoothly.

10 Tips for Homeschooling

1. Decide between formal distance education and homemade lessons. Print out curriculum documents and stock up on books and materials before setting off.
2. Be prepared to take the kids back one year after your return; hopefully you won't have to.
3. Don't underestimate the time and effort of homeschooling.
4. Stick to a firm routine, like school in the morning, sightseeing, play, or sailing in the afternoon.
5. Have star charts, incentives, rewards.
6. On some days it just doesn't work, so let it be.
7. Try and connect the lessons to your location or nature whenever you can (e.g., history, biology, physics).
8. Take atlas, encyclopaedia, travel guides, bird and fish guidebooks, art and craft material.
9. Don't leave subjects out that you don't like.
10. Make it fun!

Family Cruising and Healthy Child Development

1. Published: 2011-02-24 on Noonsite

By Ann Saitow

Family cruising presents a set of environmental conditions that contribute to healthy child development. The affirmation of family values is expressed through shared experiences that provide opportunities to live among people from other backgrounds. Theories of human development explain intellectual and emotional behavior as predispositions of age in relation to a child's surrounding environment. These milestones in maturation have become the guidelines driving school curriculum, as well as the expectations for social acceptability.

The positive psychological and emotional outcomes of family cruising potentially challenge the findings drawn by many human theorists – with cruising children exhibiting mature and compassionate behavior beyond the expectations defined in their literature. Conclusions reached in child development research appear to be more relevant to conventional school experiences and social communities where children are arbitrarily grouped together by age – rather than immersed within a heterogenic environment like a cruising setting.

Enriching a Child's Understanding

Family cruising experiences enrich a child's understanding of the world through the daily interactions that characterize the lifestyle. Arriving at a new destination becomes a chance for families to reach out to others in the sailing community, replenish provisions at a local marketplace, make boat repairs, and venture ashore to become familiar with their surroundings – each endeavor results in direct contact with the cruising and indigenous cultures. Urie Bronfenbrenner (1979) determined that "the ecology of human development involves the scientific study of the progressive, mutual accommodations between an active, growing human being and the changing properties of the immediate settings in which the developing persons lives, as this process is affected by relations between these settings, and the larger contexts in which the settings are embedded" (p. 21). The cruising family experience encompasses a broad range of relationships and circumstances that build self-confidence and healthy child development.

Widening Cultural Awareness

Cruising families become part of a larger communal network that re-forms at each new anchorage. The nature of a cruising environment inherently provides a child with a multiplicity of social and cultural resources. The access to a variety of people and situations form a basis for scaffolding – the collective structure that contributes to healthy child development. Gardiner and Kosmitzki (2005) concluded that scaffolding is an effective way to acquire specific cognitive skills. Scaffolding refers to "the temporary support or guidance provided to a child by parents, older siblings, peers, or other adults in the process of solving a problem" (p. 104).

Cruising families report improved communication between parents and children, as well as more tolerant and supportive relationships among siblings. This phenomenon is brought about by the close proximity of living aboard, and the need for cooperation in order to fulfill family endeavors. There are responsibilities associated with family cruising that are critical to the safety and well-being of each member. These everyday tasks shape a rearing environment that is founded upon a deep commitment to keeping the family together, and at the same time, allowing children to experience a broader world perspective. Super and Harkness (1986) suggested that a developmental niche defines a child's place in the world. These researchers believed the forces that influence a child's development are related to "the physical and social settings in which the child lives; the culturally regulated customs of child care and child rearing; and the psychology of the caretakers" (p. 522). The child's cultural context is formed by these subsystems.

Cruising immerses children in a series of experiences that require social and physical interaction with their immediate environment. Their desire and ability to emotionally and intellectually engage as they enter a new situation becomes a basis for adjustment. Piaget (1950) described human intelligence as a type of evolutionary biological adaptation that enables a person to interact successfully with the environment. He theorized that the ability to adapt to environmental change led to cognitive development.

As mentioned above, a cruising life presents opportunities to reach out to people as a way of becoming acclimated to a new place. By developing skills in forming these connections – cruising families become engaged in communal exchange, and subsequently learn to accept differences in cultural values. Erik Erikson (1950) endorsed a perspective on human development that was grounded in psychosocial research. He wrote that each stage of development entails a crisis in which the ego tries to find a balance between new ideas and previous assumptions. In order for healthy development to occur, the series of psychological crises require resolution. Cruising children learn to initiate friendships as a way of adjusting to an unfamiliar place. These socializing skills build self-confidence which enables them to forge new connections with their changing environment.

Cruising families returned to conventional life with perspectives and sensitivities that connected to the people and places they spent time. Often their travels took them to places where people lived at standards below their own. This direct exposure to different lifestyles nurtured an understanding of how people survive adverse conditions. Greater tolerance for what was initially unfamiliar became a basis for moral development and greater self-awareness.

Long-Term Benefits

In addition, some cruising parents shared observations about how their children adapted to conventional life upon returning home. Cruising preteens and teenagers did not participate in destructive or irresponsible behavior most commonly associated with adolescence. They retained a high level of motivation to succeed and remained focused on achieving their goals – rather than engage in "typical" risky behavior patterns. Kohlberg (1987) developed a theory of moral development that classified stages in terms of "(a) what is right, (b) the reasons for upholding the right, and (c) the social perspective behind each stage" (p. 283). Kohlberg explained that these stages show more sophistication and complex orientation toward justice and moral principles. Cruising children had the advantage of rich, life experiences to steady their transition through adolescence.

Conclusions

From the multiple theories of human development – in conjunction with feedback provided by cruising families, my study revealed that the intellectual and emotional benefit children derived from their travel experiences was directly related to the social communities in which they lived. A significant aspect of family cruising that contributed to healthy child development can be attributed to the efforts of parents – who remained dedicated to opening their children's minds to the infinite possibilities that existed beyond their lives back home. "Living the dream" was a rare gift that cruising parents shared with their children, and the positive outcomes were evidence that the experience left a sustained, meaningful impression.

REFERENCES

Bronfenbrenner, U. (1979). *The ecology of human development.* Cambridge, MA: Harvard University Press.

Erikson, E. (1950). *Childhood and society.* New York: Norton.

Gardiner, H.W., & Kosmitzki, C. (2005). *Lives across culture: Cross-cultural human development (3rd ed.).* Boston, MA: Pearson.

Kohlberg, L. (1987). *Childhood psychology and childhood education: A cognitive- developmental view.* New York: Longman.

Piaget, J. (1950). *Psychology of intelligence* (M. Percy & D.E. Berlyne, Trans.). London: Routledge.

Super, C.M., & Harkness, S. (1986). The developmental niche: A conceptualization at the interface of child and culture. *International Journal of Behavioral Development, 9*(4), 545-569.

4. BIBLIOGRAPHY

CRUISING BOOKS:

Black, Lesley: *Sea Gipsy*
Cameron, Silver Donald: *Sailing away from Winter*
Cantrell, Debra: *Changing Course: A Woman's Guide to Choosing the Cruising Life*
Cooper, Bill and Laurel: *Set up and Sail*
Copeland, Liza: *Just Cruising*
Cornwell, Doina: *Child of The Sea*
Cornell, Gwenda: *Cruising with Children*
Dearlove, Juliet: *Atlantic Children 1 and 2*
Erdman, Wilfried: *Tausend Tage Robinson*
Esterle, Paul: *Cooking Aboard a Small Boat*
Giesemann, Suzanne: *It's Your Boat Too: A Woman's Guide to Greater Enjoyment on the Water*
Gilchrist, Don and Boae, Robyn: *Here be Dragons*
Hackett, Joanna: *The Reluctant Mariner*
Hill, Annie: *Voyaging on a Small Income*
Jessie, Diana: *The Cruising Woman's Advisor: How to Prepare for the Voyaging Life*
Litzow, Mike: *South from Alaska*
Martin, David and Jaja: *Into the Light*
Neale, Tom: *All in the Same Boat*
Nicholas, Mark: *The Essentials of Living Aboard a Boat*
Pardey, Lin and Larry: *Cruising Seraffyn*
Pastorius, Kay: *Cruising Cuisine: Fresh Food from the Galley*
Patterson, Kevin: *The Water in Between*
Peterswald, Rob and Rosemary: *Sailing the Western Mediterranean*
Purves, Libby: *One Summer's Grace*

Russell, Maria: *The Best Tips from Women Aboard*
Russell, Maria: *From the Galleys of Women Aboard*
Schulz, Leon: *The Missing Centimetre*
Slavinski, Nadine: *Lesson Plans Ahoy!*
Stuemer, Diane: *The Voyage of the Northern Magic*
Thurston, Liz: *Dolphins at Sunset*
Trefethen, Jim: *The Cruising Life: A Commonsense Guide for the Would-Be Voyager*
Treleaven, Andrea: *Letters from the Med, Letters from the Caribbean*

PILOT BOOKS:

Adriatic Pilot, T. and D. Thompson
Greek Waters Pilot, Rod Heikell
Turkish Waters Pilot, Rod Heikell
Mediterranean Spain: Costas del Sol and Blanca, Robin Brandon
Windward Islands, Chris Doyle

ASPERGER BOOKS:

Atwood, Tony: *The Complete Guide to Asperger's Syndrome*
Boyd, Brenda: *Parenting a Child with Asperger's Syndrome*
Gomez/Mason: *Asperger's Syndrome for Dummies*
Greenspan, Stanley: *Engaging Autism*
Greenspan, Stanley: *Great Kids*
Matthews, Joan: *The Self-Help Guide for Special Kids and their Parents*

WEBSITES:

www.worldcruising.com
www.noonsite.com
www.womenandcruising.com

www.sailkidsed.net
www.jilldickinschinas.com
www.tutorsinternational.com
http://sdeps.net
www.calvertschool.org
www.firstcollege.co.uk
www.yachtmollymawk.com
www.sailmagazine.com/cruising-tips/crossing-seas-kids
www.wilderness-school.us
http://thegiddyupplan.blogspot.com.es/2011/04/cost-of-cruising.html

Made in the USA
Middletown, DE
30 November 2016